beauty junkies

beauty

Vermilion
LONDON

junkies

Under
the Skin of the
Cosmetic Surgery
Industry

Ⓧ

Alex Kuczynski

13579108642

Copyright © Alex Kuczynski

Alex Kuczynski has asserted his moral right to be identified as the author of this work in accordance with the Copyright, Design and Patents Act 1988.

First published in the United States in 2006 by Doubleday, an imprint of The Doubleday Broadway Publishing Group, a division of Random House, Inc., New York

First published in the United Kingdom in 2007 by Vermilion, an imprint of Ebury Publishing
Random House UK Ltd.
Random House
20 Vauxhall Bridge Road

Random House Publishers India Private Limited
301 World Trade Tower, Hotel Intercontinental Grand Complex,
Barakhamba Lane, New Delhi 110 001, India

Random House UK Limited Reg. No. 954009
www.randomhouse.co.uk

Papers used by Vermilion are natural, recyclable products made from wood grown in sustainable forests.

A CIP catalogue record is available for this book from the British Library.

ISBN: 9780091917197

Printed and bound in Great Britain by
Bookmarque Ltd, Croydon, Surrey

FOR MY PARENTS
JANE CASEY HUGHES AND PEDRO-PABLO KUCZYNSKI

Contents

Acknowledgments

My editors at the *New York Times* first directed me to some of the intriguing stories about the cosmetic surgery and beauty industries, and without them this book would not exist: Barbara Graustark, Trip Gabriel, Danielle Mattoon, Mary Suh, Anita Leclerc, Alison Silver, and Luisita Lopez-Torregrossa. I owe a great thanks to Joe Lelyveld, for hiring me; Howell Raines and Gerald Boyd, who tried to bring more popular culture reporting to the newspaper; Bill Keller and Jill Abramson, who continue to be enthusiastic and supportive; and David Smith, who taught me how to write for a newspaper. Earlier, at the *New York Observer*, Peter Kaplan, Jim Windolf, and Peter Stevenson were incredibly patient and creative mentors.

Nancy Hass and Warren St. John are terrific journalists without whose friendship and intelligence I would be lost.

Most importantly, this book owes a great debt to the medical professionals who gave me their time. The following were generous with their expertise: Dr. Sherrell Aston, Dr. Daniel Baker, Dr. Mark Berman, Dr. Alastair Carruthers, Dr. Andrew Charles,

Dr. Michelle Copeland, Dr. Terry Dubrow, Dr. Garth Fisher, Dr. Peter B. Fodor, Dr. Randal Haworth, Dr. Dennis Hurwitz, Dr. Gerald Imber, Dr. Cheryl Thellman-Karcher, Dr. Lloyd Krieger, Dr. Z. Paul Lorenc, Dr. Suzanne Levine, Dr. Stephen Marquardt, Dr. Alan Matarasso, Dr. Ivo Pitanguy, Dr. Thomas Rees, Dr. Vail Reese, Dr. Steven A. Teitelbaum, Dr. Rick van der Poel, Dr. Pat Wexler, and Dr. Harvey Zarem.

There are several excellent histories of cosmetic plastic surgery, and I encourage those who are interested in exquisitely reported historical works on the subject to read Sander L. Gilman's *Making the Body Beautiful: A Cultural History of Aesthetic Surgery* and Elizabeth Haiken's *Venus Envy: A History of Cosmetic Surgery*.

I am grateful to Irena Medavoy for sharing her story with me. Many others gave their time in other ways, including: Clare Casey, Tina Sloan McPherson, Melissa Biggs Bradley, Matthew Snyder, Jason Grunstra, Roberta Myers, Robert Emmons, Bob Roe, Peter Rawson at the Harvard Medical School's Countway Library, C. Loring Brace, Joan Kron, Lorraine Melvill, Peggy Siegal, Claudia Lowe, Peter Kaufman, Donna Zilkha, Sally Kadison, Leida Snow, and Adeena Colbert.

I interviewed many patients who were not comfortable using their names, for varying reasons. One woman did not want me to name her because she undertook an extremely private form of beautification. Another didn't want her parents to know that she started using Botox at age twenty-two. For their insight into their obsessions, I am grateful.

My thanks also to Sloan Harris of ICM for his encouragement, Stacy Creamer for her editorial skill, Laura Swerdloff for much-appreciated assistance, Bill Thomas and Steve Rubin for their patience, and production editor Bette Alexander for her careful management of the whole enterprise.

I owe the greatest debt to my husband, whose support and love have been immeasurable. You are perfection.

beauty junkies

One

Beauty Junkies

A friend of mine, a New York entertainment executive in her fifties, does not look her age. She's got the reedy, semi-starved body of an adolescent, and she has avoided the sun with a fervor bordering on religious principle. She's always impeccably turned out; she's obsessed with shoes—stilettos, kitten heels, anything to add a supple, curvaceous tightness to the calf muscle.

On a good day, she could pass for thirty-five—in dim light, possibly twenty-five. There are no telltale signs of age on her face, no wrinkles and no age spots. A dusky pink sheen illuminates her lips at all times, the work of a tattoo artist expert in the application of permanent makeup.

At the beginning of the summer, every year, my friend visits Dr. Patricia Wexler, a New York dermatologist whose clients have included Ellen Barkin, Donna Karan, Barbra Streisand, and Sean "Diddy" Combs. Everyone who goes to Wexler or who has heard of her calls her "Dr. Pat."

Prior to this visit, Dr. Pat has withdrawn fat from my friend's buttocks and siphoned out enough fat to fill twelve thick vials. The vials are labeled and stored in a freezer along with fat suctioned out of dozens of famous actors and actresses, Dallas housewives, lawyers, television anchors. My friend wears a tight-fitting set of Ace bandages for a week after the procedure. An opening at the bottom allows her to perform bodily functions and gives the outfit a distinctly S&M, Helmut Newton affect.

To subject oneself to the ministrations of a New York dermatologist can be a pricey prospect. Just to sit down and talk to Dr. Pat is $500. Laser treatments can run as high as $6,000 and liposuction as much as $11,000. A frequent guest on *Oprah* and the *Today* show, she has touted skin-tightening procedures like Thermage (about $3,500, according to the *New York Times*).

Certainly, a patient won't try everything at once. In the case of my friend and her fat, I watched Dr. Pat bring out one of the vials of fat and, using a fine subcutaneous needle, inject the contents of one of the syringes into the woman's cheeks and nasolabial folds—the lines that run from the nose to the mouth. The fat was surprisingly thick and bright yellow, a neon sludge that looks almost exactly like the lemon-flavored cake frosting you might buy in a plastic Betty Crocker tub at the supermarket. Just greasier.

The procedure is called autologous fat transfer—that is, moving fat from one part of the body to another. Peggy Siegal, a public relations executive in New York who is also a patient of Dr. Pat's, loves to joke about having had the procedure.

Siegal explains it this way: "The older you get, the more the fat gravitates to your butt. The doctor takes it out of your bottom and puts it back in your face. So when you are kissing my face, you are actually kissing my ass." Then she gives a laugh, and it is a triumphant sound.

X   X   X

When Kathleen Kelly Cregan left her home in Croom, County Cork, Ireland, early in the morning of March 14, 2005, her husband, Liam, a farmer and part-time plumber, was proud: she was going to Dublin to take a two-week business course. Life was good. In the months to come, they were going to celebrate their eight-year-old son's first Communion and take a holiday in France.

But Cregan did not go to Dublin to take a business course. She got on a plane to New York. And the next her husband heard of her was the following morning, when he got a phone call from the Irish consulate in New York. His wife was in critical condition at St. Luke's–Roosevelt Hospital in Manhattan. The day before, fresh off the plane, she'd gone to the offices of Dr. Michael Sachs on Central Park South for a face-lift and nose job.

She had planned to surprise her husband with her refreshed new look. Instead, Liam Cregan was summoned to New York. He and her two sisters were by her bedside on March 17 when she was taken off life support and died.

Dr. Suzanne Levine, a podiatrist on the Upper East Side of Manhattan, is known as the city's "foot face-lift" doctor. She shortens toes, offers microdermabrasion for feet, and will inject collagen into the sole of the foot so that it can withstand the consistent, daily pounding shock of high heels.

"People come to me and they say, 'I want to wear my Jimmy Choos, I want pretty feet, I hate that long skinny toe in the middle,'" Levine said in an interview one wintry afternoon. "'I'm divorced. I need my feet to look good. I can't get in the shower with a new man with these feet.' The foot thing is all about love, really. We live in a culture where women have to compare themselves every day to these women . . ."

Her hand swept the wall, with its framed testimonials and grinning pictures of Joan Lunden, Katie Couric, and Star Jones.

"These women are on television," the doctor continued. "Their bunions can't show."

Levine considers herself something of a romantic counselor to single women across the city, although the advice she offers is probably not that practical in the long run.

"We live in a fifteen-second culture," she said. "That's how long it takes, I believe, for a man to look at you and decide if he will be in love with you. That is it. And if you're wearing stiletto sandals and your feet look like hell, he's not even going to give you the time of day."

A man won't love you, Levine reasons, or even give himself the chance of falling in love with you, if you have a bunion peeping out of your $500 evening sandal. Tough town, I said.

"Tough town, that's for sure," she said. "It sets its own standards. People overreact. I had one woman come in who wanted me to do liposuction of the toe. I mean, that's even over the top for me."

What happened to the patient?

"I told her to go see a shrink instead," Levine said.

When I left, Levine asked me if I knew any good single men.

Fat. Happiness. Youth. Death. Wrinkles. Love. Bunions. The endless struggle against looking old, the inability to accept the changing body and face. All form a part of the mosaic that makes up the $15 billion cosmetic surgery industry in America. Our superlative narcissism extends around the planet. From Poland to Pittsburgh, most human beings on the planet, whether they know it or not, have seen pictures of people—movie stars, models—who have surgically altered themselves for the purpose of beautification.

On billboards and movie screens from Hong Kong to Bonn to Iowa, breasts are buoyant, manipulated no longer by mere padded bras but by surgically sutured underpinnings of nylon, silicone, and saline. Cheekbones are thrust forward with the help of Gore-Tex strips—the material your L. L. Bean winter jacket is made of—implanted underneath the skin. Lips the world over are plumped with collagen grown, in a football-sized petri dish in California, from the stem cells of one little boy's foreskin; or from the cadavers of people who have donated their bodies to science; or from farm animals that live in cloistered herds and flocks monitored by the Food and Drug Administration. During the mad cow disease epidemic of the late 1990s, women in Europe and the United States accustomed to routine collagen plumping sessions panicked when they were cautioned temporarily by their doctors against using the substance, much of which, at the time, was derived from cows.

In Paris, doctors sew filament into the tissues of the face—the so-called gold-thread face-lift—to hoist it up. In Los Angeles, women who have tucked and pumped and stretched every stray piece of skin back into the position it was in when they were twenty-five are no longer limiting themselves to the areas of the body that the public sees; the new operation of choice among Hollywood housewives is the labial rejuvenation, in which the lips surrounding the vagina are snipped and sculpted, giving the patient the feeling of "revirginization."

As a culture we are increasingly concerned with and insecure about looking good. In 2003, more than half of Americans—51 percent—said that they were not quite comfortable to not at all comfortable with their appearance, according to a Roper study.

Looks are the new feminism, an activism of aesthetics. As vulgar and shallow as it sounds, looks matter more than they ever have—especially for women. It's a terrifying admission. But I am a reporter, not an ideologue, and we live in a terrifying culture, a world in which images hold more power than words and language has been replaced with symbols and sound bites. For a long time it has been a part of the American spirit to embrace the world of the visual: in a caricature, Ralph Waldo Emerson was portrayed as a huge eye set atop a pair of stiltlike legs. We are, above all, creatures who arrange our world before us in visual categories. We make sense of the world by moving toward the appealing and away from the ugly. Marketers talk of getting "eyeballs" on their products and television shows. In the twenty-first century, cosmetic surgery is the embodiment of that American dream, the success story of getting eyeballs on one's self, of self-transformation.

Ordinary Americans may be flabbier and grayer than ever, but we have also never before in our history been surrounded in such completeness by images of conventional perfection. Plastic surgery, hormone replacement therapy, and other enhancement technologies now offer us a youthful fix. Specialists of all types cannot hang out their shingles fast enough. And despite the international origins of that branch of plastic surgery we call cosmetic—and its apparently increasingly international future, as Asians begin to become obsessed with the changes it offers—its story is essentially, and peculiarly, American.

Cosmetic plastic surgery today offers a particular appeal to Americans in general, not just the fashion slaves, the well-to-do, and the socially ambitious who have long sought it. We are a tribe of people who not only admire transformation but hunger for it. Easily bored, we prefer our heroes and heroines to reinvent themselves every few months. And because of programs like *Extreme Makeover* and the D-level celebrity confessionals that now fill tabloid magazines ("Kathy Griffin Shares the Pain—and Gain—of Her Recent Plastic Surgeries"), the plain members of the middle and working class can imagine what a transformation might do for them.

The makeover—the total overhaul of a woman's appearance—has become commonplace in women's magazines. On daytime television, mostly female audiences still yelp with pleasure when a woman—or man—is transformed into a new and better person through makeup, hairdo, wardrobe. There are more makeover-themed television shows than ever: *Queer Eye for the Straight Guy*, *Extreme Makeover*, *The Swan*, *A Makeover Story*, *Cosmetic Surgery Before and After*. For teenage boys, there's *Pimp My Ride*, in which a team of Southern California auto mechanics transforms the most broken-down jalopies into the most pimp ride ever. Even a television program like *Trash to Cash*—a cable program on FX in which the host, John DiResta, takes discarded belongings and makes treehouses, sewing machines, cars, anything—has gotten into the art of the human makeover. On one recent episode, Amanda, an aspiring actress, had only $250 but wanted breast implants. Fortunately, John and his brother Jimmy stopped short of performing the surgery themselves and hosted a "breastival" to raise money for Amanda's cause. When one of the brothers referred to "implants," the actress demurred.

"Enhancement," she said, speaking in the euphemistic jargon of the plastic surgeon.

Making oneself over—one's home, one's car, one's breasts—is now a part of the American life cycle. Doctors have sold us on the notion that surgery is no longer an issue as crass as mere cutting and suturing; it is merely part of the journey toward enhancement, the beauty outside ultimately reflecting the beauty within. The notion that we can enhance our looks is terrifically appealing to insecure Americans. And there are in fact more reasons cropping up to contribute to our growing self-loathing: we're getting fatter and older and more unhealthy by the minute. A wealth of mini-industries and leisure activities has sprung up around the cosmetic surgery industry, dictating everything from what we read to what we watch to how we think.

The global beauty business—an industry that includes products for the skin and hair—is growing at a rate of 7 percent a year, double the rate of the developed world's gross domestic product. The global skin care industry generates $24 billion a year, cosmetics $18 billion, hair care products $38 billion. Perfume alone is a global market worth $15 billion.

The marketing and packaging of beauty products has taken on a fetishistic cast. Cosmetics are no longer merely powder and lipstick; they are a compulsion, whether that compulsion takes the form of a $25 Chanel lipstick or $500 skin cream from La Prairie. Writing in *Allure*, Daphne Merkin remarked on her thirteen-year-old daughter's obsession with collecting new, expensive lip glosses and then leaving them pristine, in their original packaging, merely *objets* to fondle, never to actually insult with use. "She has been known to take a freshly purchased item, still nestled in its tissue paper inside a small lilac Bergdorf's bag, into the bathroom and lock the door to study it. 'Using it isn't even that great,' she explains. 'The best part is seeing it in the package, knowing you have it, and it's untouched. Once you touch it, it's all over.' "[1]

While the cosmetics industry continues to grow, it is difficult to estimate the size of the global cosmetic plastic surgery industry, although some economists put the worldwide figure at $20 billion, more than four times the gross domestic product of Somalia. Cosmetic surgery in the United States alone is an industry that as of 2005 constituted $13 to $15 billion a year.

(A brief note on terminology: *Plastic surgery* is a broad term and is often, to the dismay of plastic surgeons, a misused one. It is sometimes considered, incorrectly, to be synonymous with aesthetic, or cosmetic, surgery—that is, surgery performed solely to improve the appearance of healthy patients. Plastic surgery encompasses the subspecialties of reconstructive plastic surgery—in which, for example, a breast might be reconstructed after a mastectomy or a face put back together after an automobile accident—and what is referred to as cosmetic surgery, elective surgery that is medically unnecessary but produces pleasing aesthetic results. For the purposes of this book, I use the phrase *cosmetic surgery* to refer to elective surgery that is intended to enhance patients who are otherwise healthy.)

Addiction once meant less than desirable behavior, usually related to drugs or alcohol. But as the purveyors of American marketing learn to nurture our obsessions and nourish our compulsions, addiction is a term that is applied to not only drugs but television, food, shopping, shoplifting, chocolate, and the pursuit of beauty. We are obsessed with beauty (or what we have come to believe passes for beautiful), with attempting to create it and to hold it hostage for as long as we can. It is the nature of cosmetic surgery that, as it becomes more popular, it adjusts our standards of beauty and our expectations of appearance. Large bouncy breasts, slender hips, and blinding white straight teeth used to be the rare departures from typical human looks. Now, they are no longer rarities; they are everyday expectations. The process begins with our trying to emulate nature, but then we become greedy and try to improve on nature.

Our greed, that hunger for physical perfection, shows in the numbers. Between 2003 and 2004 alone, there was a 44 percent increase in the total number of cosmetic procedures. Surgical procedures increased by 17 percent, and nonsurgical procedures increased by 51 percent. Liposuction, breast augmentation, nose jobs, and face-lifts have been joined by a legion of wonder cures such as buttocks implants (a fad that arrived with the ascent of Jennifer Lopez and may fade when she does), Botox, and autologous fat transfer to smooth aging hands. In 2004, nearly 12 million surgical and nonsurgical procedures were performed in the United States, according to the American Society for Aesthetic Plastic Surgery—or one procedure for every single person living in Massachusetts and Washington, D.C., combined.

In 2004, 290,343 Americans had surgery to remove fat and excess skin from their upper or lower eyelids (up from 229,092 just two years before) and 166,187 had nose jobs. Liposuction was the most popular procedure: in 2004, 478, 251 Americans had fat sucked out of their bodies, up from 372,831 two years earlier, and 334,052 had breast augmentation surgery, up from 249,641 in 2002.

The American Society for Aesthetic Plastic Surgery has been compelled to add six new categories to monitor the popularity of some rather esoteric new procedures. These included umbilicoplasty, or belly button enhancement, and breast nipple enlargement. While the ASAPS considers them trends to be watched, not very many Americans got their belly buttons reshaped (2,082 procedures in 2002) or nipples enlarged (540 procedures). With the popularity of gastric bypass surgery and the dramatic weight loss that follows, cosmetic surgeons have experienced a boom in lower body lifts—multiple-operation procedures that literally remove dozens of pounds of skin that has been stretched by obesity.

From the long-term view, cosmetic plastic surgery is the Incredible Hulk of the medical industry, in a seemingly unstoppable growth spurt. Since 1997, liposuction has seen a 111 percent increase in patients, tummy tucks are up 144 percent, breast augmentations are up 147 percent, collagen injections are up 126 percent, and injections of Botox—botulinum toxin A, the neurotoxin that in larger doses causes botulism—are up 2,446 percent. And I, for one, am one of the patients who were utterly seduced by its chemical magic.

The number of patients seeing plastic surgeons has quintupled in a decade, from 412,901 patients in 1992 to 2,036,794 in 2002. Since 1997, there has been a 465 percent increase in the total number of cosmetic procedures.

Once, American women hosted Tupperware or Avon parties. Now, they invite their friends to "pumping parties," at which a doctor arrives with a bag full of Botox or some dermatological unguent with which to inject or spackle an entire roomful of women sipping white wine spritzers. For these devotees, the scowl and other unpleasant expressions have simply been banished.

Across the United States, plastic surgeons promote their work in magazine advertisements showcasing images of sculpted Grecian forms or languid, curvaceous torsos. Physicians have been allowed to advertise since a 1979 decision of the Federal Trade Commission that determined that medical advertisements should be no different from those for other consumer services. It was a decision that changed the shape of the industry. Now, even the most respected surgeons work with public relations firms to get their names—mentioned favorably only, please—in the press. Unheard of two decades ago, such self-promotion, to the chagrin of older, more traditional plastic surgeons, is considered the professional norm.

At the highest levels of the profession, the names of plastic surgeons are synonymous with their products, as in New York, where well-to-do women refer to their ultraexpensive Manolo Blahnik shoes as "Manolos." Electing to have plastic surgery has become an act of acquisition, a commercial transaction with the same appeal and same emotional patterns as shopping for a new handbag or a new pair of shoes. I will never forget going to a benefit dinner for American Ballet Theater and running into an acquaintance of mine, a woman who swims in New York social circles, in the ladies' room.

"Darling," she said, throwing open her satin wrap blouse to reveal the handiwork of Dr. David Hidalgo: two large, firm breasts held aloft by two silken straps attached to a delicate black bra. "Just look at my Hidalgos! I got them two weeks ago!"

American popular culture is saturated with references to plastic cosmetic surgery. While it was once the target of comedy, the bailiwick of aging performers like Phyllis Diller and Joan Rivers, who made mawkish fun of themselves for their surgical habits, the subject is increasingly a platform upon which popular culture is built. And the sirens singing its praises are getting younger and younger.

Cosmetic plastic surgery has inspired reality programs like *Extreme Makeover,* in which civilians with big ears or low self-esteem spend six weeks under the care of a plastic surgeon, a physical trainer, a hairdresser, a makeup artist, and a team of stylists. The program, according to the original press releases from ABC, offers the participants "a truly Cinderella-like experience by changing their looks completely in an effort to transform their lives and destinies and to make their dreams come true." In many cases, the patients undergo as many as half a dozen operations at a time. At the conclusion of each episode, the patients—after six weeks of surgery, recovery, weight training, and styling—are presented to their families, who typically sit waiting in a dimly lit restaurant or, if the hometown isn't big enough to have a fern-and-brass-rails restaurant, an enthusiastically draped municipal hall.

Typically, as the camera sweeps over the family members, viewers can see they are for the most part a saggy-eyed, double-chinned, well-padded group that pretty fairly represents the aging, ever-widening average American. The velvet curtains then rustle. The camera plays on a skittish pair of high heels, perhaps tracing tantalizingly up a liposculpted leg. The patient emerges from behind the curtains, looking entirely different. In most cases, better. Different, yes. Extremely made over? Hallelujah.

The show's participants are routinely humiliated as they enter the pupa stage of their metamorphosis. One man, a deejay for a Seattle radio station, "has a face for radio," according to *Extreme Makeover*'s voice-over. Two twins confess that one was always prettier largely because she had the benefit of braces while the other was dentally abandoned by their parents. Caroline, the twin with the snaggle teeth, weeps as she stares in the mirror and says, "I see a skinny, smushed-up-teeth person." The pretty twin, Cat, we also learn, broke Caroline's nose when they were children—hence the twisted hump on it.

The term *self-esteem* is a mantra that is repeated, yogilike, throughout the episodes. Through it all, there is never a question that the beautiful is good, a way to convey the true identity of the soul underneath, lost behind pounds of fat, submerged by a life-time of bad habits. Being beautiful is the final path to confidence and to the life that ought to have been lived for so many years. Ugliness is bad, the mark of missed potential, an all-encompassing failure to show off the true identity of the living person beneath. As the "ugly" twin, Caroline, says before her surgery, "I can't be who I am." And as Dan, with the face for radio, says after a chin implant is snuggled into his jawline, "I have the face of an action hero!"

Unfortunately, *Extreme Makeover* doesn't always end happily. In late 2005, a Texas woman, Deleese Williams, sued the program for $1 million, claiming among other things that the abrupt cancellation of her appearance on the program led to her sister's death. Ms. Williams claimed that she came to Los Angeles to be a contestant on the show after undergoing a series of medical exams to determine if her crooked teeth and droopy eyes could be fixed and her small breasts enhanced, according to the suit filed in Los Angeles Superior Court. One doctor promised her a "smile like Cindy Crawford."

To prepare for the show, the producers sent a crew to Texas in January 2004 to interview Williams and her family. Williams claimed that the crew manipulated her sister, Kellie, into making cruel statements about her looks. The night before Williams was to begin her makeover, the show's producers told her it would take too long for work on her jaw to heal. They canceled her appearance and sent her home, where Kellie, distraught over what she had said about her sister, eventually killed herself, according to the suit. (The network argued that Williams failed to allege sufficient facts to support her case. In October 2006, Ms. Williams was awarded £275,000 in damages.)

Extreme Makeover crystallizes in prime time the belief that our looks and our notions of self-esteem are matters of life and death and that change should not stop short of complete transformation. No longer is a makeover reserved for something as puny and inconsequential as your mere buttocks, your dimpled thighs, your pockmarked face, or your sparse eyelashes. The American makeover is a process that in our colloquial language now refers to a life overhaul. In the summer of 2003, when the UPN reality program *America's Next Top Model* crowned twenty-year-old Adrianne Curry of Joliet, Illinois, as the winner, *People* magazine wrote that she had "[scored] a life makeover."[2] Lives, careers, families, homes—they are no longer changed, or nosed into a new direction. They are made over.

Dramatic television programs like FX's *Nip/Tuck* aspire to do for plastic surgeons what *L.A. Law* did for lawyers or what *CSI* has done for forensic technicians: hold them up to the glittering prism of Hollywood, which will render their lives more complex and interesting, vaulting them from civilians with mere medical degrees to God-like technicians charged with the creation of all that is beautiful, youthful, and sexual.

On its program *Plastic Surgery: Before and After*, the Discovery Health channel regularly broadcasts cosmetic surgical procedures like liposuction, which highlight the violence done to the human body and, from a viewer's point of view, are as irresistible as a bloody pileup on the side of the highway. Here, however, instead of a possible glimpse of other human beings' blood, you are guaranteed the sight of their viscera. It's better than seeing them naked! Coupled with your own satisfaction (which is never uttered aloud, of course) at the humiliating "before" shot of their sagging buttocks is the assurance that yours can't be that bad—although maybe they could use a little work.

And indeed, liposuction—the suctioning of subcutaneous fat through a cannula inserted and manipulated with varying degrees of intensity beneath the skin and between layers of muscle—is bloody and visceral, an operation that combines skill with vigorous physical strength. One New York plastic surgeon told me that on the days she has liposuction procedures on her schedule, she knows she will burn thousands of calories and so doesn't bother going to the gym.

The plots of cop shows like *Law & Order* have relied on Botox as a murder weapon. The confessions of celebrities to the work they have had done on themselves are now a staple of the *People* magazine genre. In 2003, the comic actress Kathy Griffin spoke with *People* about how, despite suffering potentially fatal complications from liposuction in 1999, she decided to go for the whole enchilada in 2003, when she was forty-two. She got a nose job, a brow lift, veneers on twenty of her teeth, an acid peel, and liposuction on her waist and arms. (And a Japanese hair-straightening procedure that cost $400 and made her look like Morticia Addams.)

"I work in an industry where if you don't get a little nip and tuck, a lady of my age is going to end up playing Katie Holmes's great-grandmother in the *Dawson's Creek* reunion," Griffin said.[3] The total for Griffin's procedures would have been about $40,900, but she got what the magazine called "a celebrity discount"—the celebrity gets free or discounted work, and the doctor gets his or her name in the paper.

The mania for what those in the business refer to as "enhancement technologies" has fast spread far beyond the surgical specialty. In the case of Griffin, the veneers on her teeth alone, provided by Dr. Kourosh Maddahi, would have cost about $30,000. Dentists promote the rejuvenating effects of Chiclet-white designer smiles. Dr. Larry Rosenthal, a dentist in Manhattan, boasts of his celebrity clients and speaks of his "face-lift for your smile." Dr. Jeff Golub-Evans, another Manhattan dentist, gives interviews in which he refers to himself as a "smile designer." After all, at prices that can reach $20,000 or $30,000 a mouth, wouldn't you call yourself "designer"—a word with intimations of artistry—rather than "dentist," with its suggestion of braces, saliva, canker sores, and gum disease?

As for dentists, they're now lobbying for the right to do breast implants. Dermatologists, once relegated to the less glamorous world of acne and plantar warts and sebaceous cyst aspiration, practice liposuction. Ear, nose, and throat doctors eschew strep throat in favor of face-lifts and eye tucks. Gastroenterologists perform tummy tucks and liposuction.

It's not just legal but much more lucrative. Dr. Morris Barocas's Web site for Esthetique, "Long Island's premier center for cosmetic enhancement," reports that he is an "active member of the International Society of Cosmetic Laser Surgeons, a Fellow of the American Society for Laser Medicine and Surgery and is

Board Certified." The two organizations are not recognized by the American Board of Medical Specialties. But Barocas is board certified—just not in plastic surgery. His board certifications were handed down by the boards of internal medicine and gastroenterology. He has performed hundreds of liposuction operations, each doubtless providing a generous fee, although in 2002 one of his patients was admitted to a hospital—one at which he would not be allowed to perform liposuction because he is not board certified in plastic surgery—because of life-threatening complications. There has been no finding of negligence by Dr Barocas to date.[4]

Yet an industry that used to be reserved for the wealthy, white, famous, and female has now largely become safer—when procedures are performed by doctors with appropriate training—and much more affordable. Dr. Alan Matarasso, a plastic surgeon in New York City and a spokesperson for the American Society for Aesthetic Plastic Surgery, told the *Economist* in 2003, "Ten years ago, you could reconstruct a woman's breast for $12,000. Now it can be done for $600."[5]

Reconstruction, of course, is something that takes place after a woman has had cancer or an accident or is somehow disfigured. Yes, an insurance company might reimburse a surgeon $600 for reconstructing a woman's breast for medically valid reasons. But elective cosmetic surgery to augment a woman's breasts? In New York or Los Angeles, you're not getting out the door of a reputable surgeon's office for less than a few thousand dollars.

Nevertheless, Americans are willing to fork over the money, even if that means putting the surgery on a credit card or borrowing from a so-called beauty bank—an agency that loans money to cosmetic surgery patients who are willing to pay interest rates that make the Mafia's vig look like a great deal. More than two-thirds of Americans who now choose elective cosmetic surgery make less than $50,000 a year.

It is no accident that elective cosmetic surgery is a subject of such fascination and popularity in America today. Several tidal-force factors have collided, and their confluence has promoted a kind of golden age of cosmetic surgery. Make that the golden age in the Wild West. Every cowboy in a ten-gallon white hat is matched by a preening huckster, a snake-oil salesman, and a reckless practitioner. And for every person who is satisfied with the way he or she looks, there are just as many who are obsessed, who will stop at little to look younger, to feel anointed, to be beautiful.

Two

Surgery Safari

Claudia Lowe, a bubbly professor of physical geography, lives in Fullerton, California, a small city in Orange County about an hour's drive from Los Angeles. Lowe, who in her mid-fifties has the air of a zaftig blond Annette Funicello, looked in the mirror on a sunny spring day and decided she was unsatisfied with her looks, with her life.

So Lowe decided to embark on that most romantic odyssey of self-discovery: the African safari.

For many Americans, the word *safari*—Swahili for "journey"—evokes the most idealized, gauzy version of adventure. The mind conjures up a panorama of images and emotions ready for Ralph Lauren: crisp foreign accents, exotic locations, Hemingwayesque voyages of exploration and triumph, of spirituality and raw animal passion. Lowe, entranced by the fantasy, enlisted a girlfriend to go with her to South Africa, home to the 37,000-acre Kruger National Park, and Botswana, to the Okavango Delta in the Kalahari Desert and the Chobe National Park.

During the course of their trip, Lowe and her friend—who

did not want to be identified, so I will refer to her as "B."—would come face to face with what is known in safari parlance as the Big Five (lion, leopard, elephant, rhino, and buffalo), tour the countryside in a Nissan 4x4 (accompanied by attendants with Dakota 76 rifles, designed to penetrate the almost inch-thick hides of elephant and rhino), sleep in deluxe lodges as wild animals lulled them to sleep with their lonely calls, and enjoy the breathtaking natural splendor of a largely unspoiled and unpolluted continent.

And, at the same time, they would get cut-rate face-lifts, liposuction, and tummy tucks. The women weren't just going to see wild animals. They were going on a surgery safari.

"I guess it's a kind of modern adventure," Lowe told me several weeks before she left Los Angeles for Johannesburg.

To be sure. The tour and surgeries, arranged by an enterprising South African marketing executive named Lorraine Melvill— her company is called Surgeon & Safari—would cost them each about $12,000. The price would include round-trip airfare from Los Angeles, a stay at the four-star Westcliff hotel in Johannesburg, consultations with doctors, surgeries, anesthesia, hospital stays, medication, transportation to a game reserve, accommodations at the game reserve for a week, protection from wild animals at the game reserve, meals, painkillers, and a limo back to the airport. It sure sounded like a bargain, considering that a business-class ticket to Johannesburg from Los Angeles alone costs about $11,070.

Lowe was no stranger to the South African surgery experience. A year earlier, she had visited for the express purpose of having liposuction after reading an article in the *Los Angeles Times*. She had liposuction on her midsection and thighs, as well as a tummy tuck. Dr. Rick van der Poel, a U.S.-trained South African who with his tanned good looks and graciously graying temples has the air of a soap-star doctor, was her surgeon.

"He is marvelous," she said. "He is very personable and precise. He is very conservative about the amount of surgery he will do. And it's a private hospital so it is incredibly clean."

Her friend B. had also gone to South Africa the previous year for liposuction, a mini tummy tuck, and a breast reduction. B., who is in her sixties, was hooked.

"I wanted the face-lift this year," B. told me on the telephone from California.

"And I thought, well, if she's going back, I might as well go back and do something, get a touch-up," Lowe said.

Lowe was planning on having liposuction around her midsection again—some of the fat had crept back, she explained, and "the fat comes back to where the fat cells are, but not to where the fat cells aren't," so the overall effect was dimpled, rumpled flesh, not smooth, tight curves. She was also going to have liposuction on her back and buttocks. And she was going to have a bit of loose skin on her upper abdomen tightened. And this time, they were stopping in Botswana on their way to Johannesburg. When B. was fifty-five, Lowe told me, she had bungee jumped off the Zambezi Bridge at Victoria Falls, the waterfall between Zambia to the north and Zimbabwe and Botswana to the south that is approximately twice as wide and twice as deep as Niagara Falls.

"And by God, if she did that at fifty-five, well, I have to, too," she said.

The notion of complications didn't bother them, nor my suggestion that bungee jumping might undo some of the effects of B.'s previous surgery, nor the fact that South Africa has one of the highest AIDS infection rates in the world. Rather than be put off by notions of unknown African medications—consider African-grade Botox, I said, joking—Lowe reacted with enthusiasm. "African Botox," she said with a wistful sigh. "I'll never wrinkle again."

I hesitated before asking them if the poverty in South Africa—the per capita gross domestic product is less than $2,400 a year—would bother them. Wouldn't they feel like classic ugly Americans flying into a poor country with bags of money so that they could take advantage of the region's cheap surgery—which the actual citizens could never afford—to be beautified? But both agreed that as distasteful as it might feel to be a relatively rich American taking advantage of cheap cosmetic surgery, from an economic standpoint what they were doing could be seen as good samaritanship. After all, although in New York or Los Angeles the fee they paid wouldn't buy anyone much in the way of cosmetic surgery, it would be a welcome cash infusion into the desperately poor South African economy.

Lowe felt neither ethical nor medical qualms about traveling to South Africa for the procedures. From her previous experience, she had total confidence in the level of care she would receive. In fact, in some ways she found the care superior to the kind of treatment she could expect to receive at home. In the United States, she complained, surgeons wanted you out of the hospital or out of their offices the same day, to be offloaded onto spouses or friends, without an adequate supply of painkillers. It was a comfort to be able to stay for as long as you felt necessary in a private hospital where professionals administered heavy narcotic medication and the nurses had been trained in exquisite, soothing bedside manners.

The year before, when B. had also joined her for cosmetic surgery, she wanted to stay in the hospital an extra night or two. "And it was not a decision that was going to cost thousands of dollars. I think it cost $38, or maybe $78. And they take care of you so well. You get all the drugs you want."

I looked down at the notes I had scribbled on a yellow legal pad. Elephants. Safari. Adventure. Beauty. Bungee jumping. African-grade Botox. And then I flipped through my date book. I had no choice but to join them.

X   X   X

In 2005, Americans spent several billions of dollars on cosmetic surgery, a figure that includes only fees for surgeons and none of the attendant costs like hospital stays, postoperative garments, medications, anesthesiologists, camouflaging makeup, nursing care. But a growing number of Americans, attracted by the cheap prices and adventure, are choosing to take plastic surgery vacations outside the United States. Honduras, Jamaica, Brazil, Malaysia, and dozens of other countries offer tailored package trips.

Most cosmetic surgery patients recuperate at home, waiting until all traces of their procedures have healed. Even those patients who are open about having undergone cosmetic surgery tend to stay out of view. The surgery safari offers other practical benefits: rather than remain sequestered at home post-op, why not enjoy a vacation? Even better, when colleagues ask suspiciously why one looks so rested, patients can simply answer with the easy alibi: "There's nothing like the fresh air and vigorous exercise of the high veld to reinvigorate the body and soul."

Medical tourism first became popular in the 1970s, when inexpensive and widely available air travel intersected with deflating foreign currencies. (In the case of South Africa, the value of the rand plunged after apartheid ended, making access to the country's medical care even cheaper.) Just as some plastic surgeons are known for their breasts or noses, certain countries became known for their surgical specialties. In Brazil, it's liposuction. In Thailand, the most popular tourist procedure is gender reassignment surgery (known to the British, who invent jaunty colloquialisms for such things, as "topping and tailing"). During the Asian financial crisis of the late 1990s, as beds in Thai hospitals emptied of local patients, Thai hospitals began to aggressively market themselves abroad. Despite the tsunami of 2004, the country is still a popular destination for those seeking sex change operations as well as cosmetic plastic surgery.

And despite what seem like unnecessary risks, clinics around the world report increasing numbers of medical tourists each year. In Costa Rica, a favorite of foreigners is Dr. Arnoldo Fournier, who told a newspaper reporter of the benefits of surgery there: "We are a peaceful place, we do not have an army. We are home to roughly 4 percent of all flora and fauna on the Earth. We have seven volcanoes."[1] In Jamaica, patients can go to Dr. Z. Paul Lorenc, a well-respected surgeon whose headquarters are on Park Avenue in New York. In his Jamaican practice, far from the legal purview of the Food and Drug Administration, he can try out more experimental procedures. He also hosts "Botox weekends" at the Half Moon Club.

Most American plastic surgeons think the risks of such trips hardly outweigh the savings. Flying long distances by airplane shortly after surgery dramatically increases the likelihood that a patient will develop deep-vein thrombosis, says Dr. Alan Matarasso, a spokesperson for the American Society for Aesthetic Plastic Surgery. Deep-vein thrombosis is a blood clot that develops in the large veins in the leg. The major risk factors for developing a DVT describe a surgery tour to a T: spending lengthy periods in a sedentary position, undergoing surgery lasting longer than thirty minutes, and undertaking any kind of airplane travel. A clot in the deep veins of the upper leg can break off and travel to a lung, causing pulmonary embolism, cardiac arrest, and death. (During the Iraqi war, the condition was blamed for the death of David Bloom, an NBC reporter who spent several days cramped in a tank with soldiers.)

"Why would you go surfing in Coney Island if you live in Malibu?" Dr. Steven A. Teitelbaum of Los Angeles asked me. It sounds terrifically romantic to go on safari or go to the Caribbean to have some work done, but surgeons argue that there's a higher risk of infection, the possibility of thrombosis on the flight back, and zero chance for appropriate follow-up care. And patients don't get to sit by the side of the pool and drink mai tais while a bronzed pool boy gives massages. "You can't sit in the sun," Teitelbaum said. "It's stupid to fly. You can't drink. You'd wind up sitting in a hotel room watching cable. And then what happens if you have complications? Who do you call? Room service? 'Hello, I'd like some eggs Benedict and I'm in terrible pain'?"

X

X   X

X

The flight to Johannesburg from New York is surprisingly easy. We leave at dinnertime on Friday night and arrive at 2:00 p.m. the next afternoon after fourteen hours in the air. Further easing my journey is a five-milligram tablet of Ambien, which I take after dinner. I am not a nervous flier, but I can never get comfortable on planes, and the idea of spending fourteen hours in one room, watching an endless loop of bad movies and reruns of the *CBS Evening News* while trying to do yoga in the hallways outside the bathroom, feels like a criminal sentence. I sleep for an alarmingly comalike nine hours and arrive at lunchtime in South Africa.

On Saturday afternoon, I wander the hotel, which is set up high on a hill overlooking Johannesburg. Behind the main building, an infinity pool disappears into the horizon. On the patio, a pair of stationary binoculars set on a steel pole is trained on the elephants in the center of the two-hundred-acre Johannesburg Zoo. From the patio, their brayings and loud grunts are distant but audible. Hotel guests, however, are discouraged from walking to the zoo, the entrance of which is half a mile away. Much too dangerous, Alwynn, the cordial concierge, tells me. Too many criminals on the street.

At 6:00, I knock on the door of Lowe's hotel cottage. Over a glass of South African burgundy, she and B. talk excitedly about the coming surgical events. B., who keeps her hair in a very short crew cut, points to a spot about three inches above each ear.

"I'll have to grow my hair longer for a bit, because there will be scars right about here," she says. With stitches, she explains, you get lingering bold white stripes on the scalp. The two women speak of surgery as if it were old hat to them, tossing around jargon and phrases most people only hear doctors utter.

Lorraine Melvill has invited us for dinner. At 8:00 p.m., we arrive at her white Spanish-style house behind electric gates in a wealthy neighborhood. The house is called Manderley, after the house in *Rebecca*. Melvill is in her early forties, with a cap of brunette hair, a generous-sized nose, and a full poitrine. For dinner, she serves pasta with caviar, roast chicken with raisins and nuts, full yeasty loaves of bread, and side plates heavy with cheese. For dessert, there is a Camembert served with honey-sweetened watermelon rind and figs. And bread pudding. With cream.

"Made with eggs and cream and raisins and apricot jam and topped with double-thick cream," Melvill says as she places the pudding on the table. The guests wash down dinner with several bottles of South African burgundy. Someone passes a joint. The conversation hurtles from politics in Zimbabwe to American imperialism to Madonna to why the women on *Sex and the City* wear such expensive shoes.

"If they came to South Africa, they would never spend $500 on a pair of shoes again," says a man who grew up in a small town outside Johannesburg. But his wife quickly points out that she has known poor black residents of Johannesburg to go without food in favor of an expensive pair of Italian leather shoes.

Madonna seems to be the topic of conversation that fans the most flames. America is an up-by-your-bootstraps kind of a place, where self-invention and self-creation are signals of the meritocracy, where you get where you're going with hard work, craftiness, and charm. And what's better than self-invention? Reinvention. The ability to exchange one identity, as soon as it is the slightest bit threadbare, for the next. In 2000, you could have asked any fashion editor at almost any women's magazine in any city in the world who the most influential woman in fashion was and the response would have always been the same: Madonna. "She's so creative." "She is a genius of reinvention." She was a postpunk, a sarcastic socialite, a Brenda-Frazier-meets-Marilyn-Monroe debutante, a hippie, a Zen yoga goddess, a Kabbala-practicing Jew, a Catholic, a virgin, the class slut, a home girl, a British faux aristocrat, a space cowgirl. But by 2004, Madonna's long run of reinvention had become a kind of tired manic cycling. The editors and fashionistas and gay men who had worshipped her were now calling her by her newer, matronly sobriquet, "Madge." The dampness of English life had softened her image from a trenchant crystal-sharp edge to a hazy, less easily defined texture. She was no longer a hard body. Her movies were bombs. And—ick!—the awful, pretentious English accent.

"Do you know what happened to Madonna?" asks one of Melvill's guests, a middle-aged South African doctor. "She turned forty." Suddenly, he explains, her allotment for self-transformation was up. "It's as if the culture says, okay, now you're middle-aged, even old, and you must remain stable, in one identity, until you're in the ground." His words hang over the table. The joint goes around again. Except for the occasional hissing sound of someone sucking in marijuana smoke, the room is silent.

Lowe breaks the spell.

"Gee, that's a downer," she says.

The morning after dinner, she and B. prepare for their surgery. Melvill picks them up and whisks them off to Dr. van der Poel's. While "the girls," as Melvill affectionately calls them, have surgery, Melvill has arranged for me to visit the Entabeni Game Preserve. Entabeni is popular with the surgery safari crowd because it is one of the few game resorts in a malaria-free zone—one less shot and potential drug interaction, not to mention the disease itself, to worry about.

One of the hotel drivers, Ignatius Ndlozu, and I get into a Mercedes-Benz. Entabeni, and the Lakeside Lodge, is about two and a half hours away by car. A woman named K., swathed in bandages and a wide elastic chin strap, will be driving with us. K. explains politely that she is on some heavy narcotics and will be napping shortly. Five minutes from the hotel, K. nods off to sleep, her bandaged head lolling to one side like a doll's, her hands clasped demurely over the purse in her lap. Her mouth slides open to one side and remains that way for most of the trip.

K.'s travel so early in the recovery process is not necessarily encouraged by Surgeon & Safari, but she was on a tighter schedule than most.

As the Mercedes begins to muscle its way out of the city, it is becoming clear that very little postsurgical healing could be accomplished on such a journey. The Westcliff hotel has a fleet of Mercedes-Benz sedans, which sounds luxurious until you realize that Mercedes-Benz shock absorbers are no match for even the most accommodating of African roads. Ndlozu manages to keep his center of gravity heavy, but I feel sloshed around the car and keep reaching for a snort from my Vicks Vapo Inhaler to keep from vomiting. K. is asleep, a silvery thread of saliva working its way down her chin, her head bobbing back and forth.

After two hours, the sun has set. Ndlozu's face turns cloudy when I ask him if there's a rest stop anywhere close by. Trucks laden with cargo are roaring past us.

"Mmmmmm," he says, rubbing a finger over his lips in thought. We rumble to a stop just off the highway in front of a truck stop. K. moans and holds a hand to her face.

"You can go there." Ndlozu gestures to a yellow building with two doors. I am not a queasy person, but even my sturdy traveling mettle is tested by the room that others might describe as a bathroom but I consider more of a room-sized petri dish of biochemical sludge. The floor is inch-deep in a brackish microbial biosphere, the mucuslike sheen of which is interrupted only by brown and green chunks of—something. I don't want to look too closely. I back out the door, hand over mouth. But I'm stuck: nature is howling. If this were the United States, I would run around behind the building and squat in the bushes. But I am unfamiliar with the territory and uncomfortable with the possibility that there are predatory animals roaming in the dark lot behind the truck stop. I am hung over from the oceans of burgundy Melvill served at dinner, and jet-lagged, too, so my judgment isn't as clear as I'd like it to be. Are there criminal penalties for public urination? Will I be arrested and have my hands cut off if I am caught peeing in public?

Like a drunk heaving over the toilet bowl after a bender, I lavishly promise God that if I don't contract a scrofulous infection, I will never travel without Purell hand wipes ever again. And then I step into the void.

Here, strong thigh muscles are useful.

Fifteen minutes later, we are jouncing down a dirt road and I am wondering how postoperative patients can handle such a trip.

Ndlozu takes a few minutes to give me some pointers on driving safely in the bush. For example, don't hit an animal, because if you injure it, it will attack. But how do you see them, I ask, if it's night and there are no street lights?

"Their eyes will reflect," he says.

There is more: "Never honk at an elephant, because it will consider it a challenge."

Understood. Ndlozu pulls the car to a stop and gets out.

"You must come and see the stars," he says. I am terrified of what lies outside the safety of the car. I open the window and stick my head out, then venture forth. The sky is blacker than any night sky I have ever seen, punctuated with stars, each heavy with a pure, almost blue light. Yes, I think to myself, raising my arms heavenward and inhaling the cool clean air, this is peaceful. Despite the car ride, the nausea, the truck stop, the anxiety, I could be healed here, underneath this sky.

Suddenly, there is a sound, a whining, spectral howling that sets off pin-pricks of electricity down my spine. Ndlozu gets back in the car and tells me not to worry.

"A jackal will not eat you unless it is very desperate," he explains.

He may be joking, but my nerves are stretched. I am terrified— and ashamed of myself for being terrified. The road has gotten bumpier, and the car's wheels grind over rocks the size of Wonder Bread loaves. K.'s moans are now interspersed with tiny cries. Her meds are wearing off.

"We will be there soon," Ndlozu announces cheerfully into the rearview mirror. "Very soon."

And then we see it, lit up with stark halide lights: a sign that would strike fear into the heart of any man or woman who had just had extremely delicate facial surgery and was ready for another round of painkillers.

"Warning," the sign reads. "22 speed bumps ahead."

The next fifteen minutes are a symphony of thumps, as the car humps and dips over speed bumps, and K.'s wheezing squeals, which sound like the shee-shee-shee breathing of a woman in Lamaze class.

As beautiful as the countryside is, I cannot imagine jostling fifty kilometers over gravel roads two or even three days after a face-lift. We pull up, mercifully, finally, to the entrance. Ndlozu brings our bags to the front hallway of the lodge, a large, exquisite building on Lake Entabeni. He utters one more piece of wisdom in parting: "Lock your room when you go to breakfast or the monkeys will get in and take your things."

K. wobbles to her feet. Her cheeks are swollen, and her surgical topknot has slid to one side.

She utters her first word in two hours, one of her eyes slitting open quizzically. A silver tear of ooze shines at the top of her swollen cheek.

"Monkeys?" she says.

Traveling great distances for cosmetic surgery has its risks, but often the greatest risk is still the surgery itself. The most recent high-profile case of a surgery excursion gone wrong was the death of the Nigerian first lady, Stella Obasanjo, who died after having cosmetic surgery at a clinic on Spain's Costa del Sol, a region of Europe known best for its popularity as a playground for B-list celebrities, Arab potentates, and dignitaries from the developing world. Spain has the highest number of plastic surgeons per capita in Europe, and in recent years the Costa del Sol has become a hot spot for Europeans seeking cosmetic surgery; it is now home to dozens of rejuvenation centers, including the Molding Center, the one at which Obasanjo, fifty-nine, underwent liposuction and a tummy tuck.

The clinic is among the more luxurious looking of these centers, housed in a vast neoclassical building fronted by towering palm trees in one of the more expensive parts of Puerto Banus, an upmarket district of Marbella. Among other procedures, it advertises a facial transformation called the "Molding Mask," which, according to the center's Web site, promises to turn back the clock "at least twenty years in the age of the skin." It does not specify further what exactly the treatment is, except to clarify that it is not merely exfoliation. Not a big help, in other words. A picture of a sad-looking woman with a droopy mouth and short hair appears in the "before" photo; a gorgeous, much younger-looking woman with a big smile on her face, pink skin, and long hair appears in the "after" photo.

The clinic also offers ozone therapy, laser therapy, nutrition services, and treatment of urological disorders; it is also home to entities such as the Molding Spine Institute and the Molding Health Institute. Obasanjo underwent surgery on a Friday and at 3:00 a.m. Sunday morning was admitted, brain-dead, to a hospital in Marbella, although radio stations reported that her body was moved to the hospital after her death.

Obasanjo had become famous around the world after campaigning for the release of her husband, a former army general, who was jailed in the mid-1990s for allegedly plotting a coup. She received a number of human rights awards.

President Obasanjo received news of her death as he was dealing with a national tragedy, the aftermath of the crash of a Boeing 737 airliner that killed all 117 people aboard.

I meet Dr. van der Poel for a drink in the Polo Lounge bar at the Westcliff, which is a happening spot in Johannesburg. We sit in chairs sheathed in lizard leather, and a menu of drinks offers up caipirinhas, mojitos, daiquiris, a dizzying array of South African and French wine, and a dozen single-malt scotches. Charlayne Hunter-Gault, who made civil rights history as the first African American woman to graduate from the University of Georgia in 1962 and who later became national correspondent for the *MacNeil/Lehrer NewsHour* on PBS, walks in with her husband and they stop to chat. (They live in Johannesburg.) Dr. van der Poel wears the uniform of 1980s New York money: a blue blazer, a yellow power tie, and a gold Rolex. His hair is slick and combed back.

Dr. van der Poel interned in New York and in Brazil and knows all the old-time cosmetic surgery players. He has been in private practice in South Africa since 1989 and describes the flourishing of the cosmetic surgery industry as the result of first world medicine at third world prices, made available to international tourists once apartheid was lifted. His patients, he says, are now mostly Europeans and Americans, and the Americans want everything.

"They're the ones I have to convince to cut down on the number of procedures," he says. "They come here and want everything done, from head to toe."

While South Africa has been victim to one of the continent's worst medical brain drains, with doctors fleeing to markets where they can make more money, such as the United States, Dr. van der Poel has decided to stay.

"Do you know what it costs to have a life in New York?" he says over his glass of white wine. "I'd have to make millions of dollars there to live the way I live here. I'd never be able to afford it."

Four days after their surgery, Lowe and B. were up and about. Considering the number of procedures they had had, they looked incredibly good. B's face-lift seemed a little tight, but I guessed that after the swelling it would relax a bit. Lowe looked thinner and more streamlined—although the streamlining effect may have come more from the compression garment she was wearing to prevent bulging and dimpling of the remaining fat. We met to say good-bye on the porch of the Westcliff, where a photographer was taking pictures of a model in wedding dresses. The day was fair and sunny, and Lowe and B. were on their way to go shopping at a local mall in Johannesburg. Their procedures had gone spectacularly well, Lowe said, although there was, of course, some swelling and some residual fogginess from the anesthesia.

"In terms of recovering, that's the part that slows you down the most," she told me several months after she returned from the trip. "But in general the results were really good, and you don't actually see everything until about six months later."

The next year, Lowe and B. returned to Dr. van der Poel for a third time, for another touch-up. Lowe wanted a little more lipo on the back. She hates back fat. And she wanted Dr. van der Poel to do a little breast lift, with a bit of an augmentation.

Dr. van der Poel told her he wouldn't do it.

"He looked at me, and said, 'I won't do it.' He said, 'I won't put you under for that surgery,' " she told me. " 'Your breasts are great for your age, and the scarring wouldn't be worth it. Forget about it.' So I had some laser work on my legs for veins and got the Botox and the Restylane and all that stuff, which I just seem too lazy to get when I'm home."

Dr. van der Poel, it appeared, had reached his saturation level with Lowe.

"I think there's a limit to what he will do, and now that I've seen him three years in a row, I have reached that limit," she said.

Lowe is insistent that she could use some more work. Even after three visits in three years for major surgery?

"I've gotten a little fat," she told me in 2005. "Put on a little weight. And you know, he won't do any more lipo on me. Don't get me wrong, the places he took the weight off I look great. I'd like to go to a spa, but I want to eat gourmet food, you know, and walk around in the outdoors, not sit in some room doing Pilates." She pronounced the word like the constellation Pleiades. Plee-AH-dees.

But they are already planning a return to South Africa—their fourth visit in four years.

"Not for any surgery," Lowe said. "Just for a vacation. Like regular, normal tourists."

Three

The Rise and Fall and Rise and Fall of Botox

It's a crisp spring day in New York City just after Easter. The green heads of tulips are nosing up through the flower beds in the center of Park Avenue. The air is fresh and sweet and seems to whisper promises to everyone passing by: Your sins have been washed away. Slates are wiped clean. On a beautiful day like today, everyone has a chance to have a new beginning. I remark as much to my companion, who readily agrees—with a caveat.

"That is," says my companion, Robert, on this balmy afternoon, "everyone who has an extra couple grand lying around has a chance at a new beginning. Aren't we lucky?"

An attorney in his fifties, Robert is on his way to see Dr. Michelle Copeland, a plastic surgeon whose office is just across from the Metropolitan Museum of Art on Fifth Avenue. Robert is wearing a navy blue suit with chalk stripes, a crisp white shirt, and a lavender tie in the kind of thick silk that puckers up off the chest a bit. It is the stylized cravat of a maître d' at a very expensive restaurant, or of a chief executive on his way to trial.

For Robert, the notion of new beginnings and clean slates starts with one word, Botox, and Botox goes for several hundred dollars a shot. And several shots make up one treatment. And several shots mean a face that is as smooth and unlined as a block of marble. Which is what he wants.

In Robert's case, the expense is even more formidable. Robert, who believes that his professional success is linked to his imperturbable, placid-looking gaze, testament to his (no doubt) steely nerve and unshakeable confidence, goes more often than most Botox aficionados—the casual users—who get a dose of Botox once or twice a year.

Copeland is just one of several plastic surgeons and dermatologists Robert sees every two or three months. He does what habitual drug users of other stripes do when they've got a jones: they "double-dip," or make trips to two, three, or even four doctors so that their prescriptions can be reupped far beyond what most medical professionals would consider necessary, or good, for you. When he goes to see Copeland, he tells her he hasn't gotten any Botox since he last saw her six months ago. In truth, he went for Botox just eight weeks ago, at the office of Dr. Dennis Gross, a dermatologist in midtown.

He pays about $10,000 a year for the injections. Each visit—and he goes about six times a year—costs him about $1,800.

Botox is the commercial name in the United States for the neurotoxin botulinum toxin A. During World War II, the United States military, operating out of Fort Detrick, Maryland, investigated whether or not botulinum would be a viable chemical weapon. And during the 1980s and 1990s, botulinum toxin was a key part of Iraq's biological weapons cache.

But Robert is one of the many who see the danger commingling with the promise of beauty and succumb. A self-described Botox junkie, Robert had been introduced to me a decade earlier, in the mid 1990s, when I first wrote about the new cult popularity of Botox among well-to-do, age-anxious New Yorkers. At the time, he was just forty-two and had already been getting injections of Botox for several years. Botox had not been approved by the Food and Drug Administration for cosmetic use. Back then, his face was as unlined as a baby's, smooth and round and capped with a topping of wavy blond hair. Ten years later, his plump cheeks have shallowed with age, and the hair, which is slightly darker, has just begun to recede into the familiar horseshoe shape of male-pattern baldness. But his skin is still smooth and unlined, almost slack.

He pats his cheeks.

"I look good, don't I?" he says.

Botox has become a staple for television talking heads, ladies who lunch, affluent professionals and actors who refuse to age. Before it was approved in 2001 by the FDA for use in paralyzing wrinkles between the eyebrows, and without a whisper of promotion, it had already became the most popular cosmetic medical procedure in the country. More than 1 million people tried Botox in 2000, according to industry analysts. By 2004, that number had grown to somewhere around 8 million. Sales of Botox were $650 million in 2004. Allergan, the manufacturer, estimates that the company will have Botox sales of up to $840 million in 2005.

It has become a household word, ordained with definitions in the *Oxford English Dictionary* and *Merriam-Webster's*. When John Kerry ran for president in 2004, his campaign was dogged by rumors that he had used Botox to smooth his craggy forehead. He denied that he had ever tried Botox and in fact even said that he had never heard of the stuff. (One of Kerry's advisers told me in a confidential conversation after the election that Kerry had in all likelihood tried Botox. And he had certainly heard of it, considering his wife had given an interview to the *Washington Post* a year earlier in which she had freely admitted to using it. Her confession itself had caused a public relations headache for the Kerry campaign.)

Botox has become popular in Europe, Brazil, and the United States, according to the International Society of Aesthetic Plastic Surgery. In Germany, two doctors have even begun to chronicle the mania with which some patients lust for their Botox fix, calling the desire "botulinophilia." Not only has the public become fascinated by Botox, but so has the press. Here is a story with a ready-made if terribly clichéd conceit: a poison that promises pretty, a dangerous substance that delivers beauty. Countless editors at countless newspapers, women's magazines, and local news stations thought up the headline "Pretty Poison."

During the early years of Botox's popularity, Hollywood directors like Martin Scorsese and Baz Luhrmann complained about its use among actors, whose faces are often robbed of emotional expression. When I spoke to Luhrmann, he would not name any specific actresses, but later that year I met Nicole Kidman.[1] There has for some time been much debate in the press about Kidman's use of Botox, which she has always chosen to ignore. On meeting her, I found her face was smooth and flawless, which I expected. But her forehead was fascinating: it was absolutely motionless, except for an area right in the center about one square inch in diameter, where a tiny wrinkle writhed and wiggled like some sort of animated sea creature. For the record, Kidman has always been a critically respected actress and even if she has undertaken such procedures, it does not appear to have adversely affected her performances in any way.

In a variation on *The Stepford Wives*, it is now rare in certain social enclaves—the Upper East Side of Manhattan, Beverly Hills, Greenwich, Malibu, Dallas's Highland Park—to see a woman over the age of thirty-five with the ability to look angry. In some cases, it's easy to identify Botox abuse. There is the forehead that sits right on top of the eyebrows, a smooth slab of immutable muscle. And there is the classic telltale sign, what Dr. Michael Kane calls "bunny lines." "When so many muscles are overparalyzed," he told the *New York Observer*, the Botox recipient begins to rely on "the unusual muscles on the sides of his nose, making those little scrunchy lines on his nose like a bunny."[2] (I'm not saying that Sarah Jessica Parker in the final few seasons of *Sex and the City* had overdone Botox, but she sure does have some bunnylike lines.) No actress better exemplifies Botox abuse than Marcia Cross (although Ms Cross has never publicly discussed the use of such treatments), who plays the brittle, perfectionist Bree Van De Kamp on *Desperate Housewives*: her forehead and cheeks are as smooth and inanimate as those on a Kabuki mask. I watched her waxy face through an entire season of episodes and could not stop wondering why she looked so familiar. One night—perhaps it was the episode in which she discovers her husband has been having an affair with a hooker and still her face does not move—I hit upon why I was reminded of her. When I was fourteen years old, I visited the Soviet Union on a class trip. In Red Square, we begged our guide to let us visit Lenin's mausoleum to see the embalmed body. His face, I now realized, had the same level of animation and the same dull sheen as hers does. However, at the time, he had been dead for sixty years.

In a Botox treatment, a doctor injects a diluted form of the drug into a patient's facial muscles. Over the next few days, the toxin paralyzes the tiny muscles that control facial wrinkling, not only halting the development of more wrinkles but eradicating existing—so-called dynamic—ones. The skin does not feel numb to the patient, nor does it change in texture. Nor is there any significant risk of becoming infected with botulism—which causes respiratory failure and death in advanced cases—from Botox because the treatment is in so diluted a form. That is, if you're getting real Botox.

There is some skill involved in the injection process. Dr. Debra Jaliman, a dermatologist in New York, told me that in the hands of an unskilled doctor, Botox—which requires multiple pinprick injections with each treatment—can produce unsightly results.

"Sometimes, one eyebrow is up here and the other is down here," Jaliman said. "We had one patient who told us that she had to spend three weeks in the hospital on an IV because the doctor who injected her put the needle too deeply into her neck and she lost the ability to swallow," she said. "We had a soap opera actress who lost the ability to speak properly and had to go into hiding for three months."

There is Botox lore in every city. In Manhattan, a well-known executive at Condé Nast—the company that publishes *Vogue, Allure, Glamour,* and *The New Yorker,* among other magazines—began appearing at work with a pronounced droop to one side of her face. Her mouth sagged. Her eyelid was heavy. And the rumor mill churned: was it a "coke stroke"—a seizure caused by cocaine overuse that results in temporary nerve damage to muscles—or just bad Botox? The story circulated in gossip-column blind items and in Internet chat rooms for months, until the woman's face resumed a more normal cant. It had indeed been sloppy Botox work.

Some wealthy women begin getting Botox in their late teens and early twenties as a prophylactic measure. "This way, I'll never get wrinkles, ever," one twenty-three-year-old Ivy League graduate told me. "Plus, I can go tanning and not get wrinkly." She gets Botox three times a year in her forehead and around her eyes. Dr. Howard Sobel in New York explained to the *New York Observer* why he injected a nineteen-year-old with Botox: she was a model and some of her laugh lines were showing up in print. He also likes to inject patients in their twenties with a combination of Botox and the filler Restylane, so that lines and wrinkles are stopped before they are "etched," he said.[3]

The available assortment of prescribed treatments used by doctors to fill or correct wrinkles and pits is dizzying: AlloDerm, Autologen, Cymetra, Dermalogen, Fascian, Gore-Tex, Isolagen, Plasmagel, SoftForm, Zyderm, Zyplast, Hylaform, Restylane, Perlane, ReJuveness. But Botox remains the most popular, and most talked-about, by far.

Botox is manufactured by Allergan, the only company in the United States that is currently allowed by the FDA to market and sell botulinum toxin A. Fast on its heels is Reloxin, which was to be released by Inamed, the world's leading manufacturer of breast implants and a one-time competitor to Allergan. In the spring of 2006, however, Allergan announced a $3.2 billion bid to acquire

Inamed, making the combined entity the mother of all surgical beautification companies, and federal antitrust regulators forced Allergan to relinquish the rights to distribute Reloxin. The right to distribute the drug, now in advanced clinical trials with the Food and Drug Administration, will revert to its original license holder, a British company.[4]

(An Irish company, Elan Pharmaceuticals, manufactures a similar product, sold in the United States, that is derived from a variant of botulinum toxin. Known commercially as Myobloc, it enjoyed a brief stretch of popularity and media attention because it takes effect faster than Botox, but the shots are painful—like bee stings—and the results do not last as long. It never caught on with beauty consumers.)

Dr. Arnold Klein, a dermatologist in Beverly Hills made infamous by his association with Michael Jackson and the former actress turned Hollywood socialite Irena Medavoy, who sued him for allegedly overdosing her with Botox, told me that patients will do anything to stop wrinkles, and Botox is his preferred first line of defense. "You hear horror stories about doctors and nurses who fly into Miami and check into hotel rooms so that patients can see them for injections of an untested form of silicone," he said. "I'd so much rather use something that has been tested and is tried and true."[5]

Part of Botox's incredible popularity is that it is a cash cow for doctors. In 2005, doctors paid $488 for a vial; that one vial can generate revenue of up to $3,000. Because its use is a cosmetic procedure, there are no health insurance hassles to deal with. And it is time efficient: "You can do a patient in ten minutes, and you can run people in all day long," an analyst for the pharmaceutical industry told me.[6] "There is probably not another treatment that is so profitable for doctors." Any doctor—and in some states, dentists—can legally administer it.

For all its popularity, Botox—like so many other promising drugs that have been spectacularly well marketed—has had its share of setbacks.

In 1793, a German poet named Justinius Kerner—famous for setting his poems to music by Schumann and dabbling in medicine—deduced that a substance in spoiled sausages, which he called *Wurstgift* (German for "sausage poison"), caused botulism. The toxin was not identified until 1895, when Emile van Ermengem, a Belgian professor, isolated *Clostridium botulinum* after a group of people in a small Belgian village fell ill. He identified the sausages they had eaten at the buffet after a funeral as the source of their poisoning.

Sporadic outbreaks of botulism—the word comes from the Latin word for "sausage," *botulus*—in the United States occur after ingestion of meat products, preserved fish, and home-canned foods. (Remember when you believed that a dented Campbell's soup could mean its contents had botulism? They most likely didn't, and the idea was perhaps a remnant of your parents' or grandparents' childhood wisdom: a botulism scare in the 1930s almost annihilated America's canning industry.) The incubation period following ingestion is eighteen to thirty-six hours. In the United States, an average of about 110 cases of botulism are reported each year, according to statistics from the Centers for Disease Control. Of these, approximately 25 percent are food-borne. A large number of the cases, 72 percent, are infant botulism, which can occur when a baby ingests *Clostridium botulinum* bacteria, found in dirt and dust and occasionally in honey. These bacteria are typically harmless to older children and adults, whose mature digestive systems can move the bacteria through the body before they cause illness. In 2003, 86 cases of infant botulism were reported in the United States; none resulted in death.

The rest of the cases are wound botulism, which is frequently associated with intravenous drug use, mostly among heroin addicts. The worst recent case was in 2003, when a dozen black-tar heroin users in Washington State became infected; one person died.

Dying by botulism poisoning is an exquisite, excruciating torture. Because the botulinum toxin blocks the receptor sites for the neurotransmitter acetylcholine, which controls muscle contraction, muscles fail. Bodily functions go haywire. Bowels, otherwise held in check by constant physical contraction, open. The autonomic nervous system fails. Paralysis sets in, attacking from the cranial nerves on down, slowly, until the lungs stop working. The victim cannot breathe and, helpless, suffocates to death. Or, unable to breathe and panicking at the thought of death, suffers a fatal heart attack.

In 1946, Edward Schantz, a biochemist, purified the toxin into a crystalline form. In the 1970s, Dr. Alan Scott, an ophthalmologist, was conducting a study that involved research into squinting and pharmacological methods to stop it. He came into contact with Schantz and began testing botulinum toxin on the muscles around the eyes, called the extraocular muscles. By 1987, his work attracted the attention of a married pair of doctors in Canada, Alastair and Jean Carruthers. Jean Carruthers, an ophthalmologist, snuck some botulinum toxin into Canada and began to administer injections to patients with eye problems like uncontrollable tics and blinking. Then Alastair Carruthers, a dermatological surgeon, thought to relax muscles elsewhere on the face—specifically, on the face of his assistant, Cathy Bickerton Swann. Swann has since become something of a celebrity in the Botox community, where she is known as Patient Zero. And Carruthers is now a paid consultant to Allergan.

In 1992 he and his wife wrote "Treatment of Glabellar Frown Lines with C. Botulinum-A Exotoxin," which was published in the *Journal of Dermatological Surgery and Oncology*, and is considered seminal to the cosmetic use of Botox. By 1989, the U.S. Food and Drug Administration had approved Botox for treatment of crossed eyes and uncontrollable blinking, and in 2000 it added a neurological movement disorder known as cervical dystonia (essentially, a painfully rigid neck). In 2002, Botox's star turn came: it was approved for just a cosmetic procedure, reduction of glabellar wrinkles, also known in dermatological circles as the "elevens," between the eyebrows. Allergan was instantly transformed from a relatively small-potatoes pharmaceutical company that sold acne products and eye drops, to a hugely influential player on a billion-dollar global field.

The good news didn't stop coming. By 2003, research into how Botox could help cerebral palsy patients was proving to be encouraging. It turned out that Botox could aid patients who had had strokes and suffered from spasticity, severe and uncontrolled muscle tightness. It could also help with carpal tunnel syndrome, chronic anal fissure, hypersalivation, whiplash, migraine headaches, facial tics, back pain, club feet, female sexual dysfunction, stuttering, incontinence, and tennis elbow. One German doctor doing research in the field of incontinence compared its medical significance to that of chemotherapy. Consultants to Allergan began comparing it to penicillin. "Botox will transform the world the way penicillin has transformed infectious disease," said Mitchell F. Brin, a neurologist and vice president of Allergan, which first introduced Botox for treating spastic vocal cords in 1987.[7] Like so many other doctors who are unusually outspoken Botox fans, Brin is now on Allergan's payroll, paid to promote and market Botox.

But there were problems. Allergan went deliriously overboard in its advertising campaign. Some doctors criticized the company for saying that Botox is derived from a "natural purified protein," making it sound like health food, when in fact it is one of the most toxic agents known. Within the first year of Botox's cosmetic approval, the Food and Drug Administration charged that Allergan misled the public by claiming in its advertisements that the drug was effective for the consumer's "toughest wrinkles" and, in general, "facial wrinkles." But Botox had been approved only for use in treating one specific area—the glabellar muscles between the eyebrows. The FDA also cited the company for suggesting the product was intended to treat the general signs of aging, when Botox had only been approved for temporary and limited cosmetic use.

In a formal reprimand to the company, the FDA wrote Allergan that its magazine ads for Botox "falsely identify your product as a cosmetic treatment, fail to reveal material facts about the product's use and minimize the risk information presented."[8] Reports in the press about the FDA's reprimand also detailed the failure of physicians to disclose some of the serious potential side effects of the drug. With the reprimand came dozens of negative news reports, which caused patients across the country to ask their doctors about the safety of the drug.

Then came the saga of Irena Medavoy. Medavoy, a former swimsuit model and sometime actress, sued Allergan and her dermatologist, Dr. Arnold Klein of Beverly Hills, for giving her Botox for the wrong reasons and for not fully informing her of his paid position as a consultant to Allergan. Her lawsuit argued that Klein and Allergan were guilty, among other charges, of negligence, fraud, product liability, and improper promotion of the drug.

Medavoy, now in her late forties, is married to Mike Medavoy, the former head of Orion and TriStar Pictures and the current chairman of Phoenix Pictures, the production company behind movies such as *The People vs. Larry Flynt*, *Basic*, and *The Mirror Has Two Faces*.

The heart of the case centered on her accusation that Klein, Hollywood's most recognizable dermatologist, had treated her migraine headaches with injections of Botox to her neck and scalp, without warning her of the potential risks and without telling her he was on retainer as a consultant to Botox's manufacturer. The fact that he was paid by Allergan was a clear conflict of interest, her suit argued, rendering him too enthusiastic about experimenting with off-label uses of the drug.

In the lawsuit, Medavoy contended that on March 4, 2002, she visited Klein, who had been treating her skin since she was seventeen years old and working as a model. Medavoy complained to Klein of migraine headaches which had allegedly been alleviated by Botox injections in the past. He subsequently injected approximately 86 units of Botox into her neck, scalp, and temples. Whether it was Klein who had recommended, or Medavoy who requested, Botox injections for this off-label use was an issue of contention during the trial.

A note about what a unit means: botulinum toxin is expressed in something called "mouse units." Or, one unit is equal to the amount, when injected, that will kill 50 percent of a group of test mice in an in vivo experiment. The drug is tested in what is known in scientific research as a classic LD50 test—LD50 stands for "lethal dose, fifty percent." This is a serious procedure during which animals experience increasing paralysis over several days until the occurrence of death. (In the United Kingdom, animal rights activists have started a vocal movement against Botox and related products because animals die in the name of vanity. In the United States, where the rights of animals languish on the list of human priorities far below the right to look fabulous, this is a much less vocal movement.)

Typically, Botox injections of less than 100 units are used for cosmetic purposes (in humans, not mice). Doses of less than 600 units are used for other purposes. The dose at which Botox becomes lethal to humans is about 3,000 units. Doctors are cautioned by pharmaceutical companies that doses are not interchangeable among the different formulations of botulinum toxin, such as Reloxin, also known as Dysport, or Myobloc. To achieve similar effects, different doses must be used.

Eight days after Medavoy was injected with the 86 units, she fell ill. The injections, she said in her lawsuit, left her "with severe and unrelenting migraine headaches, upper respiratory problems, fever, weakness, fatigue, severe muscle pain, hives over much of her body and other ailments." (Her husband joined the suit, claiming his wife's illness caused the loss of her "comfort, companionship, intimacy [and] services." He later dropped out.)[9]

The suit was a public relations catastrophe for Allergan and possibly its worst nightmare: a living Barbie doll, a member of the Hollywood glitterati, someone who should have been a poster child for the product, was publicly turning against it and using her husband's money and connections in the entertainment industry to publicize the evils of Botox.

The blond and gorgeous Medavoy, no stranger to cosmetic enhancements and elaborate self-beautification techniques, appeared on *Dateline NBC* in June 2003 criticizing Allergan and the doctors who dispensed the product. The *Dateline* report featured interviews with several former Botox users who claimed the drug caused facial paralysis, nerve damage, fatigue, and other illnesses. Medavoy sent out detailed e-mails to friends and members of the press and began to wage a one-woman war against the company.

Allergan executives felt compelled to buy newspaper ads headlined "The Truth about Botox." The company sent doctors on a promotional tour of the country, with lecture dates set at doctors' offices and shopping malls, touting the safety of Botox.

The six-week trial, which began in September 2004, included testimony from Medavoy's masseuse ("She used to be so vibrant") and from *Wheel of Fortune* letter turner Vanna White (a friend). The last quarter century of Medavoy's life was laid out for jurors. There were the four husbands. Her on-and-off-again career as a model, part-time actress, and infomercial entrepreneur. Her medical history, which included testimony about her anxiety syndrome, eating disorder, and six years in psychotherapy. One of the opposing lawyers referred to her as "Mrs. Prozac" in front of the jury, although Medavoy told me she has never taken Prozac. But the jury learned that since the early 1980s Medavoy had consulted with forty-five doctors for various maladies.

None of the testimony was serving to make friends on the working-class jury. Witnesses testified about summers in Saint-Tropez, winters in Aspen, and John Travolta's birthday party.

"I missed the *Vanity Fair* Oscar party, missed going to the Oscars," Medavoy later told Ned Zeman of *Vanity Fair*. "We were going to spend June in Europe, going to Paris and then on a boat in the South of France. I missed that. People had invited me to Aspen for August. I missed that."[10]

Medavoy had asked in her suit to be paid $192,000 for medical bills and lost wages from a proposed talk show. When she fell ill, she testified, she had been trying to produce a talk show called *Behind the Gates* about the homes of the rich and famous. She left it up to the jury to determine compensation for pain and suffering.

But one of Allergan's lawyers, Robert "Hoot" Gibson, noted that although Medavoy claimed she lost income because of the symptoms she blamed on Botox, she earned just under $1,000 total in the five years ending in 2003.[11] He said that she was also working on a television project centering on the life of a Hollywood trophy wife—and that one plot featured a woman who faked an illness in order to start her own charity and focus attention on herself.

During the trial documents were presented which showed the breakdown of wages paid to Klein by Allergan for his services. The suggestion was that he was paid to attend lectures and effectively champion the drug for Allergan. Allergan and Klein fiercely denied this allegation. They claimed that Klein was only ever paid to act as a scientist and consultant and that there was nothing underhand in this arrangement.

Such arrangements are typically not revealed to patients.

Since 1999, Klein had written two dozen articles for professional journals about the use of Botox. But although he had boasted in the past to *Los Angeles* magazine that he had personally injected 90,000 people with Botox, he never told Medavoy of his links with the manufacturer.[14] Medavoy and her lawyers argued that Klein should have told her about his financial arrangement with Allergan and that by not doing so he was engaging in unfair business practices. She argued that she would not have agreed to treatment if she had known about his financial ties to the company. Instead, she testified, she felt like a "guinea pig."

But perhaps most debilitating to the defense's case was the fact that Mitchell Brin, a senior vice president of development at Allergan and a neurologist who has studied the drug for about twenty years—the one who compared it to penicillin—admitted under cross-examination that the product insert material says that the risks of Botox were unknown in doses higher than 20 units and that the drug can spread to other areas of the body, affecting neuromuscular transmission. He also admitted that Allergan's own clinical studies suggested Botox may be associated with headaches, sinusitis, pain, flulike symptoms, and respiratory problems.[15]

Klein also admitted that he knew even small doses of Botox had been reported as the cause of headaches but did not change his consent form to reflect those risks, nor did he mention them to Medavoy when she claimed Botox helped her migraines, although the form expressly outlined that Klein was prescribing, and Medavoy was agreeing to, an off-label use. It was a coup for the Medavoy side.

On the trial's closing day, as the jury left for a break, things weren't looking good for Allergan: Klein lost control of his bladder and aides went to work mopping the floor of the courtroom with paper towels.[16] Nevertheless, the jury eventually cleared Klein of all charges of unfair business practices. They also voted 9 to 3 to reject the link between Botox and Medavoy's numerous illnesses. In a statement, Douglas S. Ingram, Allergan's general counsel, said the "verdict is not merely a vindication of Allergan and Botox, it is a victory for good science and medicine. We are proud that Botox, one of the most versatile medicines in the world, has brought relief and better quality of life to millions of people suffering from serious debilitating conditions."[17]

What the trial raised were two significant issues. First, the safety of the miracle drug at what were considered tolerable, recommended doses had been brought into question. Medavoy had found women who had similar experiences to hers, and she found one whose father had died during clinical trials of the drug. None had been allowed to testify during the case.

But beneath the trial's main message—Is Botox not as safe as we thought?—was the larger issue of the relationship between pharmaceutical companies that manufacture drugs and the doctors who prescribe those drugs. Jerome Kassirer, a former editor of the *New England Journal of Medicine*, testified during the trial that Allergan was "turning doctors into sales reps."[18]

Although pharmaceutical companies clearly must rely on advice from doctors and academic professionals, recent arrangements in the industry have drawn negative attention to the closeness of some relationships. In 2003, the National Institutes of Health, the country's foremost medical research organization, was criticized for letting its scientists act as consultants for pharmaceutical companies. Pharmaceutical companies and their sales reps have come under repeated, insistent fire for giving doctors bountiful free samples of drugs and then encouraging them to distribute them for off-label use. At Allergan sales booths at medical conferences, for example, sales representatives have touted the new off-label uses that Botox can be used for—even though federal law does not allow drug companies to promote or advertise products for off-label uses.[19] In July 2002, members of Pharmaceutical Research and Manufacturers of America (PhRMA) adopted a code of ethics that is designed to help combat the image that they are bribing doctors to prescribe expensive or unnecessary drugs.

The Medavoy affair scared some patients, who had come to believe that Botox was simply too good to be true, a promised youth potion that would turn out to have serious side effects in the long term. Web sites for aficionados of the latest beauty techniques, like Cosmeticenhancementsforum.com, began chat rooms devoted to the subject.

"I have had a Botox injection 6 days ago, between the brows," reads a typical entry. "Since then, I have felt miserable. Headache, drowsiness, heavy eyes, aches and pains, blurred vision, and weird general complaints. I know definitely Botox was the cause because I felt great before the injection. Why doesn't the Dr. and assistants tell the patients the possible side effects that can happen? I guess I know the answer to that!! Never, ever, ever again!"

Or: "My doctor used Botox as an 'off label' drug for my migraines. I had one session and was given several injections in my head, face and neck. Unfortunately I do have many other health problems in addition to the migraines, maybe that contributed to the problems I had with Botox but I was not informed of how severe the side effects could be. When I watched the Medavoy case on TV I was yelling at the TV b/c she is the first person, besides myself, that I had ever heard of having the same problems with Botox that I had. My husband was just as amazed as I was since he is the one who had to watch me suffer for so long. I really thought I was all alone until seeing that program, which led me to this site, I am even more amazed now to see that I am not at all alone in this nightmare! My problems from the Botox included worse migraines, flu symptoms, nausea and complete and total exhaustion for months. That garbage stayed in my system much longer than anyone said it would. For many, many months I could barely get out of bed to work or socialize with anyone. It took my life away for a long time. I will NEVER use this product again for any reason!"

In interviews with several women who had Botox injections and complained of complications, I found similar symptoms to those of Medavoy. Sally Kadison, a forty-eight-year-old talent agent in Los Angeles, had six shots in her forehead administered by a Los Angeles dermatologist.[20]

"And then she stuck one in my chin, which I didn't ask for," Kadison told me. Three or four hours later, Kadison had difficulty breathing, her face felt numb, and she could not swallow. Two years later, she remains on blood pressure medication. A representative for the doctor later told me he believed Kadison was a copycat victim, that once she had read about the Medavoy case her symptoms appeared and she began to complain. Kadison insists her illnesses are real. Paulette Delcourt, a thirty-eight-year-old yoga teacher who lives in Illinois, told me her father had been a part of the clinical trials of the drug in 1995. He was a Parkinson's patient and suffered from cervical dystonia.

"They tried some Botox on him," Delcourt said.[21] "His head completely flopped to one side. They said, 'Well, no problem, we'll just put you in a neck brace and work with you and the stuff eventually wears off.' We thought, well, okay. He would be able to come home. Before we knew it he had atrophy down to his shoulder, then to his hands, and he couldn't move any of the muscles. You could see the bones in his skin because the muscles had become completely flaccid. And then he stopped breathing. And then he was rediagnosed. They said, 'Whoops, well, he must have Lou Gehrig's disease, not Parkinson's.' And the Botox is contraindicated for Lou Gehrig's patients." (Lou Gehrig's disease, amyotrophic lateral sclerosis, is a progressive neurodegenerative disease that affects nerve cells in the brain and the spinal cord, causing motor neurons to die. When the motor neurons die, the ability of the brain to initiate and control muscle movement is lost. Patients in the later stages of the disease may become totally paralyzed.)

Delcourt's father lived on a ventilator for two months, until he died.

Delcourt said she would never use Botox. "I just stick my head in lotion every day," she said. "I have a cousin who is using Botox. We don't speak to her anymore."

Irena Medavoy's neurologist, Dr. Andrew Charles, a professor of neurology at UCLA Medical Center, said that he does not recommend Botox for use in treating migraines and is shocked at how often Botox is cited in the popular press as a cure-all. "The surprising thing is how little background work has been done about its potential consequences," he told me. According to his own research, doses used to immobilize facial muscles can cause reactions in other muscles. "If you give cosmetic doses in the forehead, you can detect changes in muscle function in the hands and the feet. That is something that doesn't get a lot of attention in Allergan's product literature."

According to Charles, Allergan executives and salespeople promote the use of Botox to treat migraines at industry conferences and at continuing medical education seminars and CME classes. The FDA prohibits companies from marketing a drug in any way other than the manner for which it was approved. But that, Charles said, had not stopped Allergan.

"It's pretty shocking how much they have been allowed to

push the limits of the guidelines," he said. And there is not much oversight in the area. "My sense is that those guidelines are governed by more of a voluntary compliance, rather than anybody strictly enforcing it." There have been some recent cases in which pharmaceutical companies have been fined by the FDA for marketing drugs for off-label uses, "but the kinds of fines that are levied are a drop in the bucket compared to the money they're making. So I assume on the part of Allergan it is a reasonable calculated risk, and they market in a calculated way, so they will only get a slap on the wrist." Allergan have always denied unlawful practices. They differentiate between Klein and other Allergan consultants prescribing and promoting Botox for off-label uses. They argue that they only ever undertake and endorse the former, which is not contrary to FDA rules.[23]

The Medavoy trial divided Hollywood into factions: those who stood by Klein, their friend, well respected physician and the dispenser of antiaging potions, and those who defended Medavoy. As for her, she has not visited a dermatologist since her March 2002 appointment with Klein.

"I have given up," she told me, adding that she had gained weight (which translates into fewer wrinkles) and was using an all-natural skin care line.

While the trial was personally humiliating for her, she said she would do it all over again.

"I think the bigger issue here is that we've reached this point where doctors are telling us what is beautiful," Medavoy told me. "And that ideal of beauty isn't found in nature and it's not found in art. It's made up. It comes from greed, from pushing products and services we don't need. That's why it looks unnatural.

In Hollywood, Medavoy said, the standard for unnatural beauty is something she sees every day. "I look at them, and I'm thinking, look at that cheek implant, and those joker lips and that fake nose. They look like plastic dolls. They look like each other."

Now, she is no longer "about the extra ten pounds or the wrinkles on my face," she said. "I just want to be able to ride a bicycle and play with my son. I just don't give a shit anymore."

Medavoy, who has since changed her hairstyle, has a substitute for Botox.

"My new slogan is 'Bangs, not Botox!' " she said.

X X X

Just after Thanksgiving 2004, one of my editors at the *New York Times* called me in a panic.

"Botox causes botulism!" she said, breathless with excitement. "There are four people in New Jersey who got Botox and are dying from it! Get on the story!"

Botox had become an issue of such cultural and social wattage that even the *New York Times* had, wittingly or not, developed a reporter who could specialize on the Botox beat.

It turned out that a massage therapist from Florida named Bach McComb had concocted a batch of bootleg botulinum toxin at hundreds of times the strength of Botox. The week before Thanksgiving, the self-described wellness doctor injected himself, his girlfriend, and another couple with his homemade batch. He and his girlfriend then flew from Florida to New Jersey to visit his eighty-three-year-old mother and, over the Thanksgiving weekend, were hospitalized.

McComb wasn't taken off a respirator until February 2005. His girlfriend remained on one for four months longer, able to move only her eyelids and one foot. The other couple—a Florida chiropractor and his wife named Eric and Bonnie Kaplan—spent two months on respirators and, when they finally were able to breathe on their own, moved to a long-term rehabilitation center in Atlanta. At a news conference, Mrs. Kaplan, who is in her fifties, looked drawn and wizened, far older than her years.

The case revealed a glimpse of the huge growing underground market for do-it-yourself and illegally imported or manufactured antiaging compounds that are supposed to do what Botox does—at a fraction of the cost—but have not been tested for safety and have not been approved for use.

Dr. Leonard Hochstein, a plastic surgeon in Aventura, Florida, administered Botox for five years and never suspended its use because of the cases. He observed, however, "I think there will be a reduction in interest in Botox, at least for a while. Anytime we have one of these nightmare knockoff do-it-yourself surgery scares, it affects all of us."

McComb had been licensed as an osteopathic physician, but his medical license was suspended by Florida in April 2003 after he was arrested by the Sarasota County sheriff's office on felony charges of trafficking in addictive pain medications, including oxycodone. His prescription pain medications have been linked to the overdosing deaths of several people.[24]

Even after his medical license was suspended, however, he continued to see patients but changed his practice from one that dispensed painkillers to one that dispensed antiaging potions. McComb quickly became known in cosmetic surgery circles as an entrepreneur who taught at seminars that claimed to instruct doctors and others how to make their own cosmetic formulations, like collagen and botulinum toxin A. He organized conferences with two naturopathic physicians named Zahra Karim and Chad Livdahl, a married couple who had started several companies—Powderz, Inc., and Toxin Research International, among others—in Arizona.

"No need for fancy equipment, sterile rooms, etc., most physicians already have all they need," proclaimed flyers that were sent to plastic surgeons in New York City last year.[25] The flyers exhorted doctors and their staff members to attend two-day seminars where for $1,150 they would learn to formulate antiaging medications. The seminars promised to teach "simple, safe and profitable" methods. "You can prepare 100's of cc's of injectables at 1 time, in under an hour," the flyers read, at costs of as little as a dollar a dose.

In New York, Dr. Michael A. C. Kane, a plastic surgeon and the author of a book for patients about Botox, was one of the doctors who received the flyers. "It's insane," Kane said at the time. The environment and procedures used to make such pharmaceutical products, he added, "is far beyond the capabilities of a medical office, let alone people without medical degrees."

As Botox's popularity has grown so has the illegal market: in 2004, an investigation by the Food and Drug Administration found black market botulinum shipments entering the country from all over the world. Much comes from China, where botulinum toxin is sold under the brand names BTX-A and Botutox. Kane and several other surgeons said they regularly received solicitations from manufacturers promising cheap Botox and other products. One letter to Kane boasted that Botutox "is better quality, better effect and lower price than Botox" and promised savings of 70 to 80 percent. Another letter offered "a very stable Clostridium Botulinum Toxin Type A." In the fine print at the bottom of the letter was the line "Not for human use."[26]

I called the 800 number listed for the manufacturer, Toxin Research International, and got the same receptionist who had answered the phone at Powderz a few hours earlier. She was very polite and, recognizing my voice, said she would convey another message to Karim and Livdahl.

Neither returned the call. I sent faxes requesting interviews. In the evening, I called both 800 numbers again and let them ring and ring. Finally, a man picked up. He would not identify himself, nor would he answer any of my questions, but he seemed oddly thrilled. He wouldn't get off the phone. I kept asking him questions, and he would say, "No comment." Often, he accompanied his "no comment"s with an exasperated, theatrical Al Gore sigh. After fifteen minutes I realized I was just indulging the guy and ended the conversation.

It turned out that was Livdahl. Spooked by my faxes and my

phone call, he and Karim spent the night shredding thousands of pages of orders for fake Botox, a fact I learned when I was called to testify in the U.S. attorney's case against them and McComb, several months later.

Mr. McComb had been sent two vials of legitimate Botox by Allergan in the previous year. They had been sent to the Advanced Integrated Institute, the massage clinic where he kept his office in Florida. Allergan sells Botox only to licensed health care professionals, Stephanie Fagan, a spokeswoman for the company, told me. But Advanced Integrated is licensed by the state as a therapeutic massage salon, not a medical clinic, according to state records. The director of the clinic, Thomas P. Toia, is a chiropractor, not a doctor. Fagan told me that she could not comment on why Allergan shipped any Botox at all to Advanced Integrated, citing the ongoing investigation. I asked her if there was any procedure for Allergan to systematically go through their records to divine who was a doctor and who was not on their list of Botox buyers. She said she could not comment.[27]

It is next to impossible to contract a case of botulism poisoning from Botox, said several plastic surgeons and dermatologists I interviewed. Exceedingly small doses of the purified botulinum toxin are injected. The toxin binds to the nerve endings in the injected muscles, blocking the release of the chemical that would otherwise signal the muscle to contract, and typically does not enter the bloodstream. The doses necessary to produce botulism would be in the range of 100 vials of Botox.

So how did Bach McComb get his hands on botulinum toxin A?

McComb, and Karim and Livdahl, it turned out, were buying research-grade botulinum from a company in California called List Biological Laboratories. Karim and Livdahl's company paid $30,000 for 3,081 vials of the List botulinum, and resold it for $1.5 million, according to a report by federal prosecutors.[28]

The bootleg Botox was sold to more than two hundred doctors across the country. Although it is marked "not for human use," no one can say for sure that doctors won't try to fix the mistakes in McComb's failed experiment.

Anyone could manufacture botulinum toxin A, Dr. Alastair Carruthers, the pioneering doctor who injected Patient Zero, told me. "Look outside," he said. "Every shovelful of dirt contains the organism which will produce botulinum toxin." While the bacteria and spores themselves are harmless, the toxin produced when the spores are grown in an anaerobic environment is lethal. And a primitive laboratory and some scientific knowledge are all one would need to grow it.

Allergan proved to be Teflon coated once again. After a week, the company's stock had dipped and rebounded. Consumers, initially alarmed, had not stopped seeing their doctors for Botox, especially during the first weeks of December—considered by many patients and doctors as the preholiday rush (although many doctors and surgeons say that their busiest month is August, when patients have vacation time and clamor to be fixed up for the fall).

The bogus-Botox scare never created a panic among consumers. Dr. Steven A. Teitelbaum, a Los Angeles plastic surgeon, said there were several reasons. For one, the kind of person who is willing to do things to his or her body in order to look younger tends to be able to overlook risks. "It's a different personality type," he explained. Moreover, "reasonable people know that hundreds of thousands, if not millions, of people have received Botox treatments," and no one has ever contracted botulism before.

Teitelbaum suggested that patients should use common sense. "First, be sure your doctor is a doctor," he said. "Second, be sure they have actually been trained in what they are doing. Third, Google them, and if the second item on the first page of a Google of their name is a link to a story saying that they were arraigned for running a pill mill, then consider finding another doctor."

As I finished my first day of reporting on the story, Dr. Carruthers called to offer some help and left me a voice-mail message. "From what I have heard, the investigators now believe that these people are suffering from sepsis," he said, referring to the body's systemic response to infection, which is also known as blood poisoning. "It's entirely not related to botulism even. It's sepsis. Blood poisoning. It's not botulism."

I remembered Dr. Carruthers is a paid consultant to Allergan. The next day I talked to four plastic surgeons and dermatologists in New York, who told me they had all received phone calls from Allergan executives the night before, saying that the patients were suffering from sepsis. It appeared to have been a particularly clumsy attempt at brute spin control.

When McComb and the three others fell ill, Livdahl withdrew $82,000 from his company's bank account, then $312,000. By February 2005, he and Karim had purged their various bank accounts of $973,000.

In March 2005, a frail, gaunt, gray-haired McComb shuffled into a Fort Lauderdale courtroom with the aid of a walker. In the hallway, he was asked by reporters if he had any comment about his girlfriend, Alma "A. J." Hall, who remained in a hospital in New Jersey, able to breathe only with the help of a respirator. He started to cry.

He was allowed to remain free on $200,000 bond because prosecutors, considering his extreme physical frailty, could not consider him a flight risk. He faced fifteen counts of mail fraud, five counts of wire fraud, two counts of mislabeling a drug, and one count of conspiracy.

In November 2005, McComb pleaded guilty in federal court. A University of Kentucky ophthalmology professor, Robert Baker, also pleaded guilty. He was eventually sentenced to six months' home detention for mail fraud. The state of Florida revoked McComb's medical license, and he was sentenced to three years in federal prison. Livdahl and Karim pleaded guilty to federal charges involving the distribution of the Botox knockoff. Chad Livdahl, who pled guilty to one count of conspiracy to defraud the United States, to engage in mail and wire fraud, and to misbrand a drug, and one count of mail fraud, in violation of Title 18, United States Code, Section 1343, was sentenced to nine years in federal prison and was ordered to pay fines totaling $1.3 million in January 2006. Zahra Karim pled guilty to the same charges and received a five-and-a-half-year sentence and was fined $345,000.[29]

Eric Kaplan, the chiropractor who was injected with the fake Botox, had recovered by the end of 2005. His wife, Bonnie, the principal of a private school, was completely paralyzed and on a respirator for two months. Now, she can barely walk; three vertebrae in her spine have collapsed. Her face is still mostly paralyzed. They are also both suing McComb in a separate civil case. So is Hall. She is now McComb's ex-girlfriend.

After federal prosecutors reduced his sentence from twenty-three felony counts that could have led to twenty-eight years in prison, McComb pled guilty to one count of misbranding a drug in interstate commerce and was sentenced to three years' imprisonment. The judge said he received more letters supporting McComb "than practically any defendant I've sentenced."

To millions of Americans, Botox is a magic bullet. A few pinpricks and in a day the face is returned to an approximation of its teenage self, unlined and uninjured by the relentless insult of adult life.

And as the wrinkle smoother rides a wave of popularity with aging boomers, a Botox Nation of citizens with unnaturally placid expressions may find itself abandoning some old beliefs. The wisdom that a person's character can be etched on his or her face, or the observation that at twenty you have the face nature gave you and at fifty you have the face you merit, no longer applies. We are fast becoming a culture where we look at wrinkles as a remnant of the unhealthy, imperfect past, something to be fixed, like a broken tooth or bad vision, something that can be addressed in one office visit.

Or in a visit to an emergency room. In California, at Malibu Urgent Care, Dr. Jill Furgurson, the ER doctor, has started giving Botox injections. The demand for emergency Botox injections is so high that, through her Botox ministrations alone, the center has pulled itself out of debt.

X X X

I just have to have that smooth look," Robert says as we stroll past the Stanhope Hotel, the patio brimming with European tourists, their faces rumpled by travel, short cigarettes in their fingers.

"Ew," he says, catching a glimpse of one woman, about his age, who is a sun-kissed version of the actress Barbara Bel Geddes in her later years. It's not an unattractive look—robust and healthy looking, if aged—but it's too much for Robert.

"My God, she has wrinkles on her *cheeks*," he says, hissing toward me, his hand in front of his mouth and his eyes askance. "And Jesus, they all *smoke*. It's disgusting."

We talk about his habit.

"I get Botox here," he says, pointing to the area underneath his eyes, where skin gets thin with age and wrinkles more easily. "And here," he says, pointing to the triangle next to the eyes where crow's feet might have etched their way into his face by now, if the muscles hadn't been paralyzed by Botox. He also, of course, has Botox injected into the glabellar muscles between his eyebrows and into the places where lines would form on his forehead. He has also had Botox injected into the folds on his neck, on the right side of his chest (he sleeps on his right side, and so that area tends to get lines), and into the sweat glands of his armpits, which paralyzes the glands.

"I just don't sweat," he says, with a grin (no Botox around his mouth). "At all. And my dry cleaner, my God, he loves me."

And so we arrive at 1001 Fifth Avenue, where Robert will ask Dr. Michelle Copeland—a friendly, slightly zaftig brunette with wavy hair, gold jewelry, and a voice one step removed from Marge Simpson's—to inject more Botox into his face and body. He is going to ask her today to inject the palms of his hands and soles of his feet.

His goal is to live a life without wrinkles or sweat.

Four

Forefathers

I f Serbian terrorists had not assassinated Archduke Franz Ferdinand on a spring day in 1914, it is highly possible we might never have had a Pamela Anderson.

Indeed, most techniques of modern cosmetic surgery—from the facial peel to the brow lift—originated during World War I and the years immediately following, as surgeons repaired the wounds and disfigurements sustained during combat. The war was a spectacular showcase for the gruesome new forms of violence that could be done to human beings, and surgeons were forced to rely on their most creative skills to reconstruct bodies that were mangled by stronger bombs and by ammunition that traveled much faster and with greater force than any previously known weapons. The human face was a direct target: wounds were often inflicted in the close confines of trenches, and mortar and grenade fire were propelled directly into the soft tissues and delicate bones of the face. One of the war's most frequent injuries was having one's jaw simply blown off.

The war was also the first in which airplanes were used as an instrument of combat. When plane engines caught fire, soldiers belted into a cockpit seat sustained horrifying burns in the resulting chemical and gasoline blaze. If a plane crashed, the pilot's skull would catapult into the control panel, splintering the facial bones and causing massive fractures that turned human beings into Picasso grotesqueries.

In previous wars, victims of these kinds of accidents would have died or soon been left for dead. But medicine as a whole had progressed to such an extent that patients mutilated beyond recognition could be kept alive. In fact, the rate of death during wartime has continually decreased over time. In World War II, 30 percent of U.S. soldiers died from wounds inflicted during battle; in Vietnam, 24 percent of wounded soldiers died. And despite the increasingly destructive powers of weaponry, in Iraq and Afghanistan mortality has dropped to 10 percent.[1] And just as in World War I, the injuries often require cosmetic surgery.

As one British surgeon, Sir Arbuthnot Lane, remarked, "The race is only human, and people who look as some of these creatures look haven't much of a chance."[2]

French, British, and American surgeons worked together in wartime surgical services and called something of an ethical truce: they would agree that, at least for now, they would not argue about the value of reconstructive, or "serious," surgery versus the value of cosmetic, or "frivolous," surgery. The First World War marked a brief armistice in a battle that would become, and that remains, a morally charged, complex debate.

Varaztad Kazanjian, a Harvard-trained American dentist with some medical school education, was one of the war's most hardworking reconstructive surgeons. He established a plastic surgery clinic at Camiers in France that eventually treated three thousand patients, and later, when he practiced cosmetic surgery, he was often referred to as "the miracle man of the Western Front." At the Harvard Medical School's Countway Library—a fantastical place in whose lobby visitors can gaze on one of the largest hair balls ever to be extracted from a human stomach—the plaster of paris moulages of some of his work can still be seen.

On June 6, 1916, a Corporal F. N. Snowden was admitted to Kazanjian's clinic with what were described as "severe wounds to the face and jaw." That was a bit of a polite overstatement, considering that the corporal didn't really even have a jaw anymore to sustain extensive damage. Kazanjian's neatly typewritten notes indicate that the corporal had suffered a devastating shell wound: "Great loss of soft tissue including part of lower lip and chin. Mandible missing from angle on right side to second molar on left. Second and third molars present. Tongue much swollen. A small portion of shell removed from right side of neck, 1½ inch. Below ear, under Novocain."

The first moulage of Corporal Snowden, in white plaster turned yellow over the decades, looks largely normal except for the fact that there is no bottom lip or lower jaw—just a cave of lumpy flesh and protruding bone. The moulage made a year later, after extensive surgical work, shows the gap has been slightly narrowed. Finally, a photograph from 1918 shows Corporal Snowden looking relatively normal, with a jaw that has been reconstructed to give him a chin with a slightly exaggerated dimple in the center. Put it this way: he's no Brad Pitt, but he's not a complete freak.

Dr. Harold Delf Gillies, the director of the Queen's Hospital in Kent, England, was another pioneer in reconstructive plastic surgery. Born in New Zealand and trained as an otolaryngologist—an ear, nose, and throat doctor—Gillies treated patients with skeletal injuries, nerve lesions, orthopedic problems, as well as massive maxillofacial injuries. By the end of World War I, he had supervised 11,572 major facial operations at the Queen's Hospital.[3]

In 1915, Mrs. William K. Vanderbilt visited Dr. Gillies and wrote a report published in the *New York Times*, in January 1916: "I found mutilated and repulsive pieces of human wreckage taken from the battlefield and made into men again. As these men come to the Ambulance, and as they would remain for the rest of their lives if their wounds were simply left to heal, they are objects of indescribable repulsiveness both to themselves and to every one who sees them."[4] Later, in *A Moveable Feast*, Ernest Hemingway described the veterans who were marked by the war: "There were other people too who lived in the quarter and came to the Lilas [café], and some of them wore Croix de Guerre ribbons in their lapels and others also had the yellow and green of the Médaille Militaire, and I watched how well they were overcoming the handicap of the loss of limbs, and saw the quality of their artificial eyes and the degree of skill with which their faces had been reconstructed. There was always an almost iridescent shiny cast about the considerably reconstructed face, rather like that of a well packed ski run, and we respected these clients more than we did the *savants* or the professors."[5]

Think back to the last older woman you saw who looked like she had had a bit too much work done, whose face was as smooth as a freshly fired ceramic plate, and it's shocking to see how accurately that phrase "like that of a well packed ski run" resonates.

It is clear that plastic surgery didn't originate with an eye toward the flashy. It was not grounded in a woman's desire for impossibly large breasts and inflatable-doll lips. Before the First World War, plastic surgery began with the notion that social acceptance and the ability to belong to a community were inextricably related to looking like, not better than, other people.

The term *plastic surgery* comes from the Greek word *plastikos*, which means, loosely, to fit for molding. The Koomas, an ancient Indian caste of potters, were most likely the earliest practitioners of plastic surgery: among their chores was the unsavory task of fashioning new noses for women who had lost theirs as punishment for adultery. In 600 BC, the Ayurvedic surgeon Sushruta reconstructed such women's noses—along with those of prisoners and criminals—by affixing part of their cheeks to the remaining flesh. "A careful physician," he wrote, "having taken a plant leaf the size of the nose of that person, and having cut adjoining cheek tissue according to that measurement, and having scarified the nose tip should attach it to the nose tip and quickly join it with perfect sutures." This procedure left the patient with an indentation on his or her face in the shape of a flattened nose, but it was much better than having no nose at all. Sushruta described over 120 surgical instruments and 300 surgical procedures, and by AD 1000, this kind of rhinoplasty was known as "the Indian technique." According to the British *Madras Government Consultation Book*, published in 1679, the surgery addressed the injuries sustained by prisoners, adulteresses, or outcasts after undergoing the ritual humiliation of facial mutilation. It was plainly a form of social torture, designed to imprison the offender in a face that instantly signaled the person's sins.

Gaspare Tagliacozzi (1545–1599), a professor of surgery at the University of Bologna, took the nose job a step further. Tagliacozzi, who is often referred to as the father of plastic surgery, was a product of the Renaissance whose skill as a doctor was infinitely improved by the fact that his work was the first to be informed by modern anatomical studies. Before the Renaissance, repair of the face and nose was the privilege of barber surgeons, who strictly guarded their proprietary secrets. Tagliacozzi drew on the newer medical information. Most of the cases he saw involved some degree of mangling of the nose during battle. One of his patients was a Knight of Malta who had injured his nose in a duel. One Don Virginio Orsini was wounded in the hand by a harquebus, an early type of portable musket, while fighting the Turks in Hungary. Captain Flaminio Ringhiera was the victim of an assault on the streets of Bologna. Judging from Tagliacozzi's clientele, it is clear that his work was developed against a backdrop of social and military violence and disorder.

Inspired, Tagliacozzi developed a method of rhinoplasty using a flap of skin from the arm, which left the face scar-free but made some gymnastic physical demands on the patient. In his book *De Curtorum Chirurgia per Insitionem*, published in 1597 and considered the most comprehensive early plastic surgery manual, Tagliacozzi described the method, which began with the surgeon making parallel incisions on the upper arm. The doctor would loosen the skin between the incisions and place some sort of surgical dressing, such as fabric, in the wound. The fabric acted as an irritant and promoted the separation of the skin and formation of ample scar tissue. After two weeks, during which time the mass of thick scar tissue would have developed, the surgeon would bring the patient's arm to the site where the nose belonged and secure the arm in place with a sling. The patient would then spend several weeks watching the scar tissue from his or her arm meld with any tissue or cartilage material on the site of his or her nose. A few weeks later, the surgeon would cut the arm free, and a few weeks after that, he would begin the half dozen surgeries required to transform the knotty hump of flesh, which probably looked like a pale, uncooked veal meatball, into something that resembled a nose.[6]

Tagliacozzi's noses were not perfect. The long procedure itself was physically and psychologically intense. Patients were susceptible to infection or shock, and death. And when they did eventually have a nose, it was more of a gnarled stump than the pert ski jump taken for granted these days. Because Tagliacozzi noses were constructed of scar tissue—and scar tissue doesn't have a full supply of blood vessels—they tended to stiffen in cold weather, and a good hard sneeze could propel them right off the patient's face.

But people were willing to risk their lives for a nose, preferring death to life as an outcast. If you have ever seen the face of a living human being without a nose, you know that it is one of the most fundamentally disturbing aspects the human face can take. The nose is our most prominent facial feature. Without a nose, the face is merely a skull wrapped in a delicate tissue of flesh, and there is nothing more offensive to the most primitive part of our being than something that looks dead but dares to be alive. We find it a profound insult, a threat to our humanity, as well as an un-welcome reminder of mortality. On a deep subconscious level, the noseless face is a mockery of life.

In the fifteenth century, the imperfect nose was more than that: the missing, necrotic, lopped-off, or diseased nose was also the mark of the whore, the loser, and the biologically unsound. Warriors cut off enemies' noses in battle as a form of humiliation. The so-called saddle nose was a caved-in nose that was the result of cartilage eaten away by syphilis—a signal of the bearer's putre-fying bad health and his or her status as a social untouchable.

Even in the *De Curtorum Chirurgia*, published four cen-turies ago, Tagliacozzi evoked the connection between self-esteem, well-being, and beauty—or, if not beauty, at least the notion of feeling whole. The job of the plastic surgeon, he wrote, was "to restore, repair and make whole those parts of the face which nature has given but which fortune has taken away, not so much that they might delight the eye but that they may buoy up the spirits and help the mind of the afflicted."[7] Tagliacozzi con-tended that the face reflected the true nature of the bearer's soul and that to deprive people of their natural face was to deprive them of their self-esteem and self-worth. That sentiment is echoed over and over again on programs like Fox's *The Swan* and ABC's *Extreme Makeover*, when patients, at the end of their ex-pensive transformations, invariably say (or scream or shout while weeping), "Oh, my God, I finally look like me!" The notion of good looks, or whole looks, bestowing self-esteem has even made its way into the cartoons of *The New Yorker*. I keep one over my desk of a buxom blond; she wears stiletto heels and a bathing suit, and sits in a rocker on the porch of what appears to be a retire-ment home. She looks at her fellow retirees, with their white hair and false teeth, and announces: "It cost a bundle, but I can't tell you how much better I feel about myself."

Tagliacozzi defended surgery that restored patients to their whole selves "not as a mean artifice but as an alleviation of illness, not as becomes charlatans but as becomes good physicians and followers of the great Hippocrates. For though the original beauty is indeed restored . . . the end for which the physician is working is that the features should fulfill their offices according to nature's decree." In other words, form follows function, and that's beautiful.

The manuscript, a copy of which I read in the National Archives of Plastic Surgery at the Countway Library, is illustrated with care. Sketches of instruments include one of a harrowing device that combines a saw at one end with a hatchet at the other, another of a cruel-looking speculum with sharpened edges. The before and after pictures of patients are startlingly similar to the ones we see today on television and in magazines. On one page, a poignant illustration shows a man wearing elaborate robes, his hair stylishly waved. He has no nose. On the next page, he is smiling, his arm attached to his face, in the attempt to grow a new nose; in the distance, a sun sets behind a farmhouse and waving trees.

Surgeons made few significant advances beyond Tagliacozzi's work for several centuries and did nothing to bring us closer to the oversized bosoms and plump lips of the *Baywatch* babe era. But in the nineteenth century, in rapid-fire succession, doctors were able to introduce a number of operations that changed or fixed a patient's appearance.

In 1827, Dr. John Peter Mettauer, America's first noteworthy plastic surgeon, performed the first operation correcting a congenital cleft palate with instruments he designed himself. In 1881, Dr. Robert Talbott Ely performed an otoplasty—the pinning of protruding ears—on a twelve-year-old boy. In 1891, Dr. John Orlando Roe fixed the humped noses of five patients using watchspring wire to internally splint the nose. Roe also classified noses into five categories: Roman, Greek, Jewish, Snub (or Pug), and Celestial. "The Roman indicates executiveness or strength," he wrote. "The Greek, refinement; the Jewish, commercialism or desire of gain." The Snub, or Pug, and the Celestial were noses that signaled weakness.[8]

Roe speculated on the value of cosmetic surgery and on the pain of the patients who sought cosmetic surgery in an article about nose jobs titled "The Correction of Angular Deformities of the Nose by a Subcutaneous Operation." The patients, Roe wrote, had "valuable talent . . . buried from human eyes, lost to the world and society by reasons of embarrassment caused by . . . the influence of some physical infirmity, deformity or unsightly blemish." He sounded as promotional as one of the surgeons on a reality-TV makeover show.

On November 24, 1893, the course of plastic surgery was significantly altered during a single operation in Heidelberg, Germany, when Dr. Vincenz Czerny performed the first breast augmentation. The patient was a forty-one-year-old singer who had had a growth in one of her breasts removed. The result was that one of her breasts looked deflated. Luckily for her, she also had a lipoma—a growth of fat that can be as big as a head of cabbage or as small as the head of a pin—on her back. The lipoma, which must have been of a rather significant size, was drained and its fat used to plump up her breast. Surgeons continued to use fat as an alternative method for breast augmentation until the 1990s.[9]

By the late nineteenth century, a few surgeons began to think about the moral ramifications of plastic surgery, and many dismissed it as "beauty surgery" or "vanity surgery," a practice that was frivolous, wasteful, and morally objectionable. The idea of using the tools of the medical profession to make a patient more beautiful, or to somehow cheat the aging process, flew in the face of the Puritan moral codes that rejected vanity and nonessential adornment. Plastic surgery for the purposes of making a patient prettier or more handsome or more buxom, it was believed, catered to the most superficial and sinful of human impulses.

In Europe, the Viennese surgeon Robert Gersuny (1844–1924) argued that cosmetic surgery was an act of vanity. He condemned attempts to reshape the breast for purely cosmetic reasons and reviled "the hunger for beauty of old coquettes who . . . wish me to give their sagging breasts a youthful vigor."[10] Until the late nineteenth century, his attitude prevailed among most surgeons who practiced reconstructive work.

Gersuny believed that plastic surgery, because it placed higher value on aesthetic good looks than on the practice of health, defied the Hippocratic Oath, which commanded that doctors do no harm. Ask any plastic surgeon today whose business is built on face-lifts and breast augmentations, and he or she will tell you that the Hippocratic Oath also admonished doctors to never induce abortions or have sex with slaves. It is clearly a dated document. But at the time, cosmetic surgery and the attendant anesthesia and chance of infection and sepsis—the poisoned condition resulting from the presence of pathogens in the blood or tissues—did mean that patients' lives were put at substantially greater risk than they are today.

In 1900, plastic surgeons were not wealthy, nor did they often discuss with nondoctors their growing abilities to change the human face and body. Most reputable surgeons were not aggressive in marketing their new, almost magical transformational powers. Doctors were not gurus, with waiting lists two years long. Not yet.

At the end of World War I, it was assumed that plastic surgery would retreat into the obscurity of its former days. Although surgeons from around the world had worked on the injuries of the war, it was really only in the United States that the experience prompted a postwar popularity in cosmetic plastic surgery. Well-heeled women began to seek out early versions of the facial peel, which had been developed, using phenol, during the war to treat gunpowder burns. Rhinoplasty became more commonplace after World War I among American Jews and Italians who sought ways to camouflage their ethnic heritage.

In 1923, the actress Fanny Brice, fearing that she would forever be typecast in ethnic roles, had a nose job, prompting

Dorothy Parker to remark that Brice "had cut off her nose to spite her race."[11] (In the 1940s a Chicago rabbi would remind his flock of young Jewish women seeking nose jobs that "you can change your noses, but you can't change your Moses.") Brice continued to work, but her fans were never as passionate about her again. Her story was echoed in the case of Jennifer Grey, the actress who made her name in the 1987 hit movie *Dirty Dancing*. In 1989, after complaining that she was "a very small girl attached to a very large nose," she had a nose job. The result: a perky, tiny, feminine nose. However, the change was so drastic, and Grey suddenly so conventionally, generically attractive, she was no longer recognizable as Jennifer Grey. Instantly, she was almost unemployable, and she has restricted her acting mostly to made-for-TV movies (and *Bounce*, a 2000 box-office disaster starring Ben Affleck and Gwyneth Paltrow). "I thought it was like getting a tooth pulled," she told *In Touch Weekly* magazine in August 2004. "But when I came to, I didn't look like myself again. Ever."

Brice's stunt created a wave of curiosity about cosmetic surgery. The next year, a New York tabloid ran a contest offering to take "the homeliest girl in the biggest city in the country and to make a beauty of her." The *New York Times* reported that "Berlin surgeons are turning out new fashions in beaks almost daily. . . . London has its International Clinic for Plastic Surgery." The article noted that "plastic surgery in the United States has received its greatest impetus from the movies, according to a New York medical man. Hollywood has discovered that a certain ruggedness of feature is necessary for successful screen acting and it is difficult to find this quality in combination with real beauty. Thus movie directors have turned to the beauty specialists for aid in strengthening the occasional weak nose." In Hollywood, there was a plastic surgery boutique hospital known as "The House of Lost Faces," according to the *Times*, "where years may be taken off and loveliness made to appear where only plainness existed before. And from all accounts the operation for facial renovation will soon become as popular as the operation for appendicitis.

'I see you've had your ears clipped. My wife is after me to have mine attended to. Who's your surgeon?' "[12]

In the late 1920s, at the Post-Graduate Hospital in New York—which later became the Manhattan Eye, Ear & Throat Hospital, the city's popular site for elective plastic surgery—patients began flooding in, and not all were victims of accidents or fires. The success stories ended happily and sound as familiar as any on reality television. "A milliner sought an operation because a deformed nose prevented her from getting a job," the *Times* wrote. Another woman, desperate for a nose job, came in. "Three months after she had been operated on she was married," the paper reported.[13] It was as if a magic spell had been cast over these imperfect creatures, their sense of self-worth suddenly buoyant and their ability to step forward into the world with a smile and a confident stride radically enhanced. The reporter wrote that with the removal of their so-called deformities—the humped noses or narrow nostrils, which were admittedly "more distressing to the deformed than to the beholder"—there seemed to come to the reconstructed a new lease on life. As the psychologists of the time would have put it, the cause of their inferiority complexes had been removed. In 1931, a plastic surgeon, accompanied by a pianist playing show tunes, performed the first public face-lift in the ballroom of the Pennsylvania Hotel.

Once skeptical doctors had changed their minds, having listened to the growing chorus from the psychiatry field and tuned into the nascent beginnings of the self-help movement. Psychiatrists had begun to rely on the work of Alfred Adler, the Austrian psychiatrist and former colleague of Freud's whose theory of the inferiority complex as the cause of all neurosis had become widely embraced. Doctors seized on it as the psychological rationale that would allow them to develop—and, of course, profit from—cures for ugliness, not just deformity.[14] The inferiority complex became the touchstone for plastic surgeons; with the growing acceptance of psychiatry came a growing acceptance of cosmetic modification. The psychologizing of cosmetic surgery has to this day given plastic surgeons the right to feel that they are addressing patients' profound issues of self and mental health. In 1940, *Good Housekeeping* asked its readers, "Why should anyone suffer under the handicap of a conspicuously ugly feature? Why not let modern science give him a normal face and an equal chance with other people?"

With the growing acceptance of some forms of surgery came episodes of quackery. Patients who wanted to fix their noses or have their cheeks filled out occasionally wound up in the hands of doctors who would inject anything—including olive oil and Vaseline—to achieve the desired effects. A famous doctor in New York named Gertrude Steele offered a briefly popular phenol peel to diminish wrinkles and tighten the skin. Two of her patients died, and autopsies revealed poisonous levels of phenol in their brains. She fled the country.[15]

Paraffin was a popular treatment of choice until physicians and patients noticed its tendency to melt—especially as the patient enjoyed a cozy evening by the fire or leaned too close to the candles at the dinner table—and to migrate across the face or cause facial cancers called paraffinomas.

Consuelo, the Duchess of Marlborough, was one such victim. The daughter of the same Mrs. William K. Vanderbilt who visited the field hospitals of World War I, the former Consuelo Vanderbilt had been considered a great beauty in her youth. A portrait of her by Giovanni Boldini, painted in the prime of life in 1906, shows a handsome thirty-year-old woman, her young son snuggling up to her, his gaze adoring.

At the urging of her socially aggressive mother, Consuelo had married the relatively impoverished Duke of Marlborough in 1895 to add the luster of royalty to the Vanderbilt family. The Vanderbilts paid about $2.5 million for the honor of her marrying the duke and invested another $15 million or so during the course of the marriage to keep their aristocratic in-laws in high style.[16]

The marriage ended in divorce, and Consuelo gave the Boldini portrait to the Metropolitan Museum of Art, where it is now in storage. In 1935, when Consuelo was in her late fifties, she consulted with a doctor who injected paraffin—the Botox of the day—into the lines of her face. By this time, doctors knew that paraffin was inclined to harden into nodules or long, hard striations, which would drift across the face. Consuelo indeed suffered these symptoms and felt herself disfigured enough that she remained largely shut off from the world until her death in 1964.[17]

Practitioners like Consuelo's doctor served to stigmatize the profession of cosmetic surgery as an industry of pandering physicians and vain patients. In 1930, when Dr. J. G. William Greeff, the commissioner of New York City's Department of Hospitals, established a division of plastic surgery, he received a flood of letters from angry citizens who apparently misunderstood its purpose. "Those who want to improve a face not disfigured will be definitely advised against any such foolish proceedings," he told the *New York Times*. The division, he emphasized, would treat only those who had been disfigured in some way by disease, injury, burns, or "congenital deformities that hamper the mental and physical development as well as the social and economic progress of the patient." These deformities, Greeff clarified, would be determined only by a surgeon, not by the patient. That was the distinction "between cosmetic or beauty surgery and real plastic surgery." Greeff was stern in his final salvo: "Now as to beauty surgery. It is taking a reasonably normal part of the face or body and attempting to create an improvement which is against the dictates of surgical judgment. The Department of Hospitals is interested in this work only in so far as it can persuade people against this unnecessary attempt at improving upon the average natural features."[18]

By 1932, underneath a banner titled "Beauty" illustrated with a slim Art Deco model, the *Times* was regularly running ads for all kinds of beauty potions and procedures. Lincoln Stevenson, of Endicott 2-5710, advertised "face youthification," while a phone call to Circle 7-0929 would connect a client to "Eunice

Skelly's *Jeunice* Method of Rejuvenation and Face Grooming."
And Madame Peters of 30 West 55th Street, a favorite of the day,
extolled her European Face Lifting Method.

With World War II producing another wave of disfigured combat veterans and inducing surgeons to hone their skills in
even more difficult situations, the cycle of medical innovations associated with war began all over again. Again, pilots and soldiers
in airplane accidents made up a large percentage of the burn and
fracture victims. Again, injuries to pilots usually involved deep
scorching of the face and hands when flames and hot gases en-
gulfed the cockpit after the plane was hit by enemy shellfire. Sir
Archibald McIndoe, a British surgeon, compared the burns to
those inflicted by a blowtorch as they were caused by brief but
blisteringly intense heat that incinerated skin and melted bone.
Burn injuries to pilots were mostly confined to the face and hands
because, while the thick flying suits protected their bodies, the
pilots' reaction to cockpit fires was to immediately remove their
goggles and gloves for fear that they would burn and melt into
the skin. The burn, so uniquely intense it earned the nickname
"Airman's Burn," usually melted fingers and eyelids.

Amazingly, during World War II Tagliacozzi's seemingly archaic method of nose reconstruction was revived, in a just slightly
improved form, at Valley Forge General Hospital. Under Dr.
Bradford Cannon, who in 1943 joined the Medical Corps of the
U.S. Army in the plastic surgery unit at Valley Forge, over fifteen
thousand operations were performed during and after the war.
One infantryman injured in Normandy in 1944 sustained severe
soft-tissue and bony injury to the face. Nothing existed of his face
beneath the nose. A photograph donated by Cannon to the
Countway Library shows the man later staring pensively into his
arm, which is attached to his head, as tissue grows from the arm

to the site that would become his nose. The later moulage shows a man who looks relatively normal, if a bit like a roughed-up Karl Malden.

Surgeons had stopped arguing about the merits of cosmetic surgery and focused on fixing war-ravaged bodies and faces. Instead of removing injured men from the eyes of the public, they tried to restore them to status as fully visible human beings. Dr. Archibald McIndoe ministered to hundreds of the severely wounded, including one man who was so badly burned that the rescue mission could not distinguish his body parts from the pieces of twisted metal melting at the crash site.[19] McIndoe's patients spent a large part of a decade recovering from their injuries, and he began to refer to them fondly as members of his "Guinea Pig Club," offering healing therapies that ranged from the surgical to the sexual. "McIndoe made a special effort to arrange for 'fraternization' for his patients, believing that erotic attraction would prove to them their restored physical and emotional state," writes Sander L. Gilman in his history of cosmetic surgery, *Making the Body Beautiful.*[20]

Eventually, sixteen of McIndoe's patients wrote best-selling books about their experiences under his supervision, the most famous of which was Richard Hillary's memoir *The Last Enemy*, which was made into a popular and much-lauded BBC television series.[21]

Plastic surgery had succeeded in legitimizing itself in the public eye as a profession. Now, the goal was to market it to the American public, who in the heady postwar environment had become increasingly aware of the importance of youthful looks and the appearance of vitality. Postwar audiences flocked to the 1947 movie *Dark Passage,* despite its laughably implausible plot: Humphrey Bogart played a convicted murderer who, upon escaping from prison, is recognized by the taxi driver who picks him up. Instead of turning him into the police, the driver takes him to a plastic surgeon to be remade. A curiously sympathetic artist

(Lauren Bacall) nurses Bogey back to health and snips the bandages off his new face an hour into the movie.

In the new postwar America, the body became an object of physical manipulation. Waists were nipped in and buttocks thrust out as part of Dior's Corolle collection, which *Life* called the New Look. Hair was swirled into high-volume bouffants with the power of the newly popular, and newly marketed, permanent. Legs appeared in nylon stockings once again. The poitrine emerged as a practically public object as breasts were buoyed up with imaginative and radically constructed new brassieres. The voluptuous visible body was celebrated by the population at large for the first time in the twentieth century. The American Society for Plastic and Reconstructive Surgery classified small breasts as a deformity, rendering a normal body part something diseased that required medical treatment.[22]

The growing number of plastic surgeons and the growing population of financially solvent prospective patients changed the profession. The question of whether cosmetic surgery was immoral was abandoned when burn victims from Hiroshima were flown to the United States for reconstructive surgery in the mid-1950s. All women, they were known as "the Hiroshima Maidens." Because of their ages (they were all nineteen to twenty-four) and the spectacular ghastliness of their scars, the women received national attention and, as they emerged into the public eye after several operations looking markedly more attractive, generated a multitude of discussions about the wonderful restorative powers of cosmetic surgery.

Medicine and technology progressed swiftly. Through the 1960s and 1970s, developments in microsurgery and improved grafting techniques led to a new sense of comfort and ability among surgeons practicing cosmetic surgery. The number of Americans undergoing some sort of surgical cosmetic retooling rose rapidly. In 1949, about 15,000 had cosmetic surgery. In 1969, about 500,000 did.

"When I first began my practice, cosmetic surgery was almost on the same level as performing abortions in a garage on Sunday," Dr. Dorothea Weybright told the *New York Times* in 1971.[23] A surgeon in West Palm Beach, Weybright had opened her practice eleven years earlier. In 1971, there were about two hundred plastic surgeons out of about twelve hundred nationwide who practiced nothing but cosmetic surgery. The same year, another member of the Vanderbilt family—Amy, the etiquette expert—gave the *Ladies' Home Journal* an elaborate account of her own face-lift.

In 2005, 11.5 million surgical and nonsurgical cosmetic procedures were performed in the United States, according to the American Society for Aesthetic Plastic Surgery. People between the ages of thirty-five and fifty had the majority of the procedures. There are now more than five thousand members of the American Society of Plastic Surgeons. With the countless numbers of doctors performing cosmetic procedures, it's safe to assume that there may be as many as twenty thousand doctors performing cosmetic procedures. In thirty-five years, the number of doctors available to fix our noses and hoist our faces has increased by a multiple of one thousand.

Five

Boom

t is an unwritten law of the cosmetic surgery trade that the surgeon's office must employ an animal-print motif somewhere in the interior design scheme.

The animal print tells the visitor that this is not the office of a regular doctor. This is a wild place, a place of exotic qualities, a lair of feline beauty. But the color scheme—whether the print is leopard spots or zebra stripes—must be subdued, a neutralized, neutered version of its naturally occurring state. There can be no stark whites or blacks, no decisive burnt oranges, no deep, ominously sensual browns. The monotonous slate gray or desert beige tones assure patients that while this may be a doctor's office like no other, sobriety and good judgment still rule the kingdom.

Such is the decor of the subterranean office complex of Dr. Gerald Imber, across from the Metropolitan Museum of Art. A symphony of blond wood and beige-on-beige-on-cream leopard print, the waiting room is where the exotic meets the Spiegel catalog. The photographs on the wall are of painfully bland scenery, but from a distance the casual observer trained in the habits of the upper middle class can look at the black-and-white photographs, professionally matted in chic black frames, and know: classy.

Imber is himself a living evocation of the animal-print idea. He looks a bit more exotic than, say, your average cardiologist, with his tan, his fashionably chiseled Atkins diet face, and his close-cropped hair. (He shows no evidence of the dreaded puffy "carb face" tony New Yorkers and Angelenos have come to loathe.) Yet he still smells reassuringly of soap and antiseptic. His nails are manicured. He is the Platonic ideal of plastic surgeon.

"There are two reasons for the boom in plastic surgery," he said on an autumn afternoon in his consultation office, tucked at the back, past the operating room and nurses' station. "Everybody talks about it like it's going to the gym," he said. "That philosophy has pervaded society." And they're doing it younger. "I am significantly responsible for that," he added. (Like many other plastic surgeons, he projects an air of almost unreasonable confidence.) Imber has long been a proponent of doing small procedures from age thirty-five on, rather than pulling everything up at sixty. "If you do little things from thirty-five to sixty-five, you'll look like a woman," he said, "not a puppet."

The push to get work done younger is just a small part of the reason the cosmetic surgery industry is booming. The stampede of thirty-year-olds who want their upper eyelids tucked is colliding with the stampede at the other end of the age range—the older baby boomers—who are themselves increasingly aware of how easy it is to get cosmetic surgery and feel more pressure to do so.

Combine those two populations with the health care system in the United States—which has made cosmetic surgery very appealing to a broad spectrum of doctors who no longer want to harangue with insurance companies—and you have something of an explosion. There are more doctors doing cosmetic surgery–related procedures, so doctors are intensely competitive to snatch away one another's business. There are more procedures available. In a reversal of medical professional tradition, doctors advertise and surgeons market themselves. Pharmaceutical companies advertise their products directly to the consumer. Monthly magazines that used to publish articles about rosewater facials now feature ones about this month's Botox guru, or laser guru, or microdermabrasion guru. And with the popularity and public awareness of Botox, the cosmetic surgery industry is boiling at an unprecedented pitch.

Ten years ago, it would have been inconceivable for a magazine to cater to an audience interested only in articles about cosmetic surgery. Today, there are three consumer titles for the North American reader whose primary editorial focus is cosmetic surgery, modification, and enhancement. *Skin Deep* features articles on what it's like to be a collagen lip-injection addict and how new mothers can get tummy tucks to remove the stigma of having delivered a baby: "Pregnancy is a special time in a woman's life but invariably 'the mark of pregnancy' produces changes in her body which are less than desirable. Fortunately, excellent treatments are available." *New Beauty,* a thick, glossy magazine whose debut issue included 650 pages of advertising, features articles about desire. Almost all the articles in the first issue began with the directive "I want": "I want a sexy butt," "I want luscious lips," "I want a tighter tummy." Later issues featured articles like "Look Younger by Monday" and "Firm Fabulous Breasts at Any Age." A recent issue of *Elevate* magazine offered an article on "surgery slang," defining terms for the cosmetic surgery aficionado in the know such as Bowling Balls ("breasts that look like trophies from the Bowlerama"), Trout Pout ("overly prominent lips"), Wind Tunnel ("extremely tight facial skin"), and Kabuki Mask ("a largely expressionless face, resembling a ceramic or lacquered mask used in traditional Japanese theater").

X X X

The 76 million members of the baby boom generation are slowly advancing into late middle age. In 2005, the front end of the boomers, born in 1946, turned fifty-nine while those bringing up the rear, born in 1964, turned forty-one. In the next decade, the two fastest-growing household age segments will be aged fifty-five to sixty-four (52.2 percent), and forty-five to fifty-four (26.2 percent).

The boomers are more transfixed by the possibility of remaining young than any preceding generation. Their identity was built on the passionate, history-changing events of their youth: Woodstock, Vietnam, Watergate. The boomers' identities are dependent, at the profoundest personal level, on their ability to retain some aspects of youthfulness. Spending on health care and health-related items like exercise equipment and nutritional supplements will consume a higher percentage of their budgets as their ranks age. Many of their health-related expenditures will be for discretionary purchases, items acquired to enhance the quality of life, not because they were prescribed.

Boomers are willing to spend a lot to do that. Unlike any generation before them, they are prepared to spend what they've got, rather than store their savings away for future generations to squander after they've died. Instead of enacting their midlife crises or mid-to-late-life crises the way previous generations did— say, buying a sports car—boomers are choosing to buy experiences or personal enhancements that are designed to improve their emotional lives and their sense of well-being.

They are also the first generation to grasp and understand technology at its deepest levels—and they are not afraid to call on medical technology to fix themselves. "I'm fifty-seven, and I look thirty-seven," one woman who subscribes to the Web site BeautyAddiction.com wrote to me. "I'd rather spend my money on Botox and a procedure here and there than something that is not a part of me. All we have in this life is ourselves, and what we can put out there every day for the world to see. The world is not going to see my great record collection or the stuff I have at home. They're going to see me. And Me is all I got."

In the last twenty years, the advances in technology and med-

icine that boomers so value have created a culture of better—
better breasts for women, better brains for everyone, more height
for short people, and, in the future, better genes for babies. The
culture of better has its roots in the field of so-called cosmetic
pharmacology. We understand more, for example, about the
chemicals that motivate the brain to feel fear, self-esteem, and well-
being. The antidepressant Prozac, manufactured by Eli Lilly, and
drugs like Paxil, from GlaxoSmithKline, and Zoloft, from Pfizer,
are among the most popular drugs dispensed in America today.
In *Listening to Prozac*, Peter Kramer describes a patient of his
whose career is foundering and who is struggling with a series of
dead-end relationships with married men. She is depressed. After
a few weeks on Prozac, she has changed her life around entirely.
The men are gone. She is hard at work on the career.

Currently 28 million Americans take Prozac and its cousins
every day. There are women who take these drugs—selective sero-
tonin reuptake inhibitors, or SSRIs—because they have been told
they will alleviate the symptoms of premenstrual syndrome.
There are those people who take SSRIs because they just never
want to feel blue, or tired, or blah. There are those who take them
because they have social anxiety and don't make friends easily.
SSRIs have become the pathway to—again, the byword of *Extreme Makeover*—self-esteem. And many researchers argue that
millions take the drugs to mitigate minor psychological symptoms
that fall within the normal range of human behavior.

It's a way to make yourself pretty on the inside.

Cosmetic pharmacology is the interior sibling of cosmetic
plastic surgery, and together these twin forces exert their arguments on the American psyche. If I get depressed right before
my period, why not take a drug to fix that? If I get angry with
my spouse when I come home at the end of the day, why not
eradicate that? If I'm sleepless, if I'm bored with work, if I hate
my parents . . . The same thinking frequently applies to cosmetic
plastic surgery. Why suffer with this wrinkle between my eyebrows? Why allow people to think I'm angry? Why not get rid

of these bags under my eyes? Everyone says they make me look sleepy or sad. As Peter Kramer puts it, why not be "better than well"? Better than average? Better than everyone else?[1]

The "better" mentality is not confined to brains or breasts. We can cure myopia with LASIK eye surgery. Men can pop a Viagra, a Levitra, or a Cialis to—here I use the euphemism promoted by the pharmaceutical industry—enhance sexual function. Short children can now more easily be made taller: the Food and Drug Administration recently approved Eli Lilly's Humatrope, a form of human growth hormone, for treatment of the problem of being short.

The culture of better has prompted Americans to start reclassifying what is well within the range of normal as perhaps just slightly wrong, slightly diseased. Their attitude has also colored their perception of what is beautiful and even acceptable. People on one end of the distribution curve can now be seen as not quite right—whether their noses are bumpy, or their eyes are slightly asymmetrical, or they are only five foot three, or they get depressed sometimes—and their conditions pronounced fixable. Ah, that's better.

The structure of American society has somersaulted through as many revolutions in the last century as technology has. The notion of identity in America is now a fungible property, fluid and changeable from day to day.

Americans move more often than they did even fifty years ago, from city to town to suburb, wherever corporate headquarters sends them. The average American moves eleven times in his or her lifetime. According to the U.S. Postal Service, 44 million Americans (about 15 percent of the population of 280 million) move every year.

The divorce rate has septupled since 1900. During an era when it is not uncommon for people to marry two, three, even four times, Americans might find themselves single at fifty or sixty and have to get back into the dating game—and look good enough to do so successfully. Our attention spans are so shortened by the dilemmas of contemporary life that in the last decade we have invented the concept of speed dating, in which single people rotate around a room at intervals of thirty or sixty seconds, interviewing potential mates.

The average college graduate entering the job market today will hold at least seven different jobs for seven different companies during his or her lifetime. You may spend your entire work life not knowing your colleagues well, passing from city to city, with only a handful of long-term friends and family members who know your foibles, your habits, and the qualities that make you special or remarkable.

This all means that Americans living typically peripatetic American lives can no longer rely on the same set of faces around them every year. Unable to rely on their reputations as a calling card, they depend on their appearance and their ability to generate favorable first impressions.

In *The Body Project*, the historian Joan Jacobs Brumberg looked at the diaries of adolescent girls to see how their feelings about appearance had changed from one century to the next. Before World War I, girls wrote about self-improvement as an exercise that shaped their characters and intellects, not their physical selves. "Resolved, not to talk about myself or feelings," wrote one diarist in 1892. "To think before speaking. To work seriously. To be self restrained in conversation and actions. Not to let my thoughts wander. To be dignified. Interest myself more in others." By 1982, the diary of a teenage girl focused on how improving one's external self, one's physical body and face, is the goal of self-improvement: "I will try to make myself better in any way I possibly can with the help of my budget and baby-sitting money. I will lose weight, get new lenses, already got new haircut, good makeup, new clothes and accessories."[2]

In a society in which the social components of everyday life have broken down to such an extent, many of us judge a person by a new haircut, by good makeup, clothes, and accessories. Consciously or not, we no longer appraise people by their long-standing reputations or what we know about how they comport themselves.

"Is it any wonder, then, that to help them cope, people look to the new keepers of the fountain of beauty and youth—the cosmetic surgeons, the dentists, the nutritionists, the cosmeticians, the physical therapists, and so on?" Ellen Berscheid wrote in her "Overview of the Psychological Effects of Physical Attractiveness."[3] We are a nation that recognizes the importance of good looks. The American way is to couple a woman's beauty with her identity and man's virility and strength with his success. Our culture openly devalues people if their looks stray too far from the accepted standards of beauty or youth. Berscheid's studies in the 1970s and 1980s concluded that good looks had a major impact on people's lives and that attractive people were assumed to have an array of other desirable qualities, such as kindness, sincerity, and warmth. Beauty, she said, was more than skin-deep. "Genetic determinism is anathema to Americans, who want to believe everyone is born equal, with an equal chance for a happy life," Berscheid remarked to the *New York Times*. "It's simply not so."[4] The most important factors governing success in life, her research determined, were sex, height, intelligence, and appearance, factors that profoundly affected life quality as early as nursery school.

Year after year, new studies provide consistent evidence of discrimination against overweight and unattractive job applicants and employees. A 1984 study found that overweight job applicants are judged more harshly than ex-felons or applicants with a history of mental illness. A 2001 Yale study found that obesity results in clear and consistent stigmatization, and in some cases discrimination, in three important areas of living: employment, education, and health care. The study reported in part that parents provide less college support for their overweight children than for their thin ones. Not only is being fat a personal issue, it also extends to those who surround us. Two 2003 Rice University studies reported that even being seen near obese people makes others see us as inferior.

Pretty women and handsome men simply make more money than unattractive men and women. A 1991 study of 737 MBAs concluded that good-looking men were paid higher starting salaries than their less handsome counterparts and their earnings were higher over time. Attractive women, while they did not get the initial higher salaries, did earn more than their plain counterparts over the course of their careers.[5]

Of course, there are some occupations that require a generous degree of pulchritude: a Victoria's Secret model or a matinee idol is generally required to be good-looking. However, good looks matter even in fields where they should have no bearing. Studies show that good-looking auto mechanics earn more than unattractive auto mechanics, and good-looking teachers earn more than plain teachers. Daniel S. Hamermesh, a professor of labor economics at the University of Texas at Austin, and Amy M. Parker, a student, recently concluded a study titled "Beauty in the Classroom: Professors' Pulchritude and Putative Pedagogical Productivity," in which they reported that university professors whom students considered good-looking received better academic evaluations than merely plain or dowdy professors. The teachers students thought of as pretty or handsome were considered to have better intellects and to convey the information they were teaching in a more efficient and entertaining manner.

To get a good job in the United States, the scientific data suggests, you not only have to be relatively trim and good-looking but you have to be young. When *CNN Financial News* asked viewers in the summer of 2003 whether they were looking for jobs and how long they had been looking, most of the e-mails they received came from Americans in their fifties. One viewer wrote in, "I've come to find that all my years of experience don't count once you reach the age of 50. My telephone interviews go extremely well but as soon as they see me up close and personal, it's all over. There is age discrimination in this country."[6]

In Hollywood, agents encourage their writer clients over forty to lie about their age. Older credits are dropped from résumés. In 2001, fifty over-forty writers filed a class action lawsuit in federal court in Los Angeles maintaining that for the two preceding decades the television industry—fifty-one defendants, including NBC, The Walt Disney Company and its subsidiaries, Fox Entertainment, Time Warner, Universal, Paramount, Viacom, Columbia TriStar, DreamWorks, International Creative Management, and the William Morris Agency—had followed a pervasive pattern of age discrimination against writers over forty.

In one famous incident, a youthful-looking actress, Riley Weston, lied about her age, saying she was nineteen when she was actually thirty-two. Her real age was discovered after she had become a teenage phenom writing for the 1998 television series *Felicity*. "I could not be one age in the acting world and another in the writing world, so I chose to maintain the ruse," she said at the time. "In a business fraught with age bias, I did what I felt I had to do to succeed."

Women's magazines are now packed with advice and information about the latest cosmetic surgical procedures. "No Eye Lift Necessary! The New Procedure" and "The Quick-Fix Facelift" aren't headlines from a promotional pamphlet you'd find in a surgeon's office. They come from recent issues of *Elle* and *Vogue*. *More* magazine offers advice on which over-the-counter creams are good for those times when your skin is "post-procedure."

Elle's correspondent Holly Millea wrote about strategic skin lasering in a recent issue; its purpose is to make the eyes look fresher and wider without an eye lift. Millea is one of an evolving school of postmodern gonzo journalists whose métier has gone from following candidates on the campaign trail to sampling every new cosmetic surgery procedure and spreading the word about it with a kind of tempered realism. (Tempered because the kind of doctor who gives the free procedures to aging journalists expects kid-glove treatment in return.)

"Of all the Beauty Adventures I've ventured, several of which you know have left me bruised and scarred and worse for wear," Millea wrote for *Elle* readers, "I'm here to announce that the adventure I've just taken is the most excellent adventure of all." But above Millea's text fluttered a pair of smoky, smoldering eyes that belonged to a model in her very early twenties, not the rejuvenated eyes of the forty-something Millea.

Vogue regularly trumpets an issue devoted to age. On the cover of a recent "Age Issue," the headlines included *Vogue* staples such as "Chic, Sexy & Sleek from 18 to 80" and "Buy It Now, Wear It Forever." But there were also promises of much more inside. "How Old Do You Look?" blazed in hot pink capital letters. "Face, Neck, Elbows, Hands . . . What You Can Change, What You Can't. Plus, The Quick-Fix Facelift." And "Figure of Youth: Reclaiming Your Teenage Body."

Inside was a welter of information about cosmetic surgery, injectable fillers, and obscure procedures. There was an article about the fillers doctors can inject into your face to make it plumper and younger and, oh, add some extra lift to your cheekbones; another was by a woman who watched a patient get a facelift, the kind that is "definitely appropriate for younger women," according to a plastic surgeon quoted in the article.

In a section called "Going to Pieces," Nora Ephron, Penelope Green, and Dodie Kazanjian wrote that their neck, hands, and elbows—respectively—were aging. What to do? For the hands, autologous fat transfer, a procedure in which fat is siphoned out of one part of the body and pumped into another. Turkey neck? A face-lift, alas. Saggy, wrinkly elbows? Well, no one has invented the elbow lift. Yet.

But for all its catering to the aging population, *Vogue* won't let its readers stare at photographs of older women in couture clothes. It may have become in part a monthly menu of plastic surgery procedures, like many other women's magazines, but it won't let its models look like surgery is anything they will ever need. So in the fashion spreads for "The Age Issue," which the text promises will show off "the bold, statuesque looks that play up the strength and confidence of a worldly woman of 70," Carolyn Murphy, a model who was twenty-nine when the photographs were taken, wears the clothes.

In your forties, "dare to wear fishnets." And there is Murphy doing so. In your fifties, wear black leather. And there is the kittenish model with the teenage body doing so. In your sixties, "you're secure in your femininity," and a smoking jacket with crystal beading paired with a silk charmeuse pant is fresh and sexy. And there she is again, secure in her femininity but looking like a teenage gamine who has been playing in Grandma's closet.

My favorite page is Murphy, again in the section about how to dress in your sixties, in a tweed hat (Prada, $252) that looks like something my grandmother would have worn in her eighth decade to play golf. The caption reads: "You know who you are; now tell everyone else, with a trademark accessory. This jaunty chapeau says, 'I'm comfortable with attention!' "

Yes, but not with the fact that I'm seventy.

Even *O, The Oprah Magazine*, which publishes articles every month about the beauty of self-acceptance, ran a feature called "Extreme Beauty" in a recent issue that outlines everything the modern woman can do to stay young. "Did you know you can get your hands plumped, your legs lengthened, and your belly button reshaped?" the text asks. (Or, as the article goes on to report, your vagina reshaped, toes shortened, and calves augmented.) In the same issue, along with the recipe for fresh corn polenta and Dr. Phil's agony column ("If your objection is to having a stripper at the bachelor party, which your boyfriend was responsible for, you need to let him know what your expectations are"), an article describes all the physical insecurities men feel about their bodies and things they might do to fix the situation. The author, Ted Spiker, details the basis for his self-loathing and his wish to change himself: "At six feet two and 215 pounds, I'm not huge. I just carry my weight where women do—in my hips, butt and thighs. And I hate it. I hate the way clothes fit. I hate that my friends say I use the 'big-butt' defense in basketball." Spiker explains that men are threatened by today's cinematic superheroes, who more often resemble a baby-faced, unlined Tobey Maguire in *Spiderman* than the rough and wrinkled Harrison Ford of the Indiana Jones movies.

Spiker has a point. Men, like women, are increasingly worried about looking old, and they are doing something about it. From 1997 to 2001, the number of men who had cosmetic surgery increased by 256 percent. In 2004, men had 1.2 million cosmetic procedures. Men try to stop balding with Rogaine. They can develop body dysmorphic disorder or muscle dysmorphia, both of which might lead them to steroid abuse. In 2006, the actor Dennis Quaid told the magazine *Best Life* that he suffered from "manorexia" in the 1990s; many doctors now believe that men who suffer from anorexia may simply underreport the incidence. "It's not that I can't change my body; it's just that I haven't," Spiker writes in *O*. "All I do know is I'll never stop trying to shrink my hips, tighten my gut and deflate my rear tire."

Sounds like a good candidate for liposuction—which was, by the way, the most popular cosmetic surgery for men in 2004.

X X X

The flourishing of the cosmetic surgery industry owes much to the manner in which we pay for health care. The American health care system has changed dramatically over the last sixty or so years, allowing cosmetic plastic surgery and its attendant specialties to grow faster than they might have otherwise.

In the 1940s and 1950s, there was virtually no organized health care system in the United States. There were no prescription plans, and there were no shiny plastic cards to carry in your wallet that identified you as Jane Doe, protected by Blue Cross, or Harry Pincus, protected by HMO Unlimited. You got sick, you went to the doctor, and, assuming you survived, paid the bill. Patients who couldn't pay were treated in a pro bono fashion by charities or hospitals on an as-needed basis. Medical bills reflected the economic capabilities of patients and didn't scale the garish heights they do today.

This kind of system was easy to navigate for up-and-coming surgeons. A young doctor who wanted to be a plastic surgeon faced a relatively typical path after finishing medical school. His or her life was driven largely by personal choices. He or she— although surgery of all specialties is still a field largely dominated by men—finished a residency program and chose a place to live. There the surgeon would join the staff of the local hospital, open a practice, decide whether to specialize in reconstructive or cosmetic surgery or perhaps practice a combination of both, and introduce himself to colleagues and to the community.

The new surgeon would take the written and oral exams required by the American Board of Plastic Surgery and, board certified and trained in the three As taught in medical school— availability, ability, affability—continue forward for decades to come. The success or failure of the surgeon would depend on his or her abilities and the appetites and desires of the marketplace.

In the 1960s, major corporations began to recognize that ensuring that their workers had access to health care was a good idea. Employees—and their unions—were enthusiastic. Companies made arrangements with private insurance carriers, who paid the bills, and Americans began to conceive of health insurance as part of their rights as employees. With the passage of the Social Security Act of 1965 and the creation of Medicare, the federal government—and state governments, through Medicaid—became involved in the workings of health care.

As health insurance coverage mushroomed over the decades, the expense became a major part of business and government budgets. Businesses, through their alliances with the government and insurance companies, began to shoulder the burden of health insurance costs. With an aging population, huge investments in technology, and patients utterly disengaged from the concept of a bill to pay, dependence on the health care system grew. Uncontrolled, costs went through the roof. Have you ever looked at a medical bill for a serious procedure and wondered how anyone ever paid their medical bills before health insurance? Well, they didn't. The bills weren't that big.

By the early 1990s, health care costs made up about 15 percent of the nation's gross domestic product. (They are expected to rise to 20 percent by 2013.) Insurance companies began to rein in costs, working with government and corporations to place controls on the practice of medicine, no longer including procedures and care that patients saw as a basic service. And this profoundly affected the practices of all doctors.[7]

In 1992 and 1993, the federal government drafted plans for a new health care system. While it was not put into place, it did create a new way of thinking about medical care: the system needed to be more inexpensive, more accountable, more effective, leaner and tighter. But that didn't happen. The consumption of hospitals by large corporations in every state has created a finance-based mind-set in a health care setting. The health maintenance organization—known colloquially by the dreaded acronym HMO—is now the primary form of health insurance in the country. Doctors are often partnered with employees of universities, hospitals, HMOs, PPOs (preferred provider organizations), IPAs (independent practice associations), and a number of other organizations.

These insurers, responding to what are referred to in the medical community as "cost containment" guidelines, have cut back on some of the procedures and practices they will pay for.

In the case of plastic reconstructive surgeons, for example, this has meant that some states have recategorized reconstructive breast surgery for women who have had mastectomies as a cosmetic procedure and therefore no longer covered by health insurance. In turn, to boost their bottom line, insurance companies have begun to market cosmetic surgery for pay to their insured population and to contract with doctors who will perform plastic surgery—often surgeons or doctors who are not board certified in plastic surgery.

Medical specialists far outside plastic surgery have found that insurance companies are reimbursing them less often. Why let your dentistry practice suffer when you can learn to inject Botox at a weekend seminar that costs you $2,500, a fee you can make back in the first two weeks? When more doctors outside plastic surgery and its related specialties are trained in procedures that were once limited to plastic surgeons, the competition among doctors becomes intense. And for the consumer, the dividing line between the professions—dermatologist? dermatologic surgeon? cosmetic surgeon? maxillofacial surgeon? what's the big deal?—is a fuzzy one. In fact, one of the most recognized cosmetic surgeons on television, the star of E! Entertainment Network's reality program *Dr. 90210*, is not a board-certified plastic surgeon. Dr. Roberto M. Rey, Jr., forty-four, completed a two-year residency training program in plastic and reconstructive surgery but told the *New York Times* in March 2006, two years after the program first aired, that he had "postponed taking the certification exams because he has been too busy."[8] (Although a Web search using his name yields a result on HealthGrades.com reporting that his specialty is "plastic surgery," Reyes is not board certified in any medical specialty as of April 2006, according to a spokeswoman for the American Board of Medical Specialties.)

With the arrival of doctors outside the plastic surgery specialty come more in-office operating rooms. In many states, doctors who do not have hospital privileges to perform certain surgical procedures, such as liposuction, are allowed by state regulators to do so in their own in-office operating rooms. With more doctors offering cosmetic procedures and surgery outside a hospital setting, hospital-based peer review—the method of preserving professional conduct and ethical standards—is slowly disappearing. Removing the doctor from the hospital environment eliminates day-to-day contact among doctors and standard monitoring processes like the morbidity and mortality conference, a ritual of the hospital environment in which doctors meet on a regular, usually weekly, basis to discuss which patients died that week and why or which operations went badly and why. Some but not all states have passed laws requiring standards for each in-office operating facility.

There are no federal regulations governing whether a doctor (with any degree from any medical school) is practicing plastic surgery (with or without board certification in any medical specialty, with or without any skill set determined by his peers) in a facility that is filthy and unhygienic. This is bad for both the consumer and the board-certified surgeon: consumers can't tell who the good doctors are, and the good doctors get shouldered out of the way by any MD with a scalpel, a power-assisted cannula, and a nurse anesthetist.

Today, when a plastic surgeon opens a practice, he or she must decide where to locate the practice, which requires consideration of the type of insurance carriers dominating the region, the level of service provided by local hospitals, state and county taxes and regulations, regional costs for malpractice insurance, the demographics of the local patient population, the quantity of surgeons already practicing in the area, the weather, the price of real estate. Will he or she be known for breasts or eyelids? Noses or face-lifts? He or she must decide what form the business of the practice will take: will the surgeon work alone, with a partner, in a retail-style cosmetic surgery center or in a hospital setting? What relations will he or she have with third-party insurance carriers? Who will staff the practice? Who will design and construct the office and the operating theater? Who will pay the bills, subscribe to the newsletters, and order the stationery? Who will keep the surgeon informed of continuing education opportunities and new information?

In textbooks for students of plastic surgery, editions printed after the late 1990s include chapters on practice management and the value of good marketing and publicity. Every professional conference of plastic surgeons includes an ever-increasing number of forums and seminars on how to manage and market your practice, how to spread the word, whether to advertise, whether to use a plastic surgery consultant whose job is essentially to funnel clients your way, whether to hire a public relations firm, whether to appear on television, and whether to hire an image consultant to help you dress, talk, and schmooze.

Apart from the formidable task of running a business and maintaining a keen awareness of legal intricacies and medical regulations, cosmetic surgeons must keep up with new technologies and products: lasers, microsurgery, wrinkle fillers and wrinkle paralytics, power-assisted liposuction, ultrasound machines, imaging systems, endoscopic techniques.

The cosmetic surgery marketplace has become an environment ineluctably complicated by commerce, technology, and psychology. The techniques and products that make up the practices of cosmetic surgeons are in a constant state of reinvention and renewal, and consumers know more about new technologies and devices and procedures than they ever have. In other words, this fall Botox wipes away your frown lines, but by next spring it will be an injectable form of acid distilled from rooster combs. Surgeons live in a state of panic and exhaustion keeping up; if you don't have it, your patients will be seeking out someone who does.

If there were ever a set of medical professionals who could benefit from a master's in business administration, that would be cosmetic surgeons. Because at its core, elective cosmetic surgery, while completely respectable, is a medically unnecessary branch of surgical practice. Cosmetic surgeons must become masters of marketing, as well as experts in litigation and malpractice law and navigators of the complexities of small business. They must also play the important role of the psychiatrist—one who can meet with patients and turn away the disillusioned (sure to be disappointed) and the potential nutcases with wildly unrealistic expectations (those most likely to sue) in a twenty-minute consultation.

Managed care represents the corporatization of medicine, one plastic surgeon told me at a convention of the American Society for Aesthetic Plastic Surgery in Boston. "If you're a doctor working in this kind of environment, do you want to spend an hour removing a freckle and get paid $12 in two months by some insurance company?" he asked. The doctor, tall and handsomely turned out in a Louis Boston tie and suit, sipped orange Fanta from a plastic cup while we waited to go into the Adjustable Breast Implants seminar. "Or do you want to spend fifteen minutes putting Botox into someone's face and get $1,000 in cash five minutes later?"

And so doctors have converted. In Atlanta, the Glenridge Cosmetic Surgery Center is just one of many cosmetic surgery offices. Dr. Fred Petmecky, its medical director, practiced for sixteen years as a heart, lung, and blood vessel surgeon, before switching to cosmetic surgery in 1991, trading a high-pressure practice for a lower-tension field "with a high degree of patient satisfaction."[9]

The current atmosphere has caused something of an exodus from the medical profession in general. Applications to medical schools all over the country are down. Doctors across the board view HMO health plans with great wariness and have left the profession. In 2000, Merritt, Hawkins, a physician-recruiting firm in Irving, Texas, reported that in a survey of three hundred doctors age fifty or older, 40 percent said they planned to retire by 2003 and 10 percent said they planned to change careers. In a 2001 survey by the California Medical Association, 43 percent of doctors said they would not be practicing in California by 2004. One of the reasons often cited for retiring or switching careers or specialties: "HMO hassles."

There are fewer doctors overall, yet there are more doctors practicing cosmetic plastic surgery. Why? The beauty of cosmetic plastic surgery is that it is elective. No insurance company will pay for a face-lift unless it is medically necessary—which it never is. The surgeon doesn't have to deal with annoying insurance companies. The surgeon sets the fees. There is no cost containment. And it's all paid up front, in cash. Saving lives is noble, but doing so while fending off insurance carriers, monitoring costs, and paying huge insurance premiums is another matter. Cosmetic surgery has become an asylum for physicians defecting from an industry run by managed care in favor of the independence they hope to command in the free market. As a result, its economics have changed, as physicians, finance companies, and credit bureaus collaborate to extend their services to a wider sector of the population.

Most important of all, anyone with a medical degree can hang a shingle on the door that says he or she practices cosmetic plastic surgery. By the same token, a plastic surgeon can claim to do other types of surgery, but it just doesn't happen. As one well-known plastic surgeon in New York told me, "I can say to anyone, 'Hey, come to me for your cataract surgery.' Sure, I may have taken a weekend course in cataract surgery. But I'm not an eye surgeon. I don't know about all the intricacies going on in there. But no one is ever going to come to me for cataract surgery. Because no insurance company is going to have me on their list of approved doctors, and patients don't pay for their own cataract surgery. But they do pay for their own breast augmentation surgery."

And that's where the chilling economic beauty of cosmetic plastic surgery lies. Because no insurance companies are involved in paying the fees, there is no approving body involved in the transaction to demand credentials and certification—except the consumer, who is probably a little scared, a little anxious, and a little predisposed to believe that only good things will happen to his or her face. Cosmetic surgery patients are a most malleable patient population, hopeful for good results and easy to convince of good outcomes. But the fact remains that the reliability of surgeons in the field of cosmetic plastic surgery can vary greatly, especially for high-priced procedures that doctors are eager to sell. Doctors without sufficient training may try to perform operations they aren't professionally trained to do.

Unfortunately for the consumer, the information about who is qualified and who is not is difficult to come by, and often confusing. Again, unlike in any other surgical subspecialty, a plethora of boards claiming to be approving bodies for cosmetic plastic surgery have sprung up, with names like the American Board of Cosmetic Surgery and the American Academy of Cosmetic Surgery, which roll off the tongue with an authoritative-sounding Marcus Welby quality. Many doctors who don't have board certification in plastic surgery—which means the doctor has received full clinical training in that specialty—have credentials from groups with names similar to the official board's. But there is one body governing plastic surgery that is recognized by the American Board of Medical Specialties: the American Board of Plastic Surgery, which is headquartered in Philadelphia.

Some states, however, have managed to pass laws recognizing some of the nonrecognized boards. States, not the federal government, bear the responsibility for monitoring medical practice. Products, drugs, and devices, on the other hand, are regulated by the federal Food and Drug Administration. The government is reluctant to regulate medical advertising or monitor doctors too closely because the policies of the Federal Trade Commission reflect the idea that the consumer is best served by an "open field" of practitioners, which theoretically gives the consumer the widest range of choices. That leaves state medical boards—organizations that are not eager to spend their slim budgets chasing doctors who practice plastic surgery but are not board certified—to do so. What such doctors are doing is not illegal—just less than ideal medical practice.

In cosmetic plastic surgery, in particular, there are constraints impeding consumer access to good information. Practitioners facing high financial stakes who aren't board certified act aggressively to preserve their ability to attract patients. Other doctors cannot agitate to dismantle the so-called fake boards and cannot advise patients to use only board certified doctors. The government could file lawsuits against them for what is known as restraint of trade.

But the problem is that, with the flood tide of injectable fillers coming into the country and with doctors advertising products that have not been approved by the FDA for any purpose, there is an increasingly renegade quality to the cosmetic plastic surgery landscape. Many surgeons have said to me in private interviews that the FDA drags its feet in approving new drugs, and the lag has helped create a boomlet in back-room cosmetic surgery: unqualified doctors—and nondoctors—practice the medicine of beauty or inject substances that have long been banned or have never been approved for use in this country.

If there are more doctors than ever practicing cosmetic plastic surgery, there are also more patients who view aging as a medical ailment that can and ought to be treated, like arthritis or dandruff. The onslaught of television programs that show viewers how seemingly easy it all is has convinced some consumers that cosmetic plastic surgery can change their lives.

In the meantime, more and more cosmetic surgeons like Dr. Imber are encouraging patients to start getting procedures at younger and younger ages. Botox, thirty. Eye tuck, thirty-two. Brow lift, thirty-five. And still other surgeons will do anything that their pushy patients ask; this is how our culture provides us with a woman like New York socialite Jocelyn Wildenstein, who has spent a small fortune pulling her face back and her eyes up and fattening her lips so that she looks like a cat.[10] (The final look is not a good one. I found myself seated next to her at a Brazilian restaurant on Lexington Avenue, and, just imagining the details of the mutilation she must have endured to achieve her face, I found I couldn't eat my dinner.)

That, according to Dr. Steven A. Teitelbaum, "is an example of a perfect storm in plastic surgery. A patient with X desires meets up with a doctor who will do anything. It's disastrous."

It is a dance between patients and surgeons that takes place every day. Emotionally fragile patients are willing to pay anything to hear that their sagging jowls can be fixed. Doctors who have to pay for expensive public relations agents and advertising campaigns are just a tad more likely to operate on someone who doesn't need surgery. Cosmetic surgery becomes unmoored from normal economic laws and becomes an industry governed not just by money but by psychology, a conspiracy between patients who don't want to hear what they really need and doctors who won't tell them.

Back in Imber's gently exotic offices, the doctor ruminated on the subject of beauty, excess, and Hollywood. After all, so many actors and actresses have had cosmetic surgery—and their faces show it—that we moviegoers may actually perceive celebrity beauty differently. We may expect an actor of Michael Douglas's age to have eye sockets that have been hollowed out of all excess flesh. We may expect an actress like Nicole Kidman to not be able to move her forehead, except for that tiny wriggle in the center. We may expect all actresses of Melanie Griffith's age to have unnaturally pillowy lips.

"Yes, but did you see *Open Range*?" Imber asked, referring to the 2003 movie starring Kevin Costner and Annette Bening. "It was marvelous. He was wrinkled. She looked old. She looked old and tired. And God, I have to say, it was so refreshing. They looked so real."

Six

What Is Beautiful?

ecently, I was standing at the front of a crowded elevator in New York City. Just before the doors slid open, I hesitated, turning slightly to see which of the several people on board should be allowed to take the first step out.

There were five men and two other women: a pretty brunette woman in her twenties and a woman in her sixties, standing further back. Before anyone could move, the older woman sang out, "Age before beauty!" and walked boldly through the doors.

There was the briefest of mildly shocked silences, and then the rest of us filed out after her, radiating out into the city in different directions and moving on with our days. But for the rest of the afternoon, I puzzled over the incident. I had never heard anyone say the phrase in public: in my childhood, my mother had suggested it to me as a strictly tacit guideline when confronted by older people in buffet lines or getting onto escalators. I tried to avoid even mentally piecing together the phrase *age before beauty*, because my brain and mouth are connected by a perilously slim little belt of neurons, and I was sure one day it would spill out of my mouth as I stared hungrily at a plate of pasta salad at a cousin's wedding or waited to get on a bus, in the hope of urging some older person to hurry up and eat or get moving.

But this woman had actually said it, and it came out sounding quite daring and intimate. It was a command—obey this rule—and an uninvited, sudden judgment. It was a way of announcing to the five men in the elevator that she was older than I or the other woman, delineating herself as a person of age, past childbearing years, unsuitable for dating or marriage. She was also telling the collected audience that we younger women were beautiful, even if the word *beauty* is used as a merely catchy part of the phrase.

Most important, she said the phrase with a kind of pragmatic pride in her voice, as if Age knows all and Beauty, in its dumb, doe-eyed innocence, withers. There was almost an insulting feint in her authority, as if she were pronouncing her superior status in the human hierarchy. Or had she just decided to show in a public way how secure and comfortable she was with her age? Or was she trying to attract attention? I couldn't figure out the answer, and I'll never know.

What did occur to me is that the word *beauty* appears in a multitude of these daily phrases that remind us of social customs and reinforce beliefs. Beauty is as beauty does. Beauty is truth, truth beauty. My personal favorite is: Beauty fades; dumb is forever.

There are as many ways to make beauty into a political issue and a point of debate as there are definitions of what is beautiful. On a personal level, symmetrical faces, bright white teeth, shiny hair, good physical carriage are things that matter. Additionally, our lack of self-consciousness, an unawareness of our looks, plays a large role in others' perception of our beauty and always has. In the 1500s Baldassare Castiglione wrote in his etiquette manual *Book of the Courtier* that a beautiful woman appears beautiful only if it is clear that she is not seeking approval for her beauty, if her "gestures are simple and natural, without working at being beautiful." (For this reason, I have never found Madonna beautiful. There is a slightly harsh set to her face, a puritan steeliness to her jaw that shows ambition, judgment, and discipline but not the nonchalance, the self-forgetfulness, of true beauty. Admirable, yes. But relaxed, lacking in preparation and self-awareness—beautiful—no.)

Part of why beauty is so important to humans is that our depth perception allows us to see and recognize that other humans are watching us. Relatively few other species have the ability to perceive whether other members of their species are looking at them, but we as humans are acutely conscious of whether or not we are the object of someone's gaze.

Standards of beauty change over the centuries, but never so much as to elicit repulsion from era to era. There's a reason beautiful images endure: A sleeping Venus painted by Titian is different from a Brigitte Bardot or *Sports Illustrated* swimsuit model only in the percentage of her body fat and the thickness of her eyeliner. Marilyn Monroe's famous nude photographs of 1950, her pale body arched kittenishly on a red velvet backdrop, remain highly influential erotic images.

Beauty opens doors, seals marriages, disrupts dynasties, prompts war. Yet we toss around the word *beautiful* with abandon, using it to describe almost anything remotely pleasing in modern life: a pair of shoes, a photograph of wheat waving in the wind, a piece of densely marbled steak. But beauty also serves as the thrilling, exquisite counterpoint to old age and decay, as in Hans Baldung Grien's *Three Ages of Woman and Death*, painted circa 1510. A Venus, pale and slender, adjusts her long, blond hair as an infant and an old woman look on; Death holds an hourglass over her blond head, announcing her mortality, signaling that her flesh will wither like that of the old woman behind her, whose breasts have shrunk to flaps and whose teeth are rotted. Venus's beauty is a reminder of our eventual submission to time.

Biologists argue over whether beauty is an assurance of our

natural destiny, used to signal our good health and attract a mate, an invitation to breed.

Anthropologist C. Loring Brace at the University of Michigan says that what we perceive as beautiful is not hardwired into our primitive biological brain. "The idea that there is a standard desirable female body type tells you more about the libidinous fantasies of aging male anthropologists than anything else," he has said.[1] It doesn't make sense that beauty is the main driver toward reproduction. "Attractiveness has nothing to do with whether people reproduce or not. Basically, when women are capable of breeding, they will," he told me. "Birth control has changed that pretty much, and that's been a very recent development. But in the long run, in all societies, even ugly women have children. Ugly children. Who go on to have their own ugly children."

We embrace the extreme procedures that we believe will make us beautiful, that will detonate desire in others. In New York, the transvestite performer Amanda Lepore, born a man, has had operations on her nose, face, lips, and breasts, as well as having her ribs broken and pushed in for a smaller waist.[2] On Long Island, New York, girls graduating from high school receive gifts of breast implants from their parents. In China, on the island of Hainan, patients check into a 12,000-square-foot plastic surgery hospital called the Dreaming Girl's Fantasy for extensive head-to-toe cosmetic reworking. In Beijing, women from all over China compete in the Miss Plastic Surgery competition. The winner of the 2004 competition, Feng Qian, had had four surgical procedures, the first runner-up ten.

No matter how intellectually evolved we are, and no matter how primitive and vaguely immoral it sounds, beauty matters. When Eleanor Roosevelt was asked if she had any regrets in life, she said that she had one: she wished she had been prettier. Taking that sentiment a step further, Mary Tannen, writing in the *New York Times Magazine*, quoted an aging actress who is very much in favor of plastic surgery. "If Eleanor Roosevelt were alive today," the actress confidently told Tannen, "Franklin and his mother would be packing her off for a lift and a nose tip."[3]

decide to throw out the politics and ideology behind beauty and go for the numbers. It's a balmy California afternoon as I drive my rented LeSabre toward Orange County to find out exactly—down to the decimal point—what makes a person beautiful. I cruise past an endlessly repeating loop of mall plazas and low-lying exurban nothingness to the home of Dr. Stephen J. Marquardt in Huntington Beach.

Marquardt, who to some in cosmetic surgery circles is known as the "Mask Man," was trained as a maxillofacial surgeon and became an expert in fixing faces that had suffered traumas like smashing through windshields or being mangled by pit bulls. A bout of arthritis forced him into early retirement, which turned out to be a blessing. He had long yearned to do one thing, he told me on the telephone a few days before my visit: "Find out mathematically what makes someone beautiful. Find out the numbers. And then everyone can use the formula. And then everyone can be beautiful."

He sounded at first like a crude Pollyanna—or a complete crackpot—but the notion that numbers could somehow clarify who is beautiful and who isn't is not entirely without proof or precedent. Most cultures have long assigned abstract, spiritual qualities to numbers, from the sanctity of the number 3 to the bad luck associated with 13. And one number has been associated with beauty and art for two thousand years: the so-called golden section—or phi—which is an irrational number approximately equal to 0.61803. The golden section has inspired mathematicians to devise all manner of shapes and related numbers, including the golden ratio, which is 1.618 to 1. This ratio—also referred to as the golden mean or the divine proportion—is used to build what are referred to as golden shapes. A golden rectangle, for instance, is one whose width is 1 and whose length is 1.608. These are the numbers with which Marquardt is obsessed.

Artists have long considered the golden section and the golden ratio necessary for composition. During the Renaissance, artists and philosophers propounded the "grand theory," which stipulated that beauty consists in the proportion of its parts. Michelangelo's sculpture of David, for example, puts the navel at .618 of the sculpture's height. Leonardo da Vinci's studies of the ideal human figure illustrated how all its parts were related by the golden section. Painters like Seurat used the golden section in paintings such as *Bathers* and *The Parade*. Salvador Dalí poked fun at artists' reliance on the number in *The Sacrament of the Last Supper*, which features an enormous dodecahedron—a twelve-faced crystalline shape based on the golden section—floating over the table.

But what Marquardt was attempting was new: he wanted to apply the rules of the golden section to cosmetic surgery. He had invented a computer program that scans a client's face and then fits it onto a mathematical template. His objective: not only to deduce what is beautiful but to have plastic cosmetic surgeons employ it as a guide, a kind of mask they can use on the face as an overlay. The mask is, he believes, the perfect mathematical model of a beautiful face. Based on the golden ratio, it is an arrangement of forty decagons of six different sizes, aligned with our facial features.

"People have tried to understand a beautiful face for a long time, but do we know what that is?" he asked me on the telephone during our first conversation. "It is an image that is mathematically quantifiable. All life is biology, all biology is chemistry, all chemistry is mathematics." And all mathematics can be applied to cosmetic surgery.

Marquardt believes that every time we look at another human being's face, we unconsciously compare it with an ideal face that lurks in the inaccessible reaches of our deepest, most animal psyche. Since we have no direct access to this ideal face, we can't say precisely what it is; Marquardt, however, claims he has captured the ideal face in his beauty mask. "It not only shows us what is beautiful, it shows us what is human," he said. Prospective patients could simply see if their faces fit its proportions. If not, they need surgery.

There were many reasons to visit the Mask Man. The feminist in me wanted to challenge his notions of cookie-cutter beauty. After all, feminist critics of cosmetic surgery have long fastened on the notion that women use cosmetic surgery not to underscore their uniqueness or eccentricity but to conform to some broad, culturally imposed Barbie-doll notion of beauty.

The journalist in me wanted to find out if the folkloric Marquardt was a wacko or, worse, a plain old huckster trying to peddle his computer software tool to doctors practicing cosmetic surgery so they could sell more operations and procedures to more people who felt imperfect to begin with.

And the vain, irrational beauty junkie in me wanted him to scan my face into his computer—this is embarrassing—and see what I ought to get fixed.

X X X

The survival of the cosmetic surgery industry is based on the notion that a relatively specific ideal of beauty exists and that it is something that can be achieved through purchase. It has long been a commonplace of anthropology that every culture has its own standards defining beauty. But in American culture, where standards are set by a vast array of media, from reality television to airbrushed magazine covers, the parameters have been rapidly narrowing. Full lips, large breasts, a nipped-in waist, lean thighs: we're fast approaching an ideal of womanhood in which an adult female looks like a woman on top, with full breasts and large pink lips, and a twelve-year-old boy (minus external genitalia) on the bottom, with slim hips and a tiny bottom.

So just what is beauty these days? What is considered beautiful?

There is the cartoon version of beauty such as one sees on the reality programs that take pudgy, snaggle-toothed Americans and put them through a brutal round of cosmetic surgery. At the climax of each program the participants emerge, transformed, to the oohs and ahs of family, friends, and surgeons. But as the patients make their appearances week after week, viewers begin to notice an eerie similarity. "They all get a chin implant, all get a brow lift, all get their lips done," said Dr. Z. Paul Lorenc, a New York plastic surgeon.

The cheeks of the patients are all planed upward, the lips uniformly swollen to rubber-doll proportions, the breasts so ample it looks as if the women who bear them might topple over from the weight. And they all get hair extensions: scalp hair in humans grows longer than it does in other primates, and we use it to signal good health, status, and youth. Hair extensions are an überadvertisement of health and fecundity, a perfect example of the folly of attempting to outdo nature. (Folly, because eventually the extensions become stringy and loosen their bonds, and the bearer leaves trails of hair wherever she goes.) The men all receive superhero chins. Mouths are crammed with huge white Chiclets.

The look is cookie-cutter beauty, Dr. Peter B. Fodor, the president of the American Society for Aesthetic Plastic Surgery, told me. "There is a sameness to them all that is chilling," he said.

Critics of American popular culture have long looked down their noses at the quest for bland conformity. We are a nation, they say, of follow-me consumerism. We all wear the same clothes, eat at the same restaurants, and drive the same SUVs. But these television shows signal something far deeper: the herd mentality has reached alarming new levels. Are we now all going to have the same face—one that looks like whoever is on the cover of *Us* magazine?

Of course, the assembly-line look ultimately damages the notion of personal identity. When faces and bodies are remade in the image of the Platonic pop-star ideal, all ties to personal identity—even to one's own family—are lost. The husband of one of the contestants on *The Swan* e-mailed me confidentially after his wife's appearance on the program, complaining that she, while certainly looking more attractive, cried herself to sleep at night because she no longer looked like her mother or her sister. She was unmoored, physically, from her own past.

"She feels lost," he wrote.

Of seventeen candidates on the first season of *The Swan*, all received tooth veneers, sixteen had liposuction, fifteen had forehead lifts, thirteen had nose jobs, thirteen had lip augmentations, and eleven had breast augmentations. Dr. Randal Haworth, one of two surgeons on *The Swan*, said the "graduates" all bore a certain resemblance to one another partly for technical reasons. "There is a certain finite number of procedures you can do," he told me. "And when humans think of beauty, they go to those hot points—nose, brows, lips—and that's what we work hard to define."

But there may have been other reasons. Surgeons on such a program may not only listen to the patient's requests; they may also think of the show as an infomercial for their services. In other words, they are going to think of what is most broadly appealing to the mass market.

In some social sets, it is a simple fact of life that one will have some major procedure every year. In 2004, for example, when Lionel Richie's thirty-seven-year-old wife, Diane, filed for divorce in Los Angeles, her list of financial demands included $20,000 a year for plastic surgery. She also stated in her lawsuit that by her own conservative estimate she spent at least $3,000 a month on dermatology, $600 a month on hair care, $1,000 a month on laser hair removal, $10,000 to $15,000 a month on clothing, and $500 to $600 on vitamins.[4] (Later the same year, she was charged with aiding and abetting Daniel Tomas Fuente Serrano, who was using her home to host "pumping parties" and give non-FDA-approved injections to women such as Shawn King, wife of Larry King.)[5]

And who most women want to look like is no surprise.

"Our religion is celebrity, and our gods are celebrities," Haworth said. "When we conform to the dictates of taste, that's who we look to."

No better example of the celebrity notion of beauty exists than MTV's *I Want a Famous Face*, in which teenagers and people in their twenties describe to a surgeon who they want to look like. A twenty-three-year-old transsexual named Jessica wanted to look like Jennifer Lopez, so she got breast implants, cheek implants, and an eyebrow lift and had her hairline lowered. Mike and Matt, twenty-year-old twin brothers from Arizona, wanted to look like Brad Pitt. They both got rhinoplasty, chin implants, and porcelain veneers. One woman, Kacey Long, inspired by the movie *Erin Brockovich*, decided to have breast implants so she could look more like Julia Roberts (even though Roberts's ample bosoms in that movie were created with the help of push-up bras and rubber "chicken cutlet" bra inserts). *I Want a Famous Face* later broadcast the surgery Long had to remove the implants, which had created serious medical complications.

Notions of beauty are often fixed to class. Dr. Terry Dubrow, the other *Swan* surgeon, said the women on the show turned out looking alike because they are all relatively young and come from a similar socioeconomic background, so they share—and want to look like—a similar beauty prototype. "The younger girls think that beauty is raised cheeks, a higher brow, big breasts, and fuller lips," Dubrow said. "You know, Pam Anderson."

Of course, women have long tried to look like cultural icons, whether it's Twiggy or Angie Dickinson. But there is something much more chilling in the way that patients today see Pamela Anderson, an obvious and proud consumer of cosmetic surgery, as a paradigm of beauty. It is as if we have elevated artifice above humanity and the look of the fake over the natural contours of the authentic.

In the mid-1960s, the sociologist Philip Rieff put forth the notion that the average American had come to see him- or herself not as a citizen but as a patient of the culture; the way to salvation and personal fulfillment—what television's Dr. Phil might today call "ownership" of the self—was to discuss one's maladies in public and address them using therapy, medicine, and technology, he wrote in *The Triumph of the Therapeutic.* This view of the self as a patient implies from the start that the psyche or the body is somehow broken or disfigured and must be fixed if the actualized, "real" human being is to emerge. It requires constant examination of the self, and the flaws of the self, yet the patient him- or herself is not qualified to say when he or she is perfect, ready for membership in the ranks of the personally self-fulfilled. Only the judgment of our fellow Americans—or Oprah, or Dr. Phil, or a personal trainer, or our plastic surgeon—can tell us when we have reached that point. "When so little can be taken for granted, when the meaningfulness of social existence no longer grants an inner life at peace with oneself, every man must become something of a genius about himself," Rieff wrote.[6]

For Rieff, the culture of the therapeutic had replaced religion, transforming Americans from a civilization based in religious ethics and Puritan virtue into one where all concerns were of bettering the self. "That a sense of well-being has become the end, rather than a by-product of striving after some superior communal end, announced a fundamental change in focus in the entire cast of our culture—toward a human condition about which there will be nothing further to say in terms of the old style of despair and hope."[7] For us, the culture of the therapeutic—the culture of well-being—has given way to the cultures of celebrity and cosmetic surgery. We no longer focus on the bettering of the self but have gone one step further. We focus only on creating the beautiful carapace.

That hunger has translated in part into the boom in cosmetic surgery, as hundreds of thousands of Americans have sought to become patients, seeking the genius that will then allow them to become their own best self-promoters and marketers. But there is no success until the viewers applaud and the patient's happiness is allowed to become complete.

George Orwell said that at fifty, every man has the face he deserves. To erase the lines and change the contours of one's face is a way of obliterating one's history. Yet so many Americans unwittingly trivialize their identity by removing their individuality. I remember standing at a garden party during the weekend of the Oscars in Los Angeles, and as I looked across the lawn I couldn't help but notice that there were several women who were about five foot ten, looked like they weighed less than 130 pounds, and had tiny hips and large, bobbing breasts. (The look is affectionately referred to by Los Angeles cosmetic surgeons as "tits on sticks.") They all had straight blond hair. They all had full lips and large white teeth. They all had bright, open eyes. They all had small, straight noses. Their clothes were a symphony of creams and beiges. If they had been together on a stage they would have looked like a girls' doo-wop group from the sixties, just dressed by Donna Karan.

A studio executive came up to one of the women and touched her elbow.

"Time to go, honey," he said.

She turned to face him, and he realized that she was not his wife. But her silhouette was so similar to that of his wife, her breasts jutting out at the very same angle, her lips pouting in the very same way, her nose ending in the same ski jump above the same divotlike philtrum, the clothes the same Neiman Marcus uniform, it was impossible to tell from twenty feet away that she was not.

With the popularization of cosmetic surgery, there is almost a danger that beauty can be transformed into something mundane.

So how do we define beauty in an age of Botox? Is a beautiful face one without expression, a nonsmiling mask best epitomized by what some New York women call the "fashionista face"—a stony face that belies no emotion? Or is it the face presented to us by Hollywood, preternaturally wide-eyed, with lips pumped up in a cartoonish caricature of infancy?

Neither. A beautiful woman is typically a young and healthy woman—even if now the youthful-appearing face we see on Madison Avenue and Rodeo Drive and at the mall only mimics the properties of youth: bright, open eyes; full lips; clear, smooth skin free of signs of illness; a serene expression, indicating the mental well-being of the bearer; pink cheeks and full red lips, flush with vigorous circulation; strong white teeth. It makes sense that Americans are obsessed with youth. The population is aging, feeling its collective youth drain away. By 2020, more than a third of all Americans will be fifty or older. And by 2050, the population of Americans aged sixty-five or older could be bigger than that of those fourteen and under for the first time in United States history.

We have always used artifice to create what nature never gave us. In the Border Cave region of southern Africa, archeologists have found tubes of red ochre that were used forty thousand years ago for the purpose of decorating the face and body. Five thousand years ago, Egyptians ground red ochre—which gets its color from iron—with kohl and sycamore juice and applied it as blush, or they combined it with grease and used it as lip tint. Malachite, a green copper ore, and galena, a dark red lead ore, were ground into powder and used as eye shadow (with crushed beetles' wings adding an extra glittery component). These cosmetics have been found packed into graves, so the deceased could wear eyeshadow in the next life.

Unwanted body hair was removed with a combination of boiled bird bones, fly dung, sycamore juice, and cucumber, which was heated and applied—and presumably pulled off when it had congealed. Think of the agony of bound Chinese feet—imagine a grown woman with feet no longer than three inches and curled into tight pink, shrimplike forms—or the months of lip stretching endured by the lip-plate wearers of the Suri and other African tribes.

Psychology has tried to demystify beauty, to evoke it as a biological inducement to procreation, a way to weed out the infirm and gravely unattractive. Feminist philosophy has criticized it as a bland quest for conformity, often dictated by male doctors. In economic terms, the quest for beauty can be seen as a way to sell potions and devices to an easily swayed population. The flourishing of the American cosmetic surgery industry itself is the direct result of the medical profession's fleeing the bureaucracy of health insurance companies for the free market of elective surgery, where the consumer pays that day—in cash, if you'd like.

Yet beauty speaks to such basic, deep longings, that our search for it remains the most insistent force in our lives. It is an expression of the divine, a symbol we hold up against the inevitable humiliations of mortality.

X X X

The scene is one of quiet California suburbia. A dog barks as I pull up to the bungalow-style house and ring the doorbell. Dr. Marquardt's wife, a pretty woman in her forties, opens the door.

There, in the living room, sits Marquardt with his brother-in-law. He stands up, and the impression his body leaves remains silhouetted in the plump sofa pillows. Someone has just hit pause on the VCR, and the huge television in front of them plays a jittery still image from a movie.

"Oh, hi," Marquardt says. "We were just watching *Shallow Hal.*"

"That's funny," I say.

Marquardt, a fiftyish, slightly pudgy man with graying hair who that day—it's a Saturday—is wearing a T-shirt and long khaki shorts, tilts his head to the side in query. His eyes have the gauzy look of a man who has been sitting in front of a television set for a long time.

"Why?" he says.

"Well, I came from New York to talk to you about physical

perfection, and that's what this movie is about and . . . " Marquardt looks at me strangely. *What is she talking about?* I let the point drop. In Marquardt's office off the living room, we begin to discuss what makes beauty, and he starts to sift through stacks of photographs and files and sketches. The office is lined with bookshelves, neatly stacked with manila folders, videotapes, and magazines.

There is a difference between beauty and social convention, he likes to point out. "A few hundred years ago it was considered beautiful to be plump," Marquardt says. "In some societies that is still true. That is social convention. But beauty is eternity." He pauses. "I mean, you know what I mean by eternity. I'm not just spouting some commercial crap here. Eternity in the sense of something that is long-lasting. And then there is vogue, which is temporary. Like white lipstick in the sixties. And then there is fashion. High heels, say, which have been around for hundreds of years."

Marquardt tells me he has been working on his beauty research for thirty years.

"I always thought somebody would know, somewhere, that they would have written down a formula for it," he says. "But no plastic surgeon or artist was able to quantify it for me. It was all in the eye of the beholder."

At the heart of every doctor whose trade is beauty lies a definitive, sometimes searing childhood memory about the power of image or beauty or femininity, and Marquardt is no exception. When he was four years old and his mother was pregnant, he, his mother, and his father were in an automobile accident.

"My father and I were barely injured but she went through the windshield," Marquardt told me on the telephone when we first spoke. Her pregnancy remained viable but she had to have her jaw wired shut. "She had morning sickness every day. She was throwing up through her wired jaw. It was just awful."

After giving birth to Marquardt's (perfectly healthy) younger brother, Marquardt's mother was able to see her firstborn son.

"My aunt and grandmother took me to see my mother," he said. Her eyeballs, he recalled, were red because of broken blood vessels. The surrounding tissue was black and blue. The effect was horrifying. "Her face was horribly swollen and her jaws were wired shut. And my thought at the time was, 'Why are they trying to feed me to this monster?' And then she opened her mouth and said,"—here, Marquardt dropped his voice to a low, hoarse, sinister rumble—'Hi, Stevie.' "

The young Dr. Marquardt ran out of the room. He was terrified of that person in the bed. Later, his mother suffered from postpartum depression and spent a year in a sanitarium, he said. "And when she finally came back, there was this person who didn't look like my mother and didn't act like my mother," he said. "For a long time during my childhood, I wondered where my real mother was. I thought my real mother was someplace else. And it was at that time that I began to start thinking about the face, her face, and why it had scared me so. Why does the face make the person? Why is it so important? And then as I got into puberty, it was more, 'Why am I only attracted to attractive faces even if the women are jerks?' "

The face is so important, he says, because it is the center of our humanity. Its attractiveness and hence our ability to befriend fellow human beings are vital components for our survival. It is the physical portal through which we gather information about the world, and nourish ourselves, and breathe, and talk, and communicate. The skin and bones are among the most delicate on the body, the most susceptible to accident, disfigurement, and disease, and so are interpreted as the best and most immediate indicators of health. The delicate cartilage of the nose erodes with syphilis and is gnarled by leprosy. A pale cheek or eyes ringed with shadows might indicate illness. The skin of the face is thinner than skin on the rest of the body, so lesions associated with disease appear on the face more readily and scar more easily; and because the skin is thin and is frequently exposed to the sun, the face shows age first. As long as humanity has existed, the youthful, healthy face has been the best advertisement for companionship, friendship, collegiality, romance.

In medical school, Marquardt began to ask doctors about beauty. "And it was always this unknown ethereal thing," he says. "I thought, 'Bullshit.'" He believed the archetypal mask—the perfect face—was a genetic code that was programmed into human beings from birth. It told us what a human face ought to look like. There must be a formula, he thought.

Marquardt became a dentist, then trained in maxillofacial surgery, which required him to do a lot of emergency work on jaws and cheeks. "We had a tremendous ability to change the way people looked," he says. "And we usually found that when we improved the function of the face, the face would look better." He began his quest to find out what attractiveness was. With a background in math and physics, he studied the problem from a mathematical point of view. "In math, we quantify everything: light, speed, colors, sounds, odors. Everything is quantifiable. So attractiveness was not quantifiable? I began to search for a geometry of the face."

Analyzing beautiful faces to figure out if there was some mathematical configuration they all shared, he discovered the golden ratio. "Beauty could be a car," he says. "It could be a pair of shoes. It is anything that evokes a strong emotional response. *I want to be close to it. I want to be seen with it.* That is the beauty response." A beautiful face, he explains, is harmonious. The same mathematical themes occur over and over again. And there have been studies that try to quantify the components of beauty. Michael Cunningham, a psychologist at the University of Louisville, conducted a series of experiments with college students in the 1980s, asking male students to rate female faces, and discovered a list of measurements that could theoretically create a perfectly beautiful face: the ideal eye width is three-tenths of the face at the eyes' level, chin length one-fifth of the face, height of the visible eyeball no more than one-fourteenth of the face. But he did not, as Marquardt hoped to do, create a template surgeons could then use to literally cut and sew together the perfect face.[8]

Marquardt booted up his computer. He has done a particularly interesting study, he says, into how people from different cultures react to beautiful, not so beautiful, and just plain ugly faces. He asked his research subjects to look at a series of eighteen faces and rank them according to how beautiful they appeared. At one extreme, there was the model Stephanie Seymour. At the other was a woman whose face had been disfigured by neurofibromatosis, an overgrowth of fibrous tissues that made her face look like melted wax. The participants in his study—who were from several different countries and of many different ethnicities—ranked the eighteen faces in the same order, almost to a person.

"People like to say, 'There's someone out there who loves ugly,'" he says, flipping through the black-and-white photographs of faces, each uglier than the last. At first, they are just common, plain vanilla ugly: too big a nose, eyes too close together. Then they begin to mutate: there is a goiter, there are facial diseases and disfigurements progressively less tolerable to the eye. "I say that's horse manure," Marquardt exclaims. "Nobody loves ugly. And most people don't love ugly about in equal amounts. I found faces that were deformed, that were practically nonhuman. I got as great a range as possible but found that 97 percent of the people ranked them in the same order. There was one Japanese guy, and he was furious when I told him he had ranked the faces in the same order as this American woman. 'We Japanese think of beauty very differently,' he said. 'That is impossible.' He was very insulted. But the facts spoke for themselves."

We stare at the last picture, of the woman with the face seemingly melting with overgrown tissue. "Frankly, most people who survive on the planet today fit the beauty mask. Those extreme patients, no one would mate with, and the genetic mutations they carried would not be passed on." He flips the screen to his mask. "You know, I have never analyzed my own face," he says.

He picks up a pencil and a ruler and starts measuring the basic lines of mine.

"You have nice full lips and pretty eyes," he says. "Your cheekbones are well positioned. The nose is good."

Marquardt studies my face. He screws one eye shut and holds his fingers over my eye in an L shape.

"But I gotta tell you, your eyebrows aren't doing you any favors."

X
X X

The American fascination with self-improvement, inside and out, has been documented in many variations. If cosmetic plastic surgery is available to the average consumer—thanks in part to lending agencies that specialize in financing cosmetic procedures—and no longer bears the stigma of vanity, the question arises: Are we on our way to becoming a nation of the surgically enhanced? If looking beautiful becomes as easy as buying a car or a dress, will beauty—or an imitation of it—become so commonplace as to be meaningless?

"It's already happening," Marquardt told me. "It used to be that the weak of the species died. Now we have people with diabetes who are producing more people with diabetes. I have nothing against diabetics, but ultimately medicines that fix us will put a tremendous burden on us."

A theoretically possible consequence of all the surgical self-beautification is a principle marketing professionals call the "contrast effect." It is an axiom of perception that dictates that differences between things are amplified depending on which thing is perceived first and which second. Perception is, in other words, heavily colored by context. For example, if you taste a sweet drink and then set it down and taste an even sweeter drink, the second drink will seem sweeter to you than if you hadn't tasted the first one. And the contrast effect works both ways: a woman of average looks will appear to be more good-looking if she walks into a room of unattractive women. (I think this is part of the reason men are so crazy about women who play golf. Any woman on a golf course always looks gorgeous, in part because she's one of the few women out on the links. It's a desert-island effect.)

The contrast effect has taken its toll in certain quarters. Hollywood publicist Michael Levine complained in a 2001 essay that he has come to hate physical perfection and being around the Hollywood women who work all day long to keep their bodies and faces gorgeous. "There's an extraordinarily high concentration of gorgeous females in Los Angeles," he wrote. For those who don't arrive looking perfect, "whole industries exist here to render it attainable, to reshape faces and bodies to the prevailing standard of attractiveness." The final effect on him, however, is a deadening one. "But my exposure to extreme beauty is ruining my capacity to love the ordinarily beautiful women of the real world, women who are more likely to meet my needs for deep connection and partnership of the soul."[9]

I disagree with Levine's final interpretation—after all, why can't a beautiful, surgically altered woman meet his needs for eternal companionship?—but his major point holds fast. A pretty, well-coiffed, slender, toned, blond, gleaming, immaculately dressed woman in Los Angeles is just another pretty, well-coiffed, slender, toned, blond, gleaming, immaculately dressed woman in Los Angeles, in a sea of similar beauties.

The number of cosmetic procedures that Americans underwent increased by 228 percent from 1997 to 2004. The numbers are likely to rise as the population ages, prices drop, younger patients seek out surgery, technology and genetic engineering generate new techniques, and more doctors from various fields offer cosmetic surgical procedures.

Surgical procedures will inevitably become less expensive, says Dr. Lloyd M. Krieger, a plastic surgeon who also has an MBA from the University of Chicago, in part because procedures that ten years ago took place in a hospital operating room and required expensive overnight stays now take place in a doctor's office. And, like any other consumer product, as cosmetic surgery becomes more popular, the laws of economics dictate that the price will come down. "Usually that does not apply to health care, which is bound up with insurance issues, but in the case of cosmetic surgery, people are using their own money so the typical health-insurance restrictions don't apply," Krieger says. Consumers approach cosmetic surgery as a retail decision, "as if they were buying a cruise, a vacation, a car." Krieger brings that concept to the public in his own practice: he runs the Rodeo Drive Plastic Surgery Center, which is in a mall off Rodeo Drive in Beverly Hills.

It is that mind-set that seems to indicate that we have begun to think of our bodies as something like an accessory that can be modified when necessary, discarded when it is worn out, and upgraded when required, a leathery sack to transport us from one medical specialist to the next. This notion has become a theme of stylish intellectual popular culture (as opposed to *Star* magazine popular culture). In Hanif Kureishi's 2004 novel, *The Body*, for example, an affluent older playwright has his brain transplanted into a healthy, muscular, young body. In this universe of transplantees, those with new "facilities," as they are called, are New-bodies and those still stuck in their withered ones are Oldbodies. No longer doomed to the jiggles and humiliations of age, the protagonist takes a vacation from his marriage, travels through Greece, and indulges various appetites (food, sex) before concluding that even a new body is an extremely fragile entity, consigned to eventual doom.

But for a while at least, the distance between those who can afford to maintain a youthful appearance, increasingly a sign of privilege, and the merely plain, the unretouched have-nots, will likely widen.

New technologies will soon be available to draw in well-off patients who might never have thought of cosmetic enhancement. Reviewing Kureishi's novel in the *New York Times Book Review*,

Benjamin Kunkel concluded that, while we may all dream about extending our lives into healthy periods of sustained youthfulness and vigor, this is a privilege that will ultimately be reserved for the very few. "The National Institutes of Health has given grants to ethicists earnestly considering the matter, and certain scientists maintain that there are those among us who will live indefinitely," Kunkel wrote. "What they don't always mention is that these are probably the rich people."

Dr. Steven A. Teitelbaum predicts that the next milestone will be the control of tissue formation, whether to reduce scarring or to grow new tissues. When surgeons can selectively grow tissue in the breast, Teitelbaum says, patients may face less risk than if, for example, they receive breast implants, which can rupture and cause complications and must also be replaced every few years. "When we can control scarring we can do operations we don't even think of now because of the massive scar formation," he says.

Surely, a backlash against the artificial beauties will erupt. Not a chance, according to Teitelbaum. Surgical work, when well done, is now subtle. "Most people aren't getting those bad face-lifts anymore, where the eyes, lips, and cheeks are distorted," he says. "If everyone getting plastic surgery looked like that, there would be a backlash."

The aesthetically altered future would flummox Darwin. Dr. Michelle Copeland suggests that cosmetically altered couplings could create some surprises. Say a man with a big nose and receding chin has a nose job and a chin implant. With his new profile he manages to marry a beautiful woman, who, by the by, has already had her ears pinned back, her sleepy-looking eyes lifted, and her narrow lips augmented. Their child might well be a surprise package with a big nose, Dumbo ears, receding chin, saggy lids, and thin lips.

"Well then, the child will simply have to start doing all the things his or her parents did," Copeland says with a sigh. "I've already seen it happen."

Roberta Myers, the editor in chief of *Elle*, believes that there is a pretty solid standard, at least from the male perspective. "Men will always like the small waist, big breasts, curvy hips, silky hair, big eyes, big lips construction," she told me. "I'm always interested in the differences between the two coasts—which grind out all of these images for public consumption and thereby set the standards—because it's clear that the L.A. aesthetic is considered somewhat tacky and overblown by N.Y. fashion types, and California considers us to be a little wan and severe. So there's the curvy Pam Anderson, still big in Hollywood, and there's the flat-chested, almost childlike beauty of Kate Moss and Natalia Vodianova. The womanly Brazilians got bumped off the runway by the ethereal Russians."

The more power women feel they have over their own lives, Myers said, the more comfortable they seem to feel about their looks. "But it's an interesting question about whether we're more or less confident generally than we were twenty years ago," she continued. "Twenty years ago, fashion was still not mainstreamed the way it is now—everyone can have Gucci! Louis Vuitton!—and there was still a little feminist shame in seeming to care too much about your looks. But I'd say women over thirty and under sixty feel enormous pressure to avail themselves of all the intervention they can afford."

As for Marquardt, he holds fast to his dream of perfect beauty—which is, definitively and, one might add, a little narrowly, Paulina Porizkova. I didn't think he was going to hustle a lot of people with his software program, for the very reasons he described. No one can actually tell you what is beautiful. A beautiful face is symmetrical and constituted of harmonious planes and shapes. But even the artists of the Renaissance eventually abandoned their grand theory for more disquieting, complex, and surprising notions of beauty.

I did know one thing, however: I was going to have to do something about my eyebrows. They did not make me beautiful. They were painfully thin and wispy, almost patchy in places.

Later I followed the advice of an article I read in a women's beauty magazine: using a Q-tip, apply Rogaine to the bare spots of your eyebrows. I bought some Women's Rogaine and followed the advice, dutifully swabbing it every day for six months on the exact spot at the corners of each of my eyebrows where the hair is sparse.

At the end of six months, alas, my eyebrows were still painfully thin. I did, however, wind up with a wispy mustache.

Seven

Los Angeles

On a pleasant spring day, I find myself in Bel Air, just up the street from Elizabeth Taylor's house, lunching with a woman of uncertain age. She has been married to her husband, a film industry executive, for more than twenty years. But the relationship has, over time, evolved from a partnership to a *mariage de complaisance*, although it is intimate on occasion.

Mrs. X—she would talk to me about her very private cosmetic surgery only if I promised not to use her name—is the paradigm of a Hollywood housewife. In the 1980s she worked out at aerobics studios with her friends in the afternoons. In the 1990s, she and her girlfriends switched to yoga. Now, it's Pilates. If you ask her her age, she responds with a prim but witty: "Oh, I'm five foot six." She won't give it up, even off the record.

For Mrs. X, the caretaking of the body and the face is a day-long daily ritual. Her physical self encompasses all her interests: it is her profession, hobby, passion, and primary relationship. She goes to the hairdresser at least twice a week, for color or styling. She plays tennis, not for its sociability or for love of the sport but for general toning. She uses self-tanner of several varieties: one for face, one for hands, and one for body. Once a week, a facialist steams her pores and gently squeezes them. Mrs. X slathers on creams to keep her skin moist: depending on the fad of the year, that might be cream made with caviar, flecks of 24-karat gold, diamond dust, bone marrow, wild yam extract, or something promising to be human growth hormone. This year, her favorite product is Mariana Chicet Brain Lipid Serum, which is made, so the manufacturer says, from cow brain extract.

She drinks Penta water, which by virtue of a patented process using high-energy sound waves (again, according to the manufacturer), is supposed to be more effective at hydrating the body than any other water. She takes vitamins every day, including Murad Wet Suit vitamins, which are supposed to help build collagen, and she drinks a cup of probiotic blue-green algae each morning. She has her nails done twice a week (buffed, not polished: much younger looking). She is undergoing a series of Rolfing treatments.

Her policy toward body hair is scorched earth: her skin is stripped almost completely bare of hair once a week. When she goes out for an evening, her makeup is applied by a professional makeup artist who used to work on the cast of *Friends* and who arrives at her house with an assistant. She has her teeth cleaned every eight weeks, and the natural ones whitened. For those teeth with veneers, she has them checked and changed once every year or so. She has her eyebrows tweezed and tinted every week. Her vision is LASIK perfect. She visits Dr. Arnold Klein, whom she considers a family friend, once a month. She has tried Gore-Tex, Botox, collagen, Restylane, Artecoll. She says she is a member of a Restylane frequent-user awards program—a frequent-flier mile package for the beauty crowd. She sees two or three plastic surgeons about three times a year, mostly for consultation, but about once a year she finds something to be trimmed or tucked or remolded. Last year, she went with a girlfriend to see a plastic surgeon in Paris who, they had heard, had done a face-lift on Catherine Deneuve using gold threads. (She decided against it.

Deneuve has maintained that she has never had a face-lift.) Taken alone, Mrs. X's lips are beautifully full, but they nevertheless look incongruous on a woman whose age is indeterminable but who has a child from her first marriage who is thirty-three.

Over the years, she has had liposuction. She has had a tummy tuck. She has had a brow lift and two variations on a face-lift. She has had her eyes done, upper and lower, separately. And her breasts: there were implants put in, and taken out, and then larger ones put in.

She is, among her peer group, considered the norm. But last year, she went further than any of her circle of friends.

"It was after a bath, and I was looking at myself," she says with a downward-gazing delicacy that suggests "myself" actually means "my vagina." "And I noticed that the inner, you know, were protruding a bit, and the outer, you know, were looking kind of, well, droopy." She pulls her mouth down at the corners and makes a sad-clown face.

She was referred to Dr. Gary Alter, a Los Angeles plastic surgeon who is board certified in both urology and plastic surgery and is considered one of the experts in the growing field of genital cosmetic surgery. (For male patients, he can do a number of procedures, including penile implants, testicle implants, and scrotum reductions.)

"It was painful for about a week," she says. "It hurt to go to the bathroom. I had tubes for a while. And then one day, voilà. It was fresh. Clean. Tidy looking. Do you know what I mean?"

The medical term for a procedure in which the female external genital structures are surgically reshaped is labiaplasty. And while the American Society of Plastic Surgeons has no statistics yet, anecdotal evidence, according to Dr. V. Leroy Young, the chair of the organization's emerging trends committee, suggests that vaginal cosmetic surgery is one of the fastest-growing areas in the field.

In a culture so thoroughly dominated by pornography, it was inevitable that looking good would extend to every part of the body. Labiaplasty used to be terrain familiar only to sex workers, exotic dancers, and nude models, with the exception of the occasional woman who simply sought to reduce abnormally large labia. Today, images derived from pornography but stylized for mainstream consumption are a part of daily life: Abercrombie & Fitch sells thong underwear for little girls, inspired by those worn by exotic dancers. Women who would never have even uttered the phrase *bikini wax* twenty years ago now have their nether regions shaped and trimmed and cleared of hair in the style of Brazilian bikini wearers (i.e., meaning that there's no hair left or, if there is any, it is just the tiniest symbolic strip to suggest adulthood). Gyms offer pole-dancing classes as part of their aerobics programs. On prime-time network television, Julia Louis-Dreyfus's character on the sitcom *The New Adventures of Old Christine* discusses how a Brazilian bikini wax makes her look as if she has a "hair arrow" pointing to her genitalia. For my last birthday, a friend gave me a certificate for an at-home striptease lesson, taught by a professional stripper.

It is this mainstreaming of porn images, Young told me, that has changed the way women see themselves. Surgeons are receiving more requests for labiaplasty and more complaints from women of general dissatisfaction with their most personal parts. Most of the women getting this type of surgery, he said, are doing so because they or their male sexual partners compare them with images of pornography. "Women who aren't sex workers are having this kind of surgery because there's pressure from someone who is telling them they are not perfect," Young said. "I assume that their standards for labial beauty were set by a combination of the porn industry and pornography on the Internet that their male partners see and compare them to. They don't want old-looking vaginas."[1]

Gary Alter is happy to fix any number of issues pertaining to the female genitalia. And most of his clients are younger women, more easily influenced by seductive pop images. "Some women lose the fullness, and so I take fat from another part of the body and inject it there," he told me in a cheerful, businesslike tone of voice. "And then there are young women who don't like having that pad of fat on top. So I can liposuction that. It makes wearing tight dresses a lot easier."[2]

Just as with any other cosmetic surgery procedure, there are Web sites that offer graphic before-and-after images. On the site of Dr. Bernard Stern, a Fort Lauderdale gynecologist, a warning cautions, "Please enter only if this material will not offend you in any way!" And there they are.[3] A row down the left of saggy, overly pink, flushed sets of labia. They look like vaginas through which infants have passed. On the right, they are tidy, prettified, plucked of hair. Any indications of womanliness or motherhood have been snipped away so that the entire system, once a slightly rumpled flower, has been turned into a smooth pink crease between the legs.

Mrs. X feels much younger now.

"I've spent so much money for the rest of me to look like Dolly Parton," she says. "So why should that"—again, the modest downward glance—"look like Willie Nelson?"

L os Angeles is a magical crossroads of a city, a comic and tragic place where beauty, youth, sex, money, fame, and failure collide every day. Good looks are considered hard currency and, when invested properly—in a profitable marriage, a career in Hollywood or the San Fernando Valley's porn industry—more dependable than Treasury bills.

In Hollywood, thousands of working or hopeful actresses wake up every day worrying—about their weight, about the color of their teeth (three to four shades whiter than the whitest natural color works best on camera), the shape of their fingernails, the size of their pores. The perfect and slender thrive in Los Angeles; the rest wither, forgotten drones who don't care—or just don't try hard enough—to distinguish themselves by their looks. In Hollywood, a size 4 is too bulky for the camera; only size 2 or the exotic-sounding and philosophically challenging size 0 are acceptable.

A reed-slender body is so important in Hollywood and New York that many starlets have begun, on the advice of their personal trainers, taking a steroid called clenbuterol that is used to treat asthma in horses. It is called "clen," for short—as a mere abbreviation but also as a nod to the notion that being smaller, being skinnier, ingesting nothing somehow *cleanses* a girl, makes her better and shinier and just a touch more luminescent than the rest of us. The steroid, ingested in regular doses over a few weeks, rewards users with a so-called sample-size figure, a size 2 or smaller—so that the stylists who dress these mini-celebrities can get their clients' clothes for free from designers, according to Amanda Reno, a stylist who has worked with actresses Carmen Electra and Virginia Madsen.[4] Clen can also increase your risk of stroke and heart attack, destroys endurance, and stiffens the heart muscle.[5] In the end, you'll look great. But you might be dead.

The competitive stakes for good looks are so high in Los Angeles that blonds have blond insecurity. "They get nervous that they are not blond enough," one hairdresser to several famous blond actresses told me. "They'll come in week after week after week. 'So-and-so is looking awfully wheaty and buttery these days. What about me?' " The pursuit of perfection has prompted a vernacular language of its own. If a guy is not buff enough, he will be admonished by his fellow gym goers, "No pecs, no sex." Celebrities who have been famously altered become "surgery celebrities."

A small backlash has begun. A few A-list actresses such as Sarah Jessica Parker, Julianne Moore, and Jamie Lee Curtis have described the Hollywood obsession with youth and cosmetic surgery and Botox as an "epidemic." In press interviews and on red carpets, other actresses are speaking out about plastic surgery with a passion usually reserved for things like antifur campaigns. Or, depending on the year, *pro*fur campaigns. "It's out of control," Shannen Doherty, thirty-three, star of Fox's *North Shore*, told one magazine. "Why get lipo when you can work out or eat better?" Kirstie Alley, star of the Showtime series *Fat Actress*, complained: "It's sick. We should start concentrating on our lives, [not] our noses and breasts." Kate Winslet, twenty-nine, told *Harper's Bazaar* she will "never" have surgery or Botox, because "I want to be able to really show the expressions on my face." And at fifty-eight, Diane Keaton, whose brief nude scene in *Something's Gotta Give* provoked audience cheers, has declared herself against plastic surgery as a matter of "integrity. I want to express my age and be authentic. Why do so many people follow somebody else's idea of what is attractive?"

Actors still have their teeth whitened and their hair lengthened with extensions, their tans artificially applied, and their nails glued on, but some now demand that their head shots be less retouched. One reality-TV star in her forties told the *New York Times* "Fashions of the Times" magazine that she has restricted what the airbrusher can do to her image. "I give strict orders to take out every other line."[6]

Then, there are the young, who aren't quite sophisticated enough to watch out for the feelings of their elder peers. While most actresses in Hollywood have been carefully coached by their public relations handlers to take a stand against plastic surgery, one always slips through the cracks. In January of 2006, for instance, Scarlett Johansson announced that she was determined to fight the aging process with plastic surgery once her looks start to deteriorate, according to a press release sent around by a publicist for Dr. Anthony Griffin, one of the surgeons who appears on ABC's *Extreme Makeover*. The *Lost in Translation* star, who at the time of her remark had reached the ripe age of twenty-one, said she would definitely be willing to go under the knife if necessary, telling the press, "Oh, I definitely believe in plastic surgery. I don't want to be an old hag. There's no fun in that."[7]

One of the most in-demand actresses in Hollywood lives a few blocks away from me in New York. Her agent calls her two or three times a day. She has recently appeared in movies with Sydney Pollack, Ben Affleck, Amanda Peet, Kenneth Branagh, Woody

Allen, Heather Graham, and Al Pacino. Although she is much sought after by directors and producers, she is not a woman you will recognize. Her name is Tina Sloan, and the reason she is such an important actress is that she has not had any plastic surgery. She is a rare bird in the entertainment industry, a sixty-three-year-old Botox virgin. When a role calls for a mother who actually looks mature enough and old enough to be a mother, Sloan gets the call. There are simply no more actresses left in Hollywood who will allow themselves to look old enough to play someone's mother or grandmother.

We meet at her apartment on Park Avenue. She has a strong facial structure, the kind of prominent cheekbones that almost guarantee a face ages gracefully instead of sinking into itself. She is about medium height, medium weight: there is nothing dramatic. She does not wear nail polish and never will.

"People sort of allow themselves to get swept up into a tidal wave of what everyone else is doing," she says. "I look at cosmetic surgery that way. It's a tidal wave that has swallowed up every woman I know. I'm not natural entirely," she admits. "I do dye my hair. I wear makeup. I couldn't *not* wear makeup." The next character she will play is that of a miner's wife. "I couldn't play a miner's wife if I had had a face-lift," she says.

We watch her reel, which includes clips from parts on the series *Third Watch* and *Law & Order SVU* and the movies *The Guru* and *People I Know.* In Woody Allen's *Celebrity,* she plays a patient who has been frantically pacing a plastic surgeon's waiting room, eager for an appointment. In a scene from *Guiding Light,* a soap opera on which she has a recurring role, she is staring into the mirror when another woman walks in and asks her what's wrong. "I was just being overwhelmed by intimations of my own mortality," Sloan replies. "So the question is . . . " She waits a theatrical beat, and the music swells: "Face-lift?"

In real life, Sloan is radically removed from the world of cosmetic surgery. "I guess I believe in being who you are," she says. "It's that simple. I've always had my work, my family, travel, exercise, reading, theater. I don't believe in having a lot of excess stuff around," she says, her arms sweeping the living room, a clean place free of tchotchkes. "I think the more *stuff* "—her voice drips with derision at the word—"you have around, the more distracted you become from yourself. I feel the same way about my face and body. If I concerned myself with its physical perfection every day, I'd be paralyzed."[8]

While Hollywood celebrates perfection, it also yearns for the delicious, shuddering schadenfreude of imperfection. The only thing that eclipses the satisfaction of perfect beauty is beauty gone haywire, beauty that is attained only with good lighting or expertly applied pancake makeup and ultimately proved to be a fraud. And so California delivers us people like Dr. Vail Reese, a Los Angeles dermatologist who once a year awards celebrities with dermatological flaws—as he sees them—with his annual "Skinnies" awards. On his Web site, skinema.com, Reese offers his commentary on who looks great and who doesn't. In 2004, Scarlett Johansson won for "Moliest Mug," Bill Murray for the worst acne scars, and Robert Redford for sun damage. In 2005, Jamie Foxx won the award for "Pimpliest Portrayal in a Biopic."

California is a magnet for those seeking physical perfection. In *Muscle*, a memoir of his bodybuilding days, Samuel Fussell describes how at the age of twenty-six he found himself working in New York City and worrying that he would become the victim of a violent crime. Although he approached competitive weight lifting as a way to bulk up and scare off potential muggers, he became obsessed, quitting his job in publishing and moving to Southern California to perfect himself physically. Looking at before and after pictures of bodybuilders who had moved to California, he noted: "As soon as they reached sunny Southern California, their bodies seemed to explode in growth. The place had something: truckloads of anabolic steroids, variant exercise techniques, special diets—something. Whatever it was, if it worked for others, it might work for me. To the diseased there is only one Mecca, and it is nowhere near the nation of Islam."[9]

In that Mecca, one of the country's major health care providers, Kaiser Permanente, offers cosmetic surgery services to its patients. While Kaiser Permanente is not the first health care provider to do so—in North Carolina, Blue Cross and Blue Shield provide customers with some cut-rate cosmetic services—but it has made the boldest move by opening four clinics in California that are devoted exclusively to cosmetic procedures that consumers would find in any plastic surgeon's office, such as chemical peels and face-lifts. (Almost all of its twenty-two general health facilities in California also offer cosmetic procedures.) All four of the centers were profitable within months of opening, with annual revenue growth of 15 to 20 percent.[10]

And while critics love to point to the fact that the Hollywood figure seems to be shrinking every year and that Hollywood is to blame for growing rates of eating disorders, women across the country love to bring up the example of Marilyn Monroe and crow that she was a size 12. The truth is that she was not: the Hollywood figure has always been shrunken. Maybe Marilyn Monroe wore size 12 in 1950s sizes. But for an exhibition of her personal property at Christie's auction house that featured several pieces of her clothing, including the famous sheer dress in which she sang "Happy Birthday" to the president in 1962, the chief stylist, Simon Doonan, could not find a mannequin anywhere in the city of Los Angeles small enough for her figure.

"She was tiny, tiny, tiny," he told me, holding up his pinkie and shaking it. "Maybe a hundred pounds."[11]

The rest of us have just gotten fatter.

X X X

In 2004, California was the site of one of the fiercest turf battles in cosmetic surgery. In May, a subcommittee of the California legislature approved Senate Bill 1336, which proposed that dentists with training in oral surgery be allowed to perform cosmetic surgery on the face and neck and various other cosmetic procedures that doctors had long considered their territory.

The proposal was just one of many so-called scope of practice issues in California in recent years. Ophthalmologists spent a decade working to block optometrists from prescribing drugs to treat glaucoma and other diseases of the eye. (The optometrists won in 2000.) In 2001, California legislators made it easier for unlicensed aides in medical offices to perform basic procedures without a supervising physician. To the consternation of psychologists, social workers have sought to receive Medicare reimbursement for diagnosing patients with mental problems. In 2003, a proposal to allow certain holistic healers to identify themselves as "doctors of naturopathy" was opposed by medical doctors and acupuncturists. The measure was ultimately passed. In the period between 2000 and 2004, at least forty-eight measures proposing to expand one scope of practice or another came before the California legislature.

The oral surgeons wanted the same rights as doctors with MD degrees, and their argument made a kind of sense. After all, if doctors of every stripe—gastroenterologists, dermatologists, gynecologists—were cashing in all over the country by performing cosmetic surgery, why couldn't they? There are about 6,600 plastic surgeons certified by the American Board of Plastic Surgery, but most estimates suggest that three to four times that number of doctors perform cosmetic surgical procedures without being certified by the board.[12] In the United States, anyone with an MD degree can hang out a shingle and open for business as a cosmetic surgeon. The oral surgeons argued that their training in repairing the bones and structures of the face equipped them to perform the same procedures that physicians do.

Until the late 1990s, in fact, many California oral surgeons routinely did some elective cosmetic surgery, reasoning that, given their four years of training in hospital surgical residencies, they were allowed to do so. There was just one problem. They didn't have medical degrees. Oral surgeons hold DDS or DMD degrees, conferred after a four-year course of study limited to oral health, followed by another four-year period of study in dental surgery. They spend at least thirty months of their residency period in oral and maxillofacial surgery and at least four months in other surgical practices, like general surgery.[13] Although they learn how to repair damage to the jawbone and teeth, how to reconstruct facial malformations such as cleft palates, and how to treat the damage wrought by gunshot and car crashes, this period of study does not lead to a medical degree; it is considered advanced training in dentistry. (The abbreviation DMD, doctor of medical dentistry, is essentially synonymous with DDS, doctor of dental surgery, and does not mean the dentist is an MD.) Oral surgeons are traditionally considered expert in repairing fractured jaws, improperly aligned teeth, cleft palates, and related abnormalities and trauma. But even though their title includes the word *surgeon*, they hold dental—not medical—degrees.

But elective cosmetic surgery seemed to require many of the skills that their oral surgical training had given them. Also, until the late 1990s, the state Dental Practice Act was clear in saying that dentists could perform work on teeth, gums, jaws, "or associated structures." Oral surgeons interpreted those structures to be noses, lips, chins, and ears, opening them up to a world of cosmetic surgical possibilities.[14]

By 2000, however, the party was over. In the late 1990s, several patients in California died during outpatient cosmetic procedures, principally, it was found, due to faulty anesthesia procedures. Oral surgeons had nothing to do with the deaths, but in January 2000 the Dental Board of California clarified the state law in a letter to dentists and oral surgeons: the law did not permit oral surgeons to perform cosmetic procedures unless they were part of the treatment for a dental problem. No nose jobs. No lipo. No lip injections. No face-lifts.

Suddenly banned from participating in the potentially most lucrative part of their profession, the oral surgeons first lobbied the plastic surgeons, hoping to strike some sort of mutually beneficial deal. That failed. They then asked one of California's most influential lawmakers, State Senator John Burton of San Francisco, to sponsor their bill. A powerful Democrat, who had sponsored so many bills of a similar type that he was known in Sacramento as the "pope of scope," Burton held sway in the Senate.

The oral surgeons also began a major donation campaign. During the 2001–02 election cycle, the California Dental Association gave political contributions of more than $1.5 million, more than any other single group, including teachers, prison guards, and realtors, according to Common Cause California. (The California Medical Association ranked fifth.) State Senator Sam Aanestad, the Republican vice chairman of the business and professions panel—and an oral surgeon himself—received a total of $502,381 from both the medical and the dental associations during the previous election cycle, according to Common Cause California, more than any other legislator.[15]

By 2004, the oral surgeons were frustrated. The bottom line, they believed, was that oral and maxillofacial surgeons do work around the head and the neck all the time. "We are the ones called to the emergency rooms in the middle of the night to handle severe trauma," Dr. P. Thomas Hiser, president of the California Association of Oral and Maxillofacial Surgeons, told me. "And we deal with all the complex structures we would be dealing with in daylight hours if we were doing cosmetic procedures."[16] Dr. Larry J. Moore, an oral surgeon who testified before the California legislature, told me that the heart of the issue was that oral surgeons are treated unfairly, considering their level of training and skill. "Let's say you are in a horrible accident and half of your face is torn off," Moore said. "I can reattach it and then do all the follow-up surgeries to make sure it looks perfect. But I can't do that if you're born with an imperfect face. I can go in and reattach someone's nose in the middle of the night. But if somebody came in and their nose had grown that way, we are prohibited from doing the same thing. That isn't fair."[17]

Another key issue was financial, Moore explained. His voice was measured and calm. He conveyed the sense that he was a man of reason. "When you operate on a trauma patient in a Class 1 trauma center, maybe the patient has no insurance," Moore said. "You sometimes don't get paid for it. And when you do get reimbursed for it, it is about 30 percent of your actual fee."

Dr. Jack C. Lewin, a family practitioner who is the chief executive of the California Medical Association, agreed on the centrality of the financial issue. "We think this particular proposal is all about the money and not about improving health care," Lewin said. "Look. There are dentists out there who have gone through the full residency training to become plastic surgeons and we support their involvement here. But this becomes an area in which it's too easy to go after noninsurance money. We don't believe it improves quality of care. We believe it would go in the other direction."

Plastic surgeons insisted that only they could ensure the highest quality of care. Their education includes four years of medical school, in which two years are spent studying diagnosis and management of the entire patient, and seven or eight years of residency before they can be board certified. But they were clearly angry about protecting their money, too. With about fifteen hundred plastic surgeons in California and about eight hundred oral and maxillofacial surgeons in California, the proposed law would dramatically redistribute elective surgical work.

Dr. Steven A. Teitelbaum argued that the education of an oral surgeon generally does not include adequate training in all the areas essential to the treatment of a patient undergoing elective surgery. "The procedures are different," Teitelbaum said. "When you deal with a broken nose, you deal with bone. When you do a cosmetic rhinoplasty you deal with cartilage. Their bread and butter are wisdom teeth and young trauma patients with broken jaws. But do they know how to deal with IV fluids, EKGs, patients with hypertension, stroke, or blood clots? When you're talking about a sixty-six-year-old woman about to go under for a four-hour face-lift, you're talking about a patient these doctors don't usually see."

Plastic surgeons were frightened that the reputation of their profession—tarnished in recent years by high-profile deaths related to cosmetic surgery, including that of the novelist Olivia Goldsmith—would be further sullied. "There have been several well-publicized deaths, and the public is demanding higher levels of safety," Teitelbaum said. "By lowering the bar substantially, I am concerned there will be more problems."

By far the most compelling argument was offered by Dr. Jonathan S. Jacobs, both an oral and a plastic surgeon in Virginia, who told me in very plain language that oral surgery training is inadequate preparation for doctors who want to perform cosmetic surgical procedures. "They are not well trained enough to do the kinds of cosmetic procedures that they say they have expertise in," Jacobs said. A former acting head of the oral surgery training program at Vanderbilt University Medical Center in Nashville, he added that just because an oral surgeon can move a chin forward does not mean he or she can do a face-lift.[18]

More than a dozen states—including Virginia, West Virginia, Illinois, Ohio, Tennessee, and Mississippi—have in recent years adopted an expanded definition of dentistry. In those states, a nonphysican dental practitioner—someone with a dental degree and no more—can interpret the language to permit him or her to perform some cosmetic surgical procedures. In Virginia, the legislative change has led to the death of at least one patient, according to Jacobs, who was asked to be an expert witness at the malpractice trial. The patient was an eighteen-year-old, going in for a cosmetic procedure. The practitioner was an oral surgeon. But the patient had a congenital airway malformation, which the oral surgeon was unfamiliar with. The malformation required that a doctor with knowledge of complex intubation issues administer the anesthesia. The breathing tube, however, was put in improperly, and the patient died.

"The real issue, over and over again, is whether or not this is appropriate work," Jacobs said. "Is this right? Is this good? Does the doctor know how to deal with all kinds of patients? The answer is no. If you kill a patient who is eighteen years old with one minor issue who is otherwise in perfect health, then what happens when you have a sixty-five-year-old patient in your chair waiting for a face-lift? It's complete bullshit."[19]

The California legislative initiative was more alarming than the laws passed in other states (at least, according to plastic surgeons), because there were so many more prospective patients in the California marketplace. In written testimony, Dr. Jack Bruner, president of the California Society of Plastic Surgeons, called the bill "one of the most menacing pieces of legislation threatening public safety under consideration by this year's legislators." But the oral surgeons were squared off for a fight. Dr. Hiser, the California Association of Oral and Maxillofacial Surgeons president, said that oral surgeons have always been considered the poor relations of plastic surgeons. And they were sick and tired of it.

"They all say, 'Oh yeah, oral surgeons are great guys, but all they know how to do is take out teeth and treat lower jaw fractures,'" Hiser said. Unlike his colleague Dr. Moore, who had sounded calm and relaxed, he spoke through clenched teeth. His voice conveyed the tension and frustration of a man who was tired of being kicked around by the bigger kids in the neighborhood. "Well, I trained at Georgetown in the early 1970s, and in those days we learned orthognathic surgery. We learned how to separate the upper jaw from the skull and move it around and cut it into small pieces. And we did procedures up inside the nose, and we did zygomatic procedures, and we treated orbital fractures, upper jaw fractures, mandible fractures. We learned to treat all those things. We know our way around the head."[20]

Dr. Rod J. Rohrich, a Dallas plastic surgeon who was the president of the American Society of Plastic Surgeons, said he was prepared for a fight, too. "I am sorry," he said, sounding not sorry at all, "but I would not go to my dentist and ask him for a face-lift. Just as I would not expect my dentist to come to me and ask me to pull some teeth." Senator Burton never returned my phone calls. But my bet was on the oral surgeons. After all, look at Governor Arnold Schwarzenegger, several oral surgeons and plastic surgeons said. There was a guy who not only looked like a recipient of some cosmetic modifications but has admitted to taking steroids in the past and has never denied dabbling in human growth hormone—both medications that would have been given to him by a doctor or some other medical practitioner working well outside the legal limits of the law. Moreover, the sponsor of the bill was Senator Burton, with whom it was known the governor had a good working relationship. So it made sense that he might support a larger scope of practice for oral surgeons.

In September of 2004, Schwarzenegger signed several bills into law. One was to increase fines against people convicted of interfering with seeing-eye dogs. He established "Don't trash California" and "California es tu casa. No hagas de ella un basurero" as the official litter-prevention and recycling slogans of the state. And, surprisingly, he vetoed Burton's bill.

In his veto message, the Governator agreed with the plastic surgeons who had argued that oral surgeons were not prepared to do the types of operations in question, despite their work in hospital emergency rooms repairing car accident victims. "I believe this practice needs to be more carefully reviewed and evaluated to fully ensure the safety of California's consumers," Schwarzenegger wrote. "Therefore, I am directing the Department of Consumer Affairs to conduct an occupational analysis of the Oral and Maxillofacial Surgeon profession."

Four days after the veto, Dentists Insurance Company, which is owned by the California Dental Association, donated $25,000 to the governor's election committee. Concerned that the donation might violate his self-imposed ban on accepting money from single-interest trade groups, his top fund-raiser said that the governor might have to return it. (He had turned down donations from the California Medical Association.)[21]

Dr. Harvey A. Zarem, the Santa Monica physician who is president of the California Society of Plastic Surgeons, praised Schwarzenegger for "having the courage to stand up for the people of California despite the special-interest pressure." Burton offered a different explanation to a California newspaper: "It was probably all the Beverly Hills cosmetic surgeons who got a hold of their Beverly Hills clients, who got a hold of the governor. I don't know, but that's probably what happened."[22]

X X X

One afternoon I visit the man who has become the most famous plastic surgeon to television-watching America, thanks to *Extreme Makeover*: Dr. Garth Fisher. His office in Beverly Hills is decorated in a kind of French rococo meets Boca Raton motif, and the ceilings are painted with trompe l'oeil blue skies, dotted with puffy cumulus clouds.

A promotional video is playing on a monitor near the receptionist's desk when I arrive. The word *complications* is followed by *embolization*, and *revisional surgery*. A bowl of caramels sits on the coffee table, along with big books about the shape of the female breast and Corvettes. I wait. At the end of the hallway, several men bustle out of Fisher's office with camera equipment, bags, dollies, lights. Fisher walks them to the front door and gives each one a hearty handshake.

His receptionist escorts me past them into Fisher's office. Several shelves are lined with faux books—their spines are supposed to look like those of leather-bound first editions. On his desk is a square tissue holder, with the same theme: the tissues appear to be held in place by old editions of *The Great Gatsby*, *The Scarlet Letter*, and *Vanity Fair*. Unlike the false book fronts, which create a kind of Potemkin village of literary achievement, the tissue holder makes no sense in its obvious falsehood. What nineteenth-century bookbinder would have torn off the spines of his first editions to make a Kleenex holder?

Fisher walks in. He is very tan, and his teeth are very white. His hair is smoothed in a semicircle across his brow like the Ken doll I had as a child. Like many other surgeons, he became interested in cosmetic surgery for a compelling reason related to his childhood: his father died in the Vietnam War, and he grew up in a household of women. Fisher knows women.

"I had to share the bathroom with all of them," he says. "There is no better way to learn what makes women tick."

He is convinced that the Governator has done the right thing but that the issue is not gone. "There will always be doctors who say, 'Hey, baby, I can do your plastic surgery, even though I'm not a plastic surgeon really.' There are going to be more plastic surgeons. There are going to be more doctors doing plastic surgery. There are going to be more who aren't trained to do plastic surgery doing plastic surgery. And one day, something really bad is going to happen. And there will be some point when the regulatory oversight is going to have to step up."

I feel assured that Fisher is a man of some gravity.

His practice has boomed since *Extreme Makeover* began airing on ABC. His waiting list is about two years long. Dozens of hopeful patients call from all over the country every day, and the lucky pilgrims arrive in his office every week, hoping for his laying on of hands. But his intentions with the program are slightly different.

"I was kind of hoping to have the kind of practice where I can get home at 5:30 every day," he says with a grin of his big white teeth.

Before I leave, I have to ask him just one question.

"I know being tan isn't very good for you," I say. "So why is it that you guys are all so tan?" That's easy. "I am part owner of a chain of tanning salons," he says, handing me a card for Sunset Tans. "I do a spray-on tan, and then I do maybe eight minutes in a high-pressure booth," he says. "Go try it."

I have never accepted anything for free—no Botox, no facial treatment, no products, no surgery, nothing—from any surgeon, but I do accept a spray-on tan. Fisher says that he feels that owning a line of tanning salons does not cause him any shame, even if his industry is one of several that generally advocate highly restricted exposure to the sun. The beds in his salons do not emit harmful UV rays, he assures me.

No matter what any doctor says, however, tanning is not risk-free and can cause skin cancer, eye injury, and premature aging. There is no such thing as a safe tan, and those acquired in tanning beds are even less safe than those acquired by natural sunbathing. Sunlight has two types of skin-damaging ultraviolet rays, UVA and UVB. UVA rays have longer wavelengths and can cause damage to the skin's connective tissue, which can lead to premature aging and cause skin cancer. UVA rays also increase the risk of cataracts and retinal damage and are the type used in tanning salons. The tanning industry works hard to convince consumers that tanning salons are safe, but UVA rays may be as much as twenty times stronger than natural ones. UVB rays, considered the burning rays, are shorter and are primarily responsible for sunburn and skin cancer. Salons generally expose skin to a tanning unit that is ten times greater than natural light, and the beds are able to irradiate almost every part of the body. Dr. Michelle Copeland told me that she has started to remove melanomas from women in their twenties who come to her with lesions in places that don't normally see large doses of sunshine, like the buttocks.

Tanning beds have been found to increase the chances of getting dangerous cancers later in life by about seven times. One major problem of overexposure from tanning salons is a type of skin cancer called malignant melanoma. It is the number-one cancer affecting women ages twenty-four to twenty-nine and accounts for 75 percent of all skin cancer deaths. It can occur anywhere on the body and is characterized by asymmetrical moles with irregular borders. Exposure to external influences such as sunlight, heat, heavy metals, and ionizing radiation can change normal cells into cancerous cells, which often spread to other parts of the body.

But I will try the spray-on tan. That night I return to my hotel looking as if I had spent three weeks lying naked on a beach in Hawaii.

I eat lunch with a plastic surgeon at the Ivy. The Ivy is the Beverly Hills café where celebrity couples on the verge of breakup go to be photographed by the paparazzi, who will then report that they were spotted eating at the Ivy together and that rumors of their breakup must be absolutely untrue. The doctor lives in California but trained on the East Coast. We are speaking frankly, so he does not want me to use his name.

"What's most terrifying about California is that there is this cult of the body that passes for real life for a long time," he says. The notion of the real self, of one's core human nature, is a troublesome one in the era of surgical manipulation and refabrication. The body and the face have become the billboard for what we advertise our self to be. "In New York, for a woman, the notion of the self is pretty shallow, too. It's about what handbag you carry, how few wrinkles are on your face, how in shape you are, how well-dressed you are, and how accomplished you are. In Los Angeles, it's just more focused on how few wrinkles you have, how great your tits are, how great your body is, how great your hair extensions are, how great your eye job is, and how great your car is. The accomplishment thing doesn't exist. So women here live with this notion that it is all about looks. And then they hit forty, forty-five. And looks can last for a while after that, but at some point, no matter how much upkeep you do, it starts to go. And they are left with nothing. At least on the East Coast, maybe you did something. The emphasis is less on just physicality. I'm not saying it's a lot better, because most women wind up getting the same shaft, no matter if they are in Los Angeles or New York."

What shaft is that, I ask. Not because I don't know the answer but because I want to see the look of incredulity on his face when I pose the question.

"Their husbands end up trading them in for younger wo-men," he says, as matter-of-fact as if he were explaining how the force of gravity keeps his water in the glass on the table. "But here, when they get older, when they get past forty, it gets desperate on a deeply metaphysical level. I've seen it get very dark. They wake up one day and realize that they are nothing but a shell of skin. They didn't do anything on the inside. And I don't care how many yoga classes you go to, they won't be able to cope. They're not equipped. And they don't know why."

There are four reasons to have cosmetic surgery, he contin-ues. "Number one, postpartum, when the woman wants to return to her prepartum body. Number two, antiaging. Number three, ethnic issues. Number four, the freaks. And there are both ethnic and aesthetic freaks."

The freaks are the people like Michael Jackson and Jocelyn Wildenstein, patients who are decisive about what they want and who meet up with a surgeon who is willing to do what they want. Freaks, of course, occur only after the surgeon has performed a PWB.

A PWB?

"Positive Wallet Biopsy," the doctor says, munching on his salad.

If that sounds a touch cynical, he adds, well, the industry has changed. "The old model was that surgeons sold themselves in a less aggressive manner," he says. " 'Mrs. S., see how I sewed up your son's chin after that football accident? Well, I could do some-thing like that for you.' It was a soft pedal. Now there are a greater number of providers than there are patients, so they will resort to the most aggressive marketing campaigns possible."

Manufacturers can advertise directly to the public, and that creates demand from the public. Magazine readers are inundated more than ever before with articles about Botox or lasers or the newest thread face-lift. "So they see *Mademoiselle* or *Allure* and they say, 'Aha, I think I need that.' I can't tell you how many people come to my office with pages torn out from *Elle* or *Allure* or any of those magazines." Worst of all, he says, "the doctors are just greedy. I call it the battle of beauty versus blood supply."

A casino executive stops by the table to say hello to the doctor. He has just bought a casino in Las Vegas and wants to know if he should open a kind of *Extreme Makeover*–inspired boutique, a place where tourists in Vegas for a long weekend can go to get Botox, collagen, teeth veneers, hair extensions, colored contacts, a spray-on tan, maybe even boob jobs and liposuction.

"Fantastic idea," the doctor says.

"Especially since Botox will really sell in Las Vegas," the casino owner quips. "What about all the players who can't do a successful poker face on their own? This way, they can just buy a poker face."

They exchange cards. I agree. It is a fantastic idea, one with great potential commercial success. Like a safari, a trip to Vegas is considered by many Americans to be a transformative experience. The recent slogan for the city of Las Vegas—"What happens in Vegas, stays in Vegas"—implies that people arrive with the hope of something big happening to them, something slightly bad that might be best kept secret from friends back home. What better way to change oneself in some secret yet magical way than having a breast augmentation?

The doctor, too, agrees. "But, of course, the breast implants don't stay in Vegas," he says with a wink.

We leave the Ivy and walk around the neighborhood, talking about the notions of self and identity and appearance and whether plastic surgery patients change their looks to hide their inner self or more truly express it. He has always struck me as a self-assured, attractive man, and we have become friends over several interviews. I ask him how much he weighs, and his face clouds.

"Never ask a fat man what he weighs," he says.

I apologize, but I am surprised, because he isn't fat.

"In Beverly Hills, I'm fat," he says.

X X X

Mrs. X is unreflective on the subject of her cosmetic surgery habit. It is worth noting that despite all the effort she puts into maintaining her physical self, she has never seen a psychiatrist and maintains the bare minimum of a religious life. My inner armchair psychiatrist is curious: Mrs. X lives in a world of powerful men and their wives, women whose only dominion is over hairdressers, personal trainers, and housekeepers. Her ability to actually be powerful herself is so limited that cosmetic surgery appears to have become the sole area in which she can experience any feelings of self-determination.

"Is it hard being the wife of a powerful guy in Hollywood?" I ask her.

"How do you mean?"

"Do you ever wish you had had a career?"

There is the briefest of pauses.

"No, because I was never really going to be that good at anything," she says. "Or at least I was never going to be so good at anything that I would have made a difference."

Eight

You Want It, You Need It

MARKETING THE DREAM OF BEAUTY

The John B. Hynes Convention Center in Boston's Back Bay is a sprawling honeycomb, 285,000 square feet fitted with auditoriums and meeting rooms and amphitheaters larger than football fields, the floors padded with a flat, seamless ocean of industrial carpeting so thin you can feel the chill of the concrete underneath your shoes. Miles of fluorescent tube lights cast a greenish pall.

Every year, all manner of professional organizations meet here: truckers and endocrinologists, Mary Kay saleswomen and community college administrators, real estate salesmen and personal liability underwriters and electronics assembly manufacturers and members of the Yankee Dental Association. The brick and marble building huddles atop Interstate 90 and a handful of commuter rail tracks; the stream of traffic that courses through its underbelly keeps the structure humming and shuddering, as if it were a living organism.

The convention center occupies the central vacuum of an even vaster moonscape that includes a Gap, a Lord & Taylor, a

Coach, a Marriott and a Sheraton hotel, a Foot Locker, a Tie Rack, a Claire's Fashion Accessories, and a Starbucks. The sandwiches for sale at Au Bon Pain, the national deli chain, are wound so tightly in their plastic wrap that the wrinkles have been pressed out of the soft, glutinous dough. The Starbucks serves the same oily, burnt-tasting coffee they serve in thousands of other Starbucks stores around the world, a beverage brewed so dense that no amount of milk will soften the abrasive taste.

Like most other convention halls, the Hynes Center smells like an airport, thick with the intimate odors of thousands of strangers yet aggressively sanitized. Walking the thoroughfares, one is overcome with the mercantile déjà vu that haunts any business traveler in America, the regimented sameness, the automation, and the barely discernible flickers of unique detail that separate this mall from a thousand other malls in a thousand other convention complexes around the country. (In this center, that one hollow suggestion of regional identity is a booth topped with a grimy plastic swan advertising tours of the Boston Public Garden.)

It is a sunny, cold May when the American Society for Aesthetic Plastic Surgery—a group of about 2,100 plastic surgeons who are certified by the American Board of Plastic Surgery and who specialize in cosmetic plastic surgery—holds its conference at the Hynes Center. But the good people of the society have done their best to brighten the place up. A thirty-foot-high image of the bust of Nefertiti—the society's official mascot, whose name means "the beautiful (or perfect) woman has come"—is projected onto the ceilings in bright lavender and pink lights, and she swirls over the heads of the thousands of surgeons, flitting over them like the Wicked Witch of the East come to check on the Munchkins. It's a nice Vegas touch in a starched Massachusetts world.

There's a strange irony in the fact that the ASAPS chose a stylized depiction of Nefertiti as its symbol. An Egyptian queen, she was married to pharoah Akhenaten, who ruled Egypt from 1352 BC to 1336 BC. Nefertiti and her husband forced the population to convert from the existing polytheist religious system to a one-god system. (Their god was the sun.) This caused a rebellion, and the pharaoh was subsequently murdered. Nefertiti died soon afterwards—the cause of her death unclear—but her corpse and face were disfigured in order to prevent her from moving on to her next life as a great beauty.

U.S. demand for cosmetic surgery products will grow 11.2 percent yearly to 2007, to a market size of $2 billion, driven mostly by new product approvals, favorable cultural and demographic trends, and improved technology. And down in the Hynes Center's subterranean exhibit rooms, three hundred pharmaceutical companies, banks, doctors, and medical associations are eagerly showing off the wares that make up that market: pectoral implants, breast dissectors, breast retractors, tiny placement forceps used in hair transplant surgery, tummy-tuck support panties, tubes and bottles of sunblock with SPFs as high as IQ scores, skin adhesives that promise to bind postsurgical flesh and bone, nasal speculae, silicone facial implants in the shapes of anchorman-sized chins and Faye Dunaway cheeks, moisturizers made with seaweed extract, moisturizers made with copper, moisturizers made with whale feces, moisturizers made with dead chicken parts; there are tables lined with gleaming chrome nostril retainers, extremity expanders, reciprocating saws, and skin staplers.

Medical Z Corporation of San Antonio sells "the Z Bra—the only post-surgical bra that is also a sports bra." (Shouldn't you be resting, not working out, after having surgery?) Silverglide Surgical Technologies of Boulder, Colorado, features its new "SILVERGlide" nonstick bipolar electrosurgical forceps, which "eliminate the frustrating problem of tissue sticking and tissue buildup normally associated with coagulation" during surgery.

The Gebauer Company of Cleveland sells vapocoolants, or

skin refrigerants, to be applied to the skin after dermabrasion, a treatment in which the surgeon scrapes away the outermost layer of skin with a rough wire brush (or a burr containing diamond particles that is attached to a motorized handle). GVS-NY of Farmingdale, New York, sells "reconditioned" (i.e., used) surgical equipment (with a not-very-generous-sounding six-month warranty). Grams Medical of Costa Mesa, California, displays all manner of cannulae, the foot-long hollow needles that are used in liposuction, and each bears a name that sounds as if it belongs to some sort of vibrator or sex toy: there is the Mercedes, the Tiger Tip, and the PickleFork. The Sun Glitz Corporation of Energy, Illinois, is showing off "the only sponge foam bandage with sex appeal!"

If it sounds out of place to use sex to market a postoperative sponge-foam bandage, remember that many of the companies sell competing equipment that is used for the most common kinds of surgery, and so their marketing officers must find any way—even the most brazen, empty, or fraudulent ways—to differentiate their product from the crowd. There are at least a half dozen companies that specialize in wound drains—essentially, tubing with a pump attachment to suck pus and blood and other fluids out of a postoperative wound. So there is the TLS Surgical Drain, the Jackson-Pratt Drain, and the Seroma-Cath Wound Drainage System. But the most popular, according to several surgeons, is Axiom Medical's drain with the "exclusive ClotStop coating." ("It's better than the others because this one enhances flow," one of the salesmen monitoring the booth told me.)

For patients who are past the stage where their active oozing necessitates a drain, at booth 327 one can sample HK Surgical's "Super Absorbent Pad," one mother of a maxi pad that measures ten by twenty inches and can absorb up to 1,000 milliliters of fluid without leaking. (That's about the amount of fluid that would fit into a good-sized cake-mixing bowl.)

The ugly things that happen as a result of cosmetic surgery are presented with the same careful doublespeak that is used in the funeral industry. In the lingo of the business that ushers our mortal envelopes out of the world, a dead body doesn't sit in a morgue. It *rests* in a *slumber room.* A cemetery is a *memorial park.* A coffin is a *demise chest.* In the world of cosmetic surgery, the euphemisms are different but just as highly polished: Scars aren't healed, they are *managed.* Pain isn't stopped, halted, alleviated; it, too, is *managed*, as if any verb that alluded to the cessation of pain would indicate that there is also a quite formidable, offputting beginning and perhaps quite lengthy and disagreeable middle to pain as well.

Advanced Infusion of Snellville, Georgia, markets a disposable infusion pump—in the 200-milliliter or 450-milliliter size— that allows surgeons to run four or more catheters from one pump for the delivery of pain relief medication—or, as the company's pamphlet says, for "pain management." Biodermis of Las Vegas, Nevada, sells silicone gel sheeting and ointment to aid in "scar management." The I-Flow Corporation of Lake Forest, California, sells something called the ON-Q Pain Management System. Sgarlato Labs of Los Gatos, California, sells the Pain-Free Pump, again for "the management of pain." Even the aging process itself is discussed as if it is a rebellious heifer that needs to be lassoed before she busts out of the corral: VitaMedica, Inc., of Manhattan Beach, California, is hawking vitamins and so-called nutraceuticals—essentially, vitamins with a snazzy, scientific-sounding suffix—for "age management."

The little companies get little booths, manned by two- or three-person teams of men and women who beam tight, hopeful smiles. These are the companies that sell surgical dressings and postliposuction garments, the medical publishers and rinky-dink loan companies and makeup companies that manufacture foundation in bruise-obscuring shades like lime green, Bermuda pink, and bright canary yellow—depending on the shading and depth of your bruises and scars. There are tiny but vicious turf battles among the smaller booths—such as in the competition to see who

can pass out more flyers—like the guys at BreastAugmentation
.com, booth 1113, and the guys at BreastImplants411, booth
1016, both online referral sites for plastic surgeons who do breast
augmentation surgery. (BreastImplants411.com, a few doctors
decide, has a better site: its reps hand out little pink Post-it notes
in the shape of a T-shirted torso with large breasts.)

The big dogs of the convention get their own Barnum and
Bailey–style big tops, with Jetsons-like platforms and staging and
their own patches of fresh bright blue industrial carpet and
teams of bright, smiling young attendants in coordinated outfits.
These include Allergan, the belle of the ball and manufacturer of
Botox; Q-Med, the European manufacturers of Restylane; Inamed Aesthetics, purveyors of breast implants and various forms
of synthetic collagen, including Cosmoplast, which is made from
fetal foreskin stem cells. (The donor of those stem cells was a baby
boy born in the early 1990s, whose cells were harvested at birth
and were chosen to develop this artificial form of collagen because
they would not yet have been exposed to disease or inoculations
or any other contaminants. He does not, a company spokesman
told me, know that cells from his genitals now plump up the lips of
hundreds of thousands of men and women around the planet.
This is good news. One can only imagine the psychiatry bill.)

At the Inamed emporium, both saline and silicone breast implants are on display, even though silicone implants are not available for use in the United States for most patients. (The U.S. Food
and Drug Administration in January of 2004 stunned plastic surgeons when, contradicting the advice of its expert panel, it rejected Inamed's bid to reintroduce silicone breast implants. After
safety concerns arose, the FDA had banned such implants in
1992.) The implants puddle atop the up-lit countertops, looking
like perfectly symmetrical, smooth, clean jellyfish. There is something vaguely pornographic about fondling the implants at
the booth with a group of male surgeons, but I find myself doing
so nonetheless. In my palm they feel like supernaturally heavy

Jell-O. All the samples are as perfectly round as IHOP dollar pancakes and without any differentiation in shape or slope at all. The model known as McGhan Style 68 is one of the most popular; it has a slick surface and comes in twenty sizes. The textured casing of McGhan Style 168 allows it to more tenaciously adhere to the slippery smooth muscle tissues of the human body. There are rows and rows of these round implants, the kind that give a fullness to the upper breast that made Pamela Anderson's breasts look so unnatural at various points during her career.[1]

At the end of the table, there is one lonely teardrop-shaped implant, which mimics the natural shape of a woman's breast: the McGhan Style 163. It is the Diane Keaton of breast implants. An Inamed salesman explains to me at a later conference that often the comically round implants take a more natural shape when they are installed, as long as there is enough room in the cavity. But curiously, many women who get breast implants favor the slightly unnatural look; it is an obvious indication that they have received breast implants, which are a badge of honor in certain circles, and they find the cartoonish quality strangely appealing.

"I don't know why, but they like the fake shape," the salesman says, bouncing a breast implant in his hand. It makes gentle thwack-thwack noises as it lands, bonds briefly with his sweaty palm, and lifts up with a slight sucking noise.

The conventions at which plastic surgeons convene serve many gods. Just as most medical groups gather during the year to discuss, for example, improved procedures in gastroenterology, or experimental cancer drugs, or increasingly troublesome public health issues, cosmetic plastic surgeons gather to share new medical information about their profession. It's just that at their conferences the teaching courses have titles like "Lips and Lines," "Adjustable Breast Implants," and "Affordable Tattoo Removal." A convention is also an opportunity for socializing and meeting up with surgeon friends from various parts of the country. Surgeons who go to several different meetings a year in different locations refer to the routine as "same slides, different wives."

And unlike other medical professionals, cosmetic plastic surgeons must learn and perfect the art of the sale. Because of the economics of cosmetic plastic surgery, the surgeon must also act as a marketing and economics professional, skilled in the art of procuring money from a consumer who does not require surgery but merely desires it. The course curricula are thus intently focused on consumer marketing. If the surgeons are not learning new medical skills, they are learning how to market their practices (at the Boston conference, in seminars like "Web Marketing: What You Need to Know"), or how to attract the right kind of patients ("How to Read People Like a Book"), or how to attract the most patients ("How to Rise above the Competition and Maximize Staff Utilization to Increase Surgery").

Central to the search for more patients are consultants like Wendy Lewis, who has her own seminar at the Boston conference, entitled "The Art of the Cosmetic Consultation." Lewis, who goes by the sobriquet the "Knife Coach," is not the typical speaker you'd find at a typical medical convention. She is not a doctor but a nurse who was the office manager for two plastic surgeons in New York before she began her career as a consultant. Her Web site is packed with the kind of information about facelifts, liposuction, and breast implants—and nutrition and hair care and exercise—one could find in *Allure* in any given month. Her latest book, *The Beauty Battle*, is a how-to handbook divided into four areas of advice—about the body, the complexion, hair, and wrinkles (her personal favorite). Despite the fact that every piece of information in her book and on her Web site is accessible to any reader of women's magazines and daily newspapers, Lewis charges prospective patients $300 an hour for a consultation in New York, £300 for a consultation in London, and $250 for an hour-long consultation on the telephone.

I am curious. Does she actually offer some information that

is valuable or somehow protected from the general, curious public? And what can she tell doctors about what their patients want? Are they so disconnected from their client base that they cannot even conduct a simple interview?

When Lewis walks to the platform, I am surprised. She has shaggy, frosty blond hair and dark roots. She wears a shade of orangey red lipstick that is unflattering against her milky white skin. She is plump in a manner that suggests neither pleasing nor zaftig nor gemütlich, all those words that suggest fat is pleasant. The combination isn't really in keeping with the liposculpted-guru image I had in mind. After all, her nom de guerre is a play on "life coach," so one would expect her to have actually gone under the knife.

So what kind of woman would take nutrition, beauty, and cosmetic surgery advice from a woman with a bad haircut, dark roots, and a big caboose?

Lewis speaks in the animated, authoritative tone of someone who believes very strongly that she is a highly specialized expert, a revealer of industry secrets and powerful skills. Her PowerPoint presentation is a long incantation of the things plastic surgeons need to do to make their patients comfortable and their practices profitable. It is hard to believe that surgeons who specialize in appearance would need to be told that appearances—a clean office, a nice receptionist—count.

"First impressions," she says, sternly, as if addressing a fourth-grade class on a field trip to the local congressman's office. "You never get a second chance." The group nods solemnly.

Slide after slide of advice-bite mantras, in shifting tones of red and pink, appears on the screen: "The first question should be 'What can I do for YOU?' " "The first consultation should last no less than twenty minutes." "At least 75 percent of malpractice suits filed in the aesthetic field are totally preventable by adequate communication."

Another reads: "Exude an aura of patient-focussed [*sic*]

care." The Dilbertesque platitudes are more troubling to me than Lewis's appearance. The notion that a surgeon would have to exude an aura—in short, playact at creating an atmosphere—of patient-focused care doesn't make any sense. Another slide advises the surgeons to spend at least twenty minutes with a patient during a consultation. But wouldn't simple logic dictate that a surgeon who belonged to this qualified group would require at least twenty minutes to consult with a patient before the patient chose surgery? And why would any surgeon think anything other than what they can do for "YOU," unless they are planning to operate on themselves?

Later I discover that some of her messages come verbatim from a former doctor who now heads a physician-owned medical malpractice insurance provider.

Another Dilbertism flashes up on the screen. "People buy when they are understood, not when they understand.—Leonard Abrams." I wonder who Leonard Abrams is. Some consumer guru? Life coach? Car salesman? Before I can raise my hand to ask, Lewis speaks.

"I got this quote from someone I was on a panel with at an image-consulting conference," she says, her SpaghettiO-hued lips working furiously. "What Leonard Abrams—and I'm sorry, I don't know who he is—is trying to tell us is to listen more and talk less."

Later, I look up Leonard Abrams in LexisNexis. He is a dentist. She doesn't even know who he is. Why do we care what he thinks about buying habits?

X X X

Dr. Gustavo A. Colon of New Orleans and Dr. Robert Singer of La Jolla often lecture about marketing, and the title of their seminar at this conference is "Effective Marketing Techniques for Plastic Surgeons." It appears to be one of the convention's most popular seminars, and about two hundred doctors, mostly younger ones in their thirties and early forties, jam into a partitioned ballroom to listen.

"When we first went into practice, we saw ourselves as healers," Colon says, fiddling with the PowerPoint clicker. On the ten-foot-wide screen behind him a stock picture appears of a young man with a doctor's bag and a jaunty hat walking down a country road. Colon starts talking about one of his professors at medical school, a gruff general surgeon named Turk.

"He was tough," Colon says. "He looked at me and he said, 'Boy, tell me why you want to go into medicine. And don't give me any of that wanna-help-mankind bullshit.' " He describes how his mother had wanted him to be a doctor, and how he had wanted to save mankind, and how—inevitably, sadly—he fell into what he called "the cult of medicine."

"The cult of medicine is where you are told by your professors, 'Give your life up to me. Hang yourself. Or sacrifice yourself to the altar of medicine. And you are never to make money. You are to work twenty-five hours a day, et cetera, et cetera.' Well, this is what we thought we would do." But he became a plastic surgeon, attracted by the lure of helping mankind and also, perhaps, of making some money.

Colon pauses, then taps the clicker. "Unfortunately, this is how we are seen by the public," he says. On the screen an image appears: it is a cartoon of Hitler in a polka dot tie and lab coat with copies of *Seventeen* and *Vogue* on his desk. A diagram of a nose job hangs behind Hitler's desk, and the caption underneath the entire thing reads: Plastic Surgeon. Colon coughs. "We are no longer healers," he continues. "We're pseudocosmetologists, sexual, bizarre individuals who tend to operate on body images for no reason at all."

Again, there is the sense that Colon, like Lewis, is telling doctors to focus on acting competent, not necessarily being competent. "If you go to the airport, when you walk up it may be the worst airline, you may have the worst seat," he says, "but if that person behind the counter treats you right you're gonna love that airline."

A few surgeons nod in agreement. Some take notes.

"Remember, you're selling yourselves," he says, his voice taking on the urgent quality of a hell-raising evangelist. "What does a patient do when they come in? First thing is, they have to like you. Second thing is, they have to trust you. Third thing is, they have to let you operate on them." How do you, he asks, "convert might to want to will?"

Another image appears: it is a triangle, and the words *morality*, *ethics*, and *professionalism* appear at each corner. "However, the triangle gets skewered when greed enters the picture," Colon says. The word *GREED* appears in big green letters in the center of the triangle. "Greed, that's when things get ugly. 'I want to make more money,' not 'I want to be a better plastic surgeon and I want to have a better practice.' " Advertising, while not entirely unscrupulous, can often indicate that a surgeon is greedy. Plus, he adds, it's expensive. "Advertising costs money. You have to pay for it. And there's no way to do just a little bit. That's like being a little bit pregnant. You have to spend a lot of money to get name recognition. What did it take, how many times do you have to see a name on TV—twenty-seven times on TV?—to have someone ultimately remember your name. And about a hundred times in the newspaper?" Another reason not to advertise: "The bitterness of the unhappy patient remains long after the sweet lure of advertising and hype are forgotten. If you make promises, I promise you, I guarantee you, and particularly if you have it in promotional writing, the plaintiff's attorneys will take promotional writing as promises."

Consumer satisfaction cannot be guaranteed in the same manner as in the sale of a car. "It is a biologic, technical service that is inexact at times and cannot be guaranteed," Colon says. A young doctor raises his hand. Well, how inexact is it? "It's going to be more inexact when all the plastic surgeons go home because they're going to try all the procedures that they learned here and they're not going to do 'em right. That's how inexact it is."

Which leads him to another point, and another slide: "Complications happen."

"Avoid the guilt-hostility-arrogance-counterhostility cycle that is where patients come to your office and you begin to argue with them," Colon continues. He starts in on an imaginary dialogue, using the archetypal dueling voices of the mustachioed villain and the damsel lashed to the railroad tracks: " 'Do you see what you did to me?' " he says in a high, squeaky voice. " 'I didn't do anything to you,' " he replies in a low, gruff, authoritative tone. " 'Yes, you did.' 'No, I didn't. You did it to yourself because you didn't follow my rules.' 'But I didn't know what the rules were.' 'Well, I'm the doctor and you don't know any better.' 'But I'm mad at you and I'm going to sue you!' And sooner or later, they are going to sue you." He pauses. "Unless you go all the way down to the angry patient who will shoot you."

There are different patients in the world of cosmetic surgery, and in Colon's hierarchy, they go something like this: The Demanding Patient. "They always want it," Colon says. The Apologetic Patient. "Always apologizing for taking up your time." The Flirtatious Patient. This is the one "you really want to stay away from, male or female," he says, speaking in a sultry register and then, literally, batting his eyelashes. " 'Hi, you're better looking in person than you are in your picture.' Or, 'Does she have to be in here while you examine my breasts?' You really gotta be careful with that one, 'cause that one can get you into trouble."

The Hostile Patient will sue you. The Negotiating Patient will want a discount. "The Fraudulent Patient will want their insurance company to pay for their surgery." Colon, it seems, has never had an easygoing patient. He concludes his litany by observing that "patients seldom remember, never recognize limitations, and will always blame you."

Anxiety clouds the faces of the doctors in the audience.

Colon continues. The cosmetic surgery industry is under assault by all manner of doctors and gynecologists and dermatologists who are out there performing our procedures and taking our money. "We don't want to become dermato-plastic-lipo-laser-fat-injecting-peeling technicians who occasionally perform surgical procedures," he says. "We *are* plastic surgery." He holds his fist up in the air, Black Panther–style. "Remember that," he says. The doctors rise to their feet, with heavy hearts, it is clear, but they clap vigorously, resigned to their mission.

"Push plastic surgery," Colon says and leaves the stage, waving like a rock star. I half expect him to shout, *Good night, Boston.*

X X X

As any salesman knows, visual tools are essential. Pie charts sell companies. Glossy brochures sell cars. And a large part of becoming a plastic surgery salesman is learning about the new devices, products, and services that pharmaceutical, financial, and software companies manufacture every year to convert potential patients into paying ones.

To this end, Canfield Scientific, Inc., is one of the convention's big dogs. The company sells imaging hardware and software that allow surgeons to show patients what they would look like with a smaller nose and larger breasts. The software is considered one of the key components of the contemporary surgeon's office because the process is positively intoxicating to patients, who get to see themselves one way and then, magically, another—without any pain. It is considered a key marketing tool in the cosmetic surgery quiver.

The company has also cornered the market on other devices, such as ultraviolet photography, which is a tool doctors use to persuade patients to undergo treatment and surgery. UV photography works like this: the UV camera takes pictures that show the melanin clusters in the skin, making it easy to capture an image of the mottled, blotchy hyperpigmentation that has yet to appear.

"The results can often be quite shocking for patients, heightening their awareness of the need for sun protection and raising a desire for treatment," the sales material reads. Of course, most patients would have to lie in the sun every day for fifty years before their skin became as blotchy as the UV photos indicate. (To be fair, the camera can indicate large amounts of early skin damage, such as that suffered by serious sun worshippers and tanorexics, the men and women who visit tanning salons frequently.)

The hot marketing tool Canfield is introducing at the convention is an imaging system called Visia, a diagnostic tool that costs $10,700. An attractive woman in her late twenties named Geana Smalls beckons me over. She is five months pregnant, she tells me, but the tiny mound is barely noticeable, a fashionably miniature basketball of a baby. Visia takes the UV camera concept several gargantuan steps further. While UV photography can only show you what you might look like in fifty years without sunblock, Smalls explains that this new device takes pictures of the patient's face, calculates the amount of bacteria and the number of wrinkles, spots, and other nefarious age-related splotches, and then compares the patient with other members of his or her age group.

The competition the machine encourages is, of course, where the product is most compelling, where it can wave the hand of morality across the patient population. Which fifty-year-old has been more vigilant over the years? Which thirty-nine-year-old stayed out of the sun, didn't drink too much wine, never took up smoking or ate fatty cheese, and wore sunblock every day like their dermatologist told them to? And which one ignored all the sage medical advice, drank, smoked, ate cheese, and went to tanning booths?

This is the Visia's genius: while the UV camera is able only to demonstrate to patients the amount of sun damage they have perpetrated on themselves, this machine actually compares patients to their peers. And there is no more effective way to sign up clients than to make them feel as if they are falling behind their neighbors or their classmates or the Jones family down the street.

The Visia is a white cube mounted so that a patient can sit with his or her chin balanced in a little cup that holds the face in position for a short burst of photographs. At the conference in Boston, I sit down and place my face into the chin holder, and Smalls instructs me to look into a tiny white box in the corner. The interior of the Visia looks like a diorama of the all-white Wonka-vision studio in *Willy Wonka and the Chocolate Factory*, where greedy Mike Teevee is accidentally shrunk to doll size so he will fit in a television set. ("I'm famous! I'm a TV star!") Once he has been shrunk, Mrs. Teevee deposits him in her handbag and the Oompa Loompas take mother and son away to the taffy-pulling room.

The light flashes. Then another. I pull back and look at the image on the monitor. My eyes are open, theatrically blue, my lips pink and glossed, cheeks rosy. It is actually quite a generous portrait.

Smalls moves her mouse around and shows me the next picture. Oh. It is me, but this version of me has a nose dotted with gaping pores, welcome vessels waiting for bacteria. Smalls asks my age. I am thirty-six. We enter the information in the computer.

"Now we get to contrast your results with those of your peer group," she says. The categories I will be judged on include spots, pores, wrinkles, and porphyrins. Spots and pores, I get. Porphyrins need a little explaining: they are molecules in the body that combine with iron to produce heme, which is responsible for giving blood its red color and aids in the creation of hemoglobin. A related porphyrin can also stimulate acne production on the skin. A disorder of renegade porphyrins causes porphyria, which some historians believe was the cause of George III's mental instability. He ruled during the American Revolution, and his episodes of constipation, his rashes, pimples, and manic ravings were thought to have had a significant impact on Britain's defeat. In 1811, he suffered an especially severe attack, was dethroned, and spent the rest of his life wearing straitjackets, becoming progressively more insane, rashy, pimply, and blind until he finally died in 1820.

I guess checking for nasty porphyrins is a good thing.

Despite the gruesome depictions of my face, I am feeling pretty confident about my skin. My peers, surely, would not measure up to me and my scrupulous skin-maintenance regimen, the thousands and thousands of dollars I have spent on creams, sprays, mists, facials, and injections during my life. My vigilance is surely demonstrated by the fact that I was the first of my friends to start getting Botox shots at twenty-eight. Maybe I didn't score highest in my class on the SATs, but here, under Visia's calculating eye, I am confident that all my prophylactic work will finally be rewarded with high scores.

A sheet of paper unfurls from the computer.

"On spots, you score in the 18th percentile," Smalls says. Eighteenth, I ask, is good? "Um, no, that would be toward the bottom of the scale." That means, she says, that 82 percent of women my age are less spotty than I am. In other words, I am as spotted as an old banana. On my right cheek alone, she points out, I have twenty-six visible blotches and thirty-two invisible ones—the nascent blotches ready to become visible if I step outside into the sunshine without sun protector.

My other scores are higher but still no good. I score in the 68th percentile on wrinkles, meaning that 32 percent of my peers are less wrinkly than I, and have they gone out and spent four thousand dollars on Botox? Doubtful. I rank in the 51st percentile on evenness of skin tone. (Strange, considering my spottiness.) But the worst is my porphyrin level, which is rated by Visia on a scale of 0 to 350, 350 meaning the skin is home to teeming colonies of bacteria ready to chew your face apart with a tsunami of pimples.

My score is 318, or the equivalent of the Black Death. It is shocking to me, suddenly, that I have not already been devoured by scrofulous infection.

"Oh, my," Smalls says, her voice suddenly brittle with politeness. She begins to look at me as if I were the Nazi with the melting face at the end of *Raiders of the Lost Ark*, and gets a queasy little half smile on her face, the kind that says: *I am smiling because I don't want to be unkind, but I'm afraid you might pass some flesh-eating disease to me so I am just going to stand back a bit, say, over here. After all, I'm pregnant and must protect my unborn child.*

A year later, I attend the conference of the International Society of Aesthetic Plastic Surgery in Houston. In the intervening fourteen months, I have spent $8,000 on microdermabrasion to even out my skin tone and scrub away the scourge of spots, pits, dents, and miniature lipomas (tiny white fat nodules); collagen injections to fill the deepening nasolabial canals coursing from my nose to the outer sides of my mouth; Botox to get rid of wrinkles on my forehead, furrows between my eyebrows, at the sides of my nose, and at the corners of my eyes; and Restylane, the substance that is related to the viscous goo that allows human cartilage and rooster combs to be flexible and bendy.

No one can accuse me of not trying. So when I see the Canfield booth, looming like Valhalla in the corner of the refrigerated convention hall in the Houston Hilton, I have no choice but to square my shoulders and march into battle. Wander Rodrigues, the director of international sales for Canfield, is showing surgeons from around the world the new, improved Visia, which now costs $17,000. Rodrigues has just returned from a sales junket to China, where he sold fifteen of the devices. He speaks five languages fluently. He lives in suburban New Jersey.

His colleague, Tom Moog, snaps my pictures. This time, the results spool out on photographic paper, with my face and all of its atrocities sketched out six times. I score in the magical 99th percentile on pores, meaning that 99 percent of women have more visible pores than I do. Wow, I could get into Harvard with scores like these. On spots, I score in the 32nd percentile. Moog explains to me that last year Smalls had been wrong about my 18th percentile score, which actually meant that I had *fewer* spots than 82 percent of women my age. This year, my score is up, in a bad way, to the 32nd percentile, meaning that I have fewer spots than just 68 percent of the female population my age.

I score in the 73rd percentile on wrinkles, meaning that I am less wrinkly than 73 percent of the population my age, an improvement from last year's 68th percentile but, shockingly, not as great as I might have thought, considering how many thousands of dollars I have spent. And on porphyrins, I score 258 out of 350, and there in the picture, the porphyrins shine, angry hot-pink dots on a mottled gray surface, looking like a NASA map of the eastern seaboard at nighttime. My nose is New York City on New Year's Eve. My cheek, way out near the earlobe, is calm, quiet, darker Maine.

"Gee, when was the last time you washed your face?" Moog asks.

Nine

Fat Is Not Beautiful

Outside, it is almost 100 degrees Fahrenheit, muggy, hot, and so steamy the wrinkles in my cotton dress fall out as soon as I leave the door of my hotel, a block from the Hilton. This humid circle of hell is Houston, Texas, in August. Outside on the sidewalk in front of the Hilton, a couple of homeless men shuffle along with grocery carts piled with garbage; they are clothed in dark green plastic garbage bags thumbprinted with dirt.

The glass doors of the hotel slide open with a soft hissing sound, and I step six inches into another world. The air is refrigerated. Every pore on my skin clamps up, and the hairs reach outward. An enormous Dale Chihuly sculpture hangs from the lobby ceiling, a spectral glass man-o'-war angling its multiple eyeballs down onto the crowds milling below. Here, plastic surgeons from around the world have converged for the annual meeting of the International Society of Aesthetic Plastic Surgery. Outside: homeless men, slick with fat and grimed in streaky dirt. Inside:

surgeons, cool and clean and slender, seemingly vaporous in the chilled air.

There are plastic surgeons from Dubai, Iran, Mexico, Israel, South Africa, Thailand, New Zealand, and one from Cambodia. I arrive at the free lunch held in the exhibit hall and introduce myself to a table of Czech surgeons who are sitting off in a corner, not mingling with any other doctors. They are complaining about how they are not able to perform as complex operations or procedures as American surgeons are. This is the source of their unhappiness. It's really unfair, one of them says.

"Why can't you?" I ask, unwrapping the carefully Saran Wrapped ham sandwich, apple (also Saran Wrapped), and chocolate chip cookie. "Surely, you have good training, good educations. What's the problem?"

"The instruments," one says. "We just can't get them sharp enough. Sharp instruments cost a lot, you know. We don't make that much money. And when they are dull—how you say—they do not cut so well." He draws his right hand up in the air, as if holding a scalpel, and slashes it downward, pausing to tug through an imaginary tough piece of flesh. The other surgeons laugh.

Memo to self: do not travel to the Czech Republic for cosmetic surgery.

I excuse myself. I am late for a seminar that these doctors are not attending because the topic is an almost exclusively American procedure, the full body lift. "Not our problem," one of them tells me with a wave. The body lift—a kind of macro-face-lift for the torso, stomach, back, neck, arms, and thighs—is a procedure in which surgeons remove the extra, now irrelevant flesh and yards of skin that hang from the bodies of patients who have rapidly lost extreme amounts of weight as a result of gastric bypass surgery. As liposuction became one of the cosmetic surgery industry's fastest-growing procedures when it was introduced in the 1970s, the full body lift is among the fastest-growing procedures today. Its popularity speaks, of course, to the rising levels of obesity in this country: where surgeons could once siphon out a few ounces or pounds of fat, now they have to choke off the stomach and literally starve patients, who then lose so much weight they require a half dozen plastic surgical procedures to correct the deformed skin and muscle.

In 2004, about 140,600 Americans had gastric bypass surgery according to the American Society for Bariatric Surgery—up from 16,000 ten years before. The surgery typically reduces the size of the stomach, thereby limiting the body's ability to accept excess amounts of food and hampering its ability to absorb nutrients from food. After the procedure, a patient is left with a stomach pouch often described as the size of a thumb. The size of the stomach forces people to dramatically limit the amount of food they eat, and patients—consuming as little as four hundred calories a day—lose huge quantities of weight, often between a hundred and two hundred pounds within the first year after surgery.

Gastric bypass first dazzled the popular imagination in 1999 when the pop singer Carnie Wilson declared that she would undergo the procedure. Wilson was a long-term warrior in the battle against obesity. By age nine, she weighed 110 pounds. By thirty-three, at five foot three, she weighed 300 pounds. Exhausted and suffering from a number of weight-related ailments, she signed up for the ninety-minute operation, which she and her doctors agreed to broadcast on a Web site called Adoctorinthehouse.com. On the day of the surgery, I eagerly logged into the site, but I was one of thousands who couldn't get in because traffic was so heavy. More than 250,000 Web viewers watched. She lost 152 pounds.[1] (She later had a child and gained seventy-five pounds with the pregnancy but has been working with a trainer and nutritionist to lose the weight again.)

Once Wilson shared her dramatic experiment with weight-reduction surgery, the floodgates opened. Celebrities like Sharon Osbourne, Al Roker of the *Today* show, Congressman Jerrold Nadler, and others have come out about their own gastric bypass surgery.[2] The opera singer Deborah Voigt has lost 130 pounds;

immediately after her 2006 appearance on *60 Minutes* to discuss her weight-loss surgery, ticket sales for her future performances at the Metropolitan Opera in New York skyrocketed.

Most people who undergo gastric bypass surgery do not do so to become supermodels. They do it to save their lives, reduce their levels of hypertension, save the bones and joints that support their enormously outsized weight. They want to walk down the street, sit on a bus, take an airplane. They don't want to be diabetic. They want to live past their fortieth or fiftieth birthday. They don't want to die before their parents do.

The surgery is not without risk. Roughly 10 percent of patients suffer serious complications. Between 0.1 and 2 percent of patients die during or following the procedures, and for the rest complications after surgery include infections resulting from gastrointestinal leaks, abdominal hernias, metabolic bone disease, anemia, osteoporosis, gallstones, blood clots, bleeding, and respiratory failure. Patients have trouble absorbing nutrients for the rest of their lives and so must carefully monitor the few calories that are allowed into their systems. Nearly 30 percent of bypass patients develop osteoporosis, anemia, and malabsorption problems caused by nutritional deficiencies. According to the National Institutes of Health, 10 to 20 percent of patients require additional surgery to address complications.

There is no doubt that, despite the complications, more Americans will choose gastric bypass as a way to lose weight. Almost a quarter of the population is obese. Fat Americans are on display everywhere, from Disney World, where the structural engineers have been forced in recent years to make the seats on rides wider to accommodate ever-spreading American bottoms, to the Wal-Marts of the Midwest, where the best-selling sizes are all in double digits. Even in cities like New York, where not only is thinness prized but frequent walking is part of the daily routine, you can't help but notice the office workers who line the Avenue of the Americas in the afternoons, their necks choked with rings of fat, as they smoke the cigarettes no longer allowed in their office buildings or walk back to their offices holding their pizzas and calzones aloft in front of them like slaves merely doing the food's bidding.

And we will only get fatter. A Boston University study released in late 2005 and published in the *Annals of Internal Medicine* suggested that in the long term nine out of ten men and seven out of ten women will become overweight. Half of the men and women in the study who had made it well into adulthood without a weight problem ultimately became overweight.[3] A third of those women and a quarter of the men became obese. Ramachandran Vasan, an associate professor of medicine at Boston University and the study's lead author, studied data gathered from four thousand white adults over thirty years. Participants were between the ages of thirty and fifty-nine at the start and were examined every four years. By the end of the study, more than one in three had become obese.

We are so fat, in fact, that even our feet have grown from the force of our extra weight. In the 1960s the average American woman wore a size 5½ or 6, according to the *Professional Shoe Fitting Manual*, the bible of shoe-size training written by podiatric historian William Rossi. Adults are only about an inch taller than they were in the 1960s, but they are also twenty-five pounds heavier. The extra weight, podiatrists say, has caused the American foot to widen and spread significantly.[4]

Seats in automobiles and on amusement park rides, subways, and airplanes have gotten wider. Caskets are now available in triple-wide sizes, about forty-four inches across, to accommodate bodies of up to 700 pounds. Many funeral homes now discourage cremation of such large patients, because during the process, the vast amounts of fat often leak and cause fires outside the cremation device. Hospitals can now purchase diagnostic equipment such as CAT scans that can accommodate patients weighing up to 800 pounds, according to Dr. Lee Kaplan, director of the MGH Weight Center at Massachusetts General Hospital.

Obesity—and concomitant illnesses such as diabetes—is now an affliction of the very young. There is no more grippingly sad television commercial than the recent one for a diabetes blood-monitoring system in which a young boy, barely a teenager, is playing guitar with B. B. King, his idol. They have a lot of things in common, the child's voice-over announces: their love of music—and their diabetes. In every demographic group, children are getting fatter. A 2003 report from the Federal Interagency Forum on Child and Family Statistics found that, from 1976 to 1980, 6 percent of children ages six to eighteen were overweight. From 1999 to 2000, 15 percent were.

As more of us get fatter, the more we hate fat. If beauty is a religion, fat is a cardinal sin. To be fat is to be perceived as weak and morally lazy. Women who belong to the cult of the beauty junkie will resort to any means to remain thin. Thin is beautiful. Thin means you are smart, sexy, powerful, and in command of your own destiny. In New York, the lower your body mass index, the better a person you are. In fashionista circles, anorexia and bulimia are not illnesses but conditions that make life fun and sample-size clothing wearable. I once visited a friend on the editorial floor of *Vogue* and needed to use the bathroom. A handwritten sign, scrawled on yellow notebook paper, was taped to one of the stalls: "Please do not use this ladies' room as your personal vomitorium. Go barf up your lunch elsewhere!!!"

As the number of weight-reducing procedures increases, several other kinds of problems have emerged. On the psychological level, newly slim patients must now face a world that has always perceived them as fat, unnoticeable, objectionable. They must learn to cope with jealousy, with changing family dynamics, with skepticism from friends and acquaintances. After a time, they must overcome the initial euphoria that comes with the dramatic weight loss and realize that life isn't just about being slender, a contest to be thin. The rest of life eventually charges back in all its colloquial numbness, and the lives of extreme-weight-loss patients begin to resemble those of lottery winners. Maybe having all this money, or losing all this weight, hasn't changed them.

Maybe their faces didn't turn out so pretty after all. Maybe their husbands are still jerks. (Three-quarters of bariatric surgery patients are women.) Maybe their kids are mean, and maybe their jobs are still terribly unfulfilling. Maybe they had other problems, problems that being slender just won't ever fix.

But on the physical level, there is an equally profound, more immediate and embarrassing problem. What happens when a body shrinks from 400 pounds to 150 in a dramatically short period of time? The patient is left swimming in a sack of skin, the hide of the former fat person in which they are literally trapped. The results—depending on the swiftness of the weight loss, the patient's age, and his or her genetic heritage—can be devastating. Studies are under way to see whether the amount of loose skin that results from gastric bypass surgery is because of the speed with which patients lose the weight. Most plastic surgeons I spoke to who make a substantial income from plastic surgery on bariatric patients told me that the speed with which patients lose weight is most definitely not the cause. And most plastic surgeons I have spoken to who do not attend to the problems of bariatric patients say that slower weight loss, over several years, results in less droopiness.

Cosmetic surgery of such intricacy and scale isn't cheap. Most bariatric patients who choose plastic surgery have two to three separate operations at $10,000 to $15,000 per procedure. Insurance rarely covers the cost. Nearly 70 percent of all upper-arm and thigh lifts performed in the United States in 2003 were on patients who'd had weight-loss surgery, according to the American Society of Plastic Surgery. With an estimated 144,000 people expected to undergo bariatric surgery this year, weight-loss-specific plastic surgery operations are likely to increase by 36 percent, the ASPS predicts.

Carnie Wilson had the excess flesh and skin excised during an eight-hour operation in the office of Beverly Hills plastic surgeon Dr. Steven Zax, who removed the excess skin on her stomach, repositioned her belly button, lifted her breasts, and suctioned fat out of her hips and torso. He also removed a pound of skin from underneath her armpits.

Extensive scarring follows such operations. While the scars fade a bit over time, and surgeons do their best to position them where they are least noticeable, it is not an exact science. Prospective patients must also realize that the results may fall short of what they expect. No matter how talented, surgeons can't always get rid of every piece of sagging skin or pocket of fat. There are other complications, as well. Often the belly button is simply lost and a surgeon must refashion and reposition one in the place that nature first placed it.

For many patients, this sudden laxity of skin—the plastic surgeons call it skin redundancy—forces them to confront the friends and acquaintances who were skeptical of gastric bypass surgery in the first place. I spoke to one woman from a prominent New York family who asked that she not be identified because she did not want to embarrass her family members, all of whom are relatively slim and athletic. She was always the fat outlier, and choosing to have gastric bypass surgery was a decision she came to after ten years of dieting and spa visits. At first, the weight loss seemed like a miracle. But then she realized that her white Anglo-Saxon heritage had not prepared her skin well for this resolution. She looked, she told me, like a hammock of flesh, after losing 115 pounds.

"I lost all the weight," she told me as we ate lunch at Via Quadronno, the socialites' coffee shop on the Upper East Side of Manhattan. The chairs are tiny, the tables are tiny, and the food is tiny. I feel like I am sitting on dollhouse furniture when I eat there. She reveled in the fact that she could fit in the front door, and the bite-size miniature sandwiches were too much for her. She ate a quarter of one sandwich and used a tiny spoon to sip mint tea. "And then I had these flaps of skin hanging off of everywhere. I had this flap that hung down over my belly. I wouldn't be able to show off my new body because then all the assholes who told me gastric bypass would never work, that there were no quick fixes, would be able to look at me and say, 'Ha! You traded one set of problems for another. And now you look even more hideous!' "

She had not yet gone in for the surgery to correct the folds of hanging skin but was contemplating it.

X X X

In Houston, at the afternoon seminar on the full body lift—the procedure that addresses the issue of extra skin after weight-loss surgery—Dr. Dennis J. Hurwitz, a charismatic surgeon from Pittsburgh, begins to rattle through a series of slides. In the late 1990s, Hurwitz, a trained reconstructive plastic surgeon and former head of the craniofacial center at the University of Pittsburgh, began to see referrals from some of the top local bariatric surgeons. The biggest problem, he saw at the time, was that the patients needed multiple surgeries to address the excess skin—abdominoplasties, thigh lifts, neck lifts, arm lifts, liposuction, face-lifts, breast lifts—a round of surgery that could take each patient somewhere between eighteen and thirty-six months.

He developed the total body lift, in which the patient undergoes a circumferential abdominoplasty, a lower body lift, an inner thigh lift, a reverse abdominoplasty, a back-roll removal, and a breast reshaping. All are performed in a single surgical session that lasts nine or ten hours. Throughout the procedures, Hurwitz handles only the cutting, liposuctioning, and repositioning; he has a team of surgical sous-chefs who perform most of the suturing as he moves on to the next portion of the body.

"Here is the patient before the gastric surgery," Hurwitz says in Houston, speaking with the same glottal vocal inflection that identifies former New York mayor Rudolph Giuliani's speech patterns. And there on the screen in the air-conditioned ballroom is a picture of an enormously obese person, so bloated with fat it's impossible to tell if the torso belongs to a woman or a man. Some of the rounded softness in the hips suggests it is a woman, but obese men produce abnormal quantities of estrogen and often develop gynecomastia, the condition of male breasts. And there are breasts here.

Some Brazilian surgeons sit in front of me. They lift their hands to their mouths and stifle laughter. After all, there isn't much gastric bypass surgery in Brazil. There just aren't that many obese people in Brazil. It is the first time I have, over the course of five years of attending medical conferences, ever seen surgeons stifle giggles at something they found so utterly outlandish and foreign. Surgeons tend to conduct themselves in a most professional manner when they are at conferences of their peers, and to watch a group of cosmetic surgeons from Brazil suppress a nervous laugh means that they are seeing something completely strange and grave. They have been shocked out of their professionalism by American fat.

"Here," Hurwitz says, switching slides, "is the patient after gastric bypass surgery. She has lost 280 pounds."

The slide appears. A gust of air goes out of the room as a thousand people simultaneously sip in an amazed gasp. There is the merest suggestion of a skeleton, the dimly hinted shadow of a regular-sized human being, but this person is draped behind curtains of yellowed skin. Her breasts—because now you can see that she is a woman—sink to the midportion of her thighs as if they were weighted flaps. They put me in mind of canvas bags filled with boating or fishing equipment.

Each leg is wrapped in folds of skin, whorled in tissue. Two full foot-long overhangs of skin descend from her upper torso and midtorso, and one puddles over her pubic area, draping it like a flesh miniskirt.

In the next slide, she holds her arms out to the side. The skin falls in crepe layers that accumulate into thicker flesh formations, enthusiastic cataracts of skin sluicing out from her body like a heavy liquid. She is a wax figure held to heat; she is melting. I imagine myself briefly as that woman and decide that I would rather have remained obese, or would rather have died, than look like a figure out of a horror movie.

The Brazilians gasp out loud in horror, their mouths falling open. This time, they are so shocked they don't even bother to cover their mouths.

n New York City, I spend an afternoon with Dr. Mark Lidogaster, who operated several times on Stacy Halpern, an actress who lost almost 200 pounds, going from 550 to a relatively svelte 277. "The skin issue is a big issue in massive weight loss," he says. "If the skin were an envelope made of something like Lycra, it would snap back. But skin is skin. Once it's stretched, it's stretched. The patients end up with folds and aprons of skin, and the only way to address the issue is to, well, darn the sock."

Stacy had so many folds of skin around her genital area, Lidogaster tells me, she couldn't even get a Pap smear at her gynecologist's. A male patient had "a volleyball-sized mound of fatty, swollen infected skin," Lidogaster says. He removed it. "Now he can get up and play volleyball," he says, "instead of carrying one around all day." He chuckles. Lifting the skin around the abdomen in these patients, he explains, isn't like a run-of-the-mill tummy tuck. In a tummy tuck, he explains, you don't go past the firm internal envelope that houses the viscera. "With this, it's much more involved. Skin has grown over the vagina and the penis. They get an apron of skin or a second apron. This prevents a patient from taking care of herself or himself. They can't keep themselves clean. They get infections. It's not a happy thing."

Lidogaster, a Russian émigré who learned to speak English in the United States, likes to pepper his speech with American idiomatic expressions. When we are discussing Jocelyn Wildenstein, whom Lidogaster has met, he says, "She is as happy as a clam in a sand bank!"

He tells his body-lift patients to hope for the best and prepare for the worst.

"I give them the Grim Reaper speech," he says, his voice

rising to a theatrical pitch. "This is not going to be all peaches and cream. You are not waltzing into a field of roses. This is not a field of daisies. This is no day in the park. Are you going to have a scar? Why, yes. Yes, indeed. By golly, you are going to have the mother of all scars! Pardon me, the *mothers*! Because you will have many, *many* scars. Will you recover quickly? Hmmm." He taps his temple and pushes his mouth up to one side, in a gesture that resembles deep thought. "You think a week is a long time for recovery? Try a year. Try two years. Try two years, and scars up and down your legs, and scars on your arms, and on your back, and a fleur-de-lis scar running circumferentially around your body."

Lidogaster pauses for a breath.

"And then tell me you're ready for this."

When Lidogaster was a resident, plastic surgery, he explains, "was the happiness surgery. It was something people did for happiness, plain and simple. Now, at least in this work, it strikes me as more of quality-of-life surgery. Let's see. 'If I weigh 450 pounds am I going to be able to get into and out of a car? Would I feel better if I could do that? Would I like to be mobile, in the most moderate way imaginable?' The answer is probably yes."

Of course, some people screw up the surgery and gain the weight back by sitting around all day sipping milkshakes. "And there's your 7,000 calories," he says, blowing out his cheeks like Louis Armstrong. "And there goes the happiness."

Four months after the conference in Houston, Dr. Hurwitz comes to New York to show off one of his prize patients at a conference held at the Plaza Hotel by the Manhattan Eye, Ear & Throat Hospital. This is the hospital where the novelist Olivia Goldsmith died the year before while having a cosmetic surgical procedure on her neck and lower face. Some doctors assumed the conference, in its third decade, would not go on this year, but it did.

Hurwitz's patient is a thirty-six-year-old lawyer, an intelligent woman from Pennsylvania with bright eyes, a good education, and a great job as a litigator.

"I want you to meet her," he says enthusiastically to me on the telephone, sounding like a young man bringing his first girlfriend home from college.

"I'd like to," I say. "Where?"

He gives me the number of his room in the Plaza. It is a Sunday afternoon, chilly and bright. I enter the Plaza—home to so much glamour and nostalgia, a place echoing with memories of martinis and elegant women and black-tie parties—and take the elevator up to Hurwitz's tiny room. The Plaza will close in a few months and the room shows signs of the disrepair of the place. The headboard is stained from the grease of the heads of a thousand guests sitting up in bed watching Johnny Carson, then Jay Leno. The carpet is worn.

A heavyset woman sits on the side of the bed. Hurwitz introduces us. We all sit on the bed, folding our bodies into positions that feel demure and professional and appropriate, even though there are three of us sitting on a queen-sized mattress in a tiny hotel room. Hurwitz takes out several large photographs. They are of the lawyer, the woman sitting next to me. In the pictures, she wears no clothes. I cross my legs and hug my arms to my chest, trying to be respectful.

In the photos, the flesh hangs curtainlike off her arms and back, her thighs. A skirt of skin hangs over her genitals. Her breasts hang, empty stretched flaps of skin with a distended purple area at the bottom. *Aha! I recognize that! A nipple!* I glance at her. She looks at me. She does not wince. She has seen these pictures before. She has lived these pictures.

"And now look at her," Hurwitz says.

She looks—slimmer. Chunky still, but not obese.

"Do you mind if she takes off her shirt?" he asks me.

And so there I am in a tiny hotel room with a doctor and his patient. She is stripping down. He takes a pen, and as she removes her shirt to reveal her body, he draws a line in the air outlining where he and his team cut and sewed the skin and where they reattached the muscles and resutured the flesh.

"Doesn't this look great?" he asks. We stare at her chest. She is unself-conscious. She does indeed look a lot better than in the photographs. But to be honest and brutal and bitchy, she doesn't look that great. The lawyer can now wear a bra. She can now fit her arms into shirts. She can bathe and not have to spend an hour drying beneath every fold of skin on her body and then putting antibacterial diaper cream into every crevice that might rub and chafe and retain moisture and get infected. But her body has been traumatized. I look at her face. She is my age, midthirties, a chronological place that can either look freakishly teenage or haggard and geriatric. The skin on her face hangs; her cheeks, once plump, are slack and heavy. In her face, I see decades of struggle. The skin has been ballooning out for so long it has no sense of where to go. She has struggled so hard to lose this weight, paid so much money to lose it and then paid so much more to have all of her skin repositioned, but she still looks old. It's a chilling disappointment. Plastic surgery can't do everything.

But she is happy.

"I never wanted to be a model," she says. "But I took the train here. I took the train to New York. And you know, I have never taken the train anywhere before."

Ten

Harvey Weinstein's
White, White Teeth

When doctors provide services that are not medically necessary, they must rely on good word of mouth and good references to attract new patients. In 1982, the Supreme Court upheld a 1979 order by the Federal Trade Commission requiring the American Medical Association to allow doctors to advertise, but advertising isn't enough. After all, it's just an ad, and pretty much everyone knows an ad is written and paid for by the company doing the advertising. Wouldn't it be so much better, so much classier, to be quoted in a newspaper or on the local evening news?

So doctors hire publicists. The publicist's job is to call up reporters and writers at creditable news organizations and ask them to produce something favorable about his or her client. At women's magazines, men's health magazines, and some city magazines, the writer often receives a service for free and then writes something wonderful about it. In the fashion industry, the same thing happens: a fashion editor is sent a free pair of Jimmy Choo shoes and puts something nice in the magazine about Jimmy

Choos. Why? Not because they are the best shoes, not because they are the sexiest shoes or the best-made shoes, but because if she puts them in the magazine, she will get more free shoes.

Like chefs and hairstylists, fashion designers and handbag purveyors, surgeons and other doctors have become more daring and aggressive about attracting new clients. They are no longer barred from advertising their services and there are few ethical constraints against hiring public relations firms. Whether or not a doctor hires a public relations firm is a matter of taste. With help from publicists, doctors now market themselves aggressively to magazines like *Harper's Bazaar*, *New York*, *Elle*, *Self*, *Vogue*, and *Good Housekeeping* and shows like *Good Morning America* and *Today*, hoping to reach the millions of readers and viewers who might want to try their wares.

But medicine is not fashion. A woman is not going to be seriously hurt if she buys a pair of poorly made shoes for $600 or spends her life laboring under the delusion that a $12,000 Hermès handbag is a cool purse to own. It seems harmless at first: the doctor gives a free service and the journalist gets a free face-lift. But the arrangement leaves the reading and viewing public in a difficult position: how do they know when a journalist has received some form of plastic surgery payola and thus feels pressure to produce something favorable about the doctor? Are they getting the most accurate and fair information on an expensive procedure that could change the way they look forever?

The practice has influenced even the way journalists conceive of stories. Doctors now complain about journalists requesting free treatments. Dr. Laurie Polis, a Manhattan dermatologist, told the *New York Times* that a writer for *More* magazine called her up and requested a day of treatments that included Botox, a facial, and a dermabrasion treatment. Polis complied lest she alienate someone who could make readers aware of her services. "I feel strong-armed," she said. "I can't bite the hand that feeds me."[1] Shortly afterwards, the writer requested a series of laser treatments. Polis was unpleasantly surprised. "Some of these people are so entitled," Polis said about the writer, who she said "threw a hissy fit" when she hesitated. "Laser treatments are expensive, and what she wanted would have taken six treatments."

Every week, I receive at least two solicitations from publicists hawking the wares of a doctor who specializes in some form of cosmetic beautification: they are selling face creams and sun-blocks, face-lifts using wires, face-lifts using acupuncture, fat re-moval using tiny needles. I have in the last couple of years received letters exhorting me to write about elastomer transduc-tion therapy, in which putty is applied to the skin and then ener-gized with electrical charges; a grapefruit-scented fragrance that will change other people's perception of your age by at least five years; injections of herbal tonics that dissolve fat; a one-day face-lift using tissue glue; cosmetic surgery for pets; adult circumci-sion; snap-on temporary teeth, dental Potemkin villages that are supposed to make you look like Julia Roberts for a night; the Russian thread lift, in which barbed threads are pushed beneath the skin, pulled back, and anchored to provide a lifting effect; the feather lift (same thing); the Aptos thread lift (same thing); the contour thread lift (same thing but with a competing company's thread); the Gerut lift (same thing but performed by a doctor named Gerut); a wonder pill to transform Manhattan drinking water into an antiaging elixir; a foot surgeon who does Botox in-jections; a cream that contains "liquid oxygen" and does the same thing as liposuction; a doctor who specializes in eyebrow hair transplants for women with thinning brows; a doctor who changes the shape of the toes to better fit pointy high heels. (That was fascinating: the pitch described how the toe is cut open and some bone is removed, then sewn back up, leaving the tip of the toe to shrink. It is a method similar to the one used by Amazon tribes to make shrunken heads, in which the skull was removed, leaving the soft tissue to contract.) Usually the pitcher of such sto-ries informs me that I can try any of these services for free. (How-ever, the *New York Times* does not allow reporters to receive anything from any news source for free—no free face-lifts, no free shoes, not even a bottle of champagne at Christmas that costs more than $25. I confess that I did succumb to the one free tan in L.A. Forgive me.) Occasionally, the doctors are trustworthy, talented professionals who aren't guilty of anything but a little attempt at self-promotion. Just keeping up with the times, they say when I speak with them on the telephone.

But more often than not, they turn out to be more complex creatures. Hiring publicists to get exposure for services is a quick fix, so it makes me wary. These doctors just don't have the patience to build a practice through patient word of mouth—which signals to me they don't have the patience to do anything to my body. And the publicists and the doctors are frequently hawking some radical new device or surgery that is untested and has no track record. Finally, I find that doctors hire publicists when they've got something to hide. The publicist can act as spin control and handle all the uncomfortable questions, if they ever arise.

In my personal estimation, of the approximate six hundred solicitations from public relations executives I have received about surgeons and other doctors practicing new cosmetic procedures, I would consider becoming a patient (if I were so inclined) of perhaps five of them—less than 1 percent. But I was curious about how the public relations message worked. Take the case of Dr. Larry Rosenthal, a dentist who was promoting his "smile lift" a couple of years ago. Using porcelain tooth veneers, and positioning them in certain spots and varying their thickness, his publicist told me, he could achieve something of a so-called lift around the mouth. Building out the size of the teeth in the mouth essentially reduced the number of small lines around the mouth and added fullness to the cheeks. It was so much better than cosmetic surgery that it was going to make cosmetic surgery totally unnecessary. It seemed like an extravagant and unnecessary way to achieve such a subtle effect, but I was intrigued. And I liked the publicist, Matthew Snyder, who was starting out in his own business. It wouldn't kill me to talk to the guy for an hour.

Snyder meets me outside what he calls The Building. The Building is 36 East 72nd Street, an office building that is a kind of Beauty Central to New York, just as North Rodeo Drive or Bedford are to Beverly Hills—home to dermatologists and surgeons and home to the John Frieda private salon, where celebrities come to have their hair done while the schlubs like me have to go to the salon on Madison Avenue, where you sit in the window and passersby can look up and see you with tin foil in your hair. Oh, to be Fergie, Duchess of York, who gets to sit in her own private booth at John Frieda!

Rosenthal is running late. We wait in his office. Snyder, who is about thirty-five but looks about twenty-five, tells me that Dr. Larry has done everyone's teeth.

"Everyone," he says.

A receptionist brings us water bottled in blue glass and we sip it out of elaborately hand-painted stemmed glasses. Snyder tells me that Dr. Larry has even done Harvey Weinstein's teeth. (Harvey Weinstein was the famously fiery cochairman of Miramax Films, now cochairman of the Weinstein Company.) "That shows he's brave, too," Snyder says of Dr. Larry. "Would you want to stick your hand inside Harvey Weinstein's mouth? Not me."

We gossip about doctors. Snyder calls a dermatologist with offices in Miami and New York who has undergone several of his own dermatological procedures "a living portrait of Dorian Gray." He points to a framed *Vogue* article about Dr. Larry by Tama Janowitz, a novelist of the *Bright Lights, Big City* era who made her name chronicling the go-go party life of the 1980s and who is in my mind inextricably linked with youth, glamour, recklessness, and what the Italians call *menefreghismo*, a word that in Sicilian dialect means not giving a fuck.

I peer at the article, titled "Oral Fixation," in its neat frame. It is all about how Janowitz—wild-haired rebel, bad girl, provocatrice—

was given lovely new white teeth by Dr. Larry. "I've always wanted big white teeth, the kind that movie stars and fashion models have," the first line reads. "There is something trustworthy about people when their teeth are clean. They somehow look more . . . honest."[2] The thought of *Vogue* sending glamorous Tama Janowitz off to get free teeth—which they were, Snyder tells me—from Dr. Larry is depressing. Had she not taken good care of her teeth? She couldn't afford new ones on her own? Does writing pay that little? A year later, I meet her for the first time, and she is vibrant, pretty, and engaging, but her teeth are as white as refrigerator paint—and big. Instead of looking younger, or more honest, she looks like a youngish middle-aged woman with Grandma's dentures in her mouth.

Dr. Larry arrives an hour late. He is, as Snyder describes him, a Jewish version of Michael Douglas, just slightly more built, with a slightly more pronounced nose and a better head of hair. He begins a top-speed public relations spiel. The spiel is something I have become accustomed to, especially writing about the business of cosmetic surgery. The kinds of dentists and doctors who have public relations people working on their images are the kinds of people who can listen to themselves expel hot air for hours. They also tend to have a typical rap, which they crank up and let loose by rote until the reporter they are talking to holds up his or her hand and says, Enough.

Dr. Larry is typical, if a bit more theatrical. "It was 1981, 1982, and my travel agent needed some bonding," he starts. "She had on these thick, thick veneers. God, they were thick. She needed some new bonding. I remember in the process of taking those teeth off—Phew. You usually get the crown off in one piece. And let me tell you, underneath a crown, it is not pretty. Even a good crown, boy, does that smell bad."

I look at Snyder. He doesn't move, but his eyes briefly enlarge at Dr. Larry, as if to say: *Do not mention how the teeth smell bad, do not mention anything ugly. Only mention the pretty things.* Dr. Larry recomposes his face, reverses course, and starts to sell me on his smile lift. "It all started way back before anyone had even heard of veneers," he says. "I'd ask a taxicab driver, 'Have you ever heard of porcelain laminate veneers?' They'd say no." I am curious: how many taxicab drivers today would have heard of porcelain laminate veneers? Dr. Larry explains that he has become so successful at his new craft and changed so many lives, basically—by the way—making cosmetic surgery obsolete, that he has decided to honor his profession with a new name, one that more appropriately describes the work he is doing now. "Now we call it facial aesthetics."

Dr. Larry flips on a video presentation. "This will rock your world," he says as a picture of a woman with unnaturally large white teeth flashes onto the screen. Then a picture of Dr. Larry appears, wearing what he describes as his "big white Chiclet teeth." Those, he explains, are the teeth he made for Matt Dillon in *There's Something about Mary*. "There I am wearing them." There's Daniela Pestova, the model: "We raised the gum line on her. So much better." Kylie Bax, the pop singer: "There she is kissing me. Hot, right?" Kathie Lee Gifford. A New York Socialite: "There she is before. There she is after. Why is she wearing sunglasses? Because she can't stand herself she is so beautiful. Why? Because she has now gone Hollywood." He talks about all the other celebrities he has done. Wayne Gretzky. Michael Bolton. Bruce Springsteen. Sumner Redstone. Tommy Hilfiger. Bridget Hall. Natasha Richardson.

(I called and wrote agents and press representatives for several of the above-named celebrities, but only two returned my calls or e-mails. Kathie Lee Gifford's assistant told me that Gifford still sees Rosenthal on a regular basis. But David Brokaw, the press agent for Michael Bolton told me: "As far as I can tell, and I know what dental work looks like, Michael hasn't had any work done," he said. "I am pretty sure that what he has is a set of God-given choppers.")

(Later, Dr. Rosenthal would not confirm he had treated any of these patients—even though he had felt free to bandy their names about with me previously—citing the medical privacy laws of the United States Department of Health & Human Services Office for Civil Rights.)

And, then, of course, there's Harvey.

"Harvey loves me," he says, pausing the tape. We stare at Harvey's picture. He is smiling, a broad carnivorous grin distinguished by rows of large white teeth. "We hang out. He comes here. We watch movies together right here in this very room." Dr. Larry is like a little kid fantasizing about how his favorite sports hero is coming over to visit him *right in his own room.* "Just look at those," Rosenthal continues. "Harvey's white, white teeth."

A picture of a man—not a celebrity—flashes up on the screen next. His teeth are stained and brown, and one of them curls out front like a curvy fingernail. "He must be English," Snyder comments. In the after shot, the man looks normal.

Dr. Larry's voice-over rolls. On the tape, he is silhouetted by bright light in a dark room. Shadows move theatrically across his face. "In a short period of time, we believe we can change your life," he says, staring soulfully into the camera. *Beat.* His voice drops. "I had no idea it would change a profession." Then, soaring inspirational music. Dr. Larry's voice continues: "Pride. Passion. Dedication." The Rolling Stones' "Under My Thumb" plays as background music. Patients on the tape talk about how the shape of their faces has changed, how they look younger, how their lives have improved. The video shows a waiting room full of happy customers and smiling, pretty nurses. The voice-over makes a promise about how lives are changed when patients get a smile lift, how patients feel happier, and how they even make new friends.

Dr. Larry leans over to me and whispers: "Actually, friendship is extra."

He snaps the lights back on.

Some patients are intolerable, he explains. He was late to our meeting because he had come from a patient who in her initial consultation was fidgety, insecure, and too demanding. She wanted too much. He could see that she was a high-maintenance client who asked too many questions and wanted too much from him. He wasn't sure he had the energy to deal with her. "And you know what, I said to her, your expectations are unrealistic and I am afraid I can't take you on as a client at this time." The work she wanted would normally cost $16,000. If he had the time and inclination to do it, he adds.

"Well, what happened?" I ask.

"Oh, she's been waiting next door this whole time," he says, flicking his hand in the direction of the next room. "Now she's been waiting and thinking. She really wants this. So I'll go back and say, Guess what, I've changed my mind. I can do this, but I'll have to charge you 25 percent more. And you see. She'll go for it." But she'll have to stew a bit longer. "Oh God, let me tell you the story about Faye Dunaway," he says. "She comes in and same thing. Demanding, pushy, wants too much, thinks too much, talks too much. And I send her away. She sends me this letter: 'Dear Dr. Rosenthal. Was it the way our eyes met? Did I intimidate you? Did I scare you?' Oh my God, it was hilarious."

Snyder is beginning to look frightened. The last thing he wants is to have to deal with an angry Faye Dunaway. (Dunaway's manager did not respond to a telephone message nor to an e-mail request for comment.)

Dr. Larry explains that he went to dental school to avoid going to Vietnam. He's not sure what his future plans are—whether to expand the business or sell it and move on. "I might sell the business," he says. "Next year, I am going to be executive producer of a movie. Harvey loves me. He's my buddy. He says, 'Larry, I'm your poster boy.'" Weinstein's spokeswoman, Julie Cloutier, did not comment on whether Weinstein had ever been a patient of Rosenthal's. A source close to Weinstein, however, added that he had no recollection of ever telling Rosenthal he could be executive producer of a movie.

Rosenthal was amusing, certainly. I wasn't sure how much positive press he would get if he felt free to tell reporters that he liked to charge patients unfairly and manipulate their expectations.

A few months after our interview, various press accounts reported that Rosenthal had been suspended from practicing for six months in 1987 after New York State officials found that he had bought or dispensed controlled substances without keeping patient records. Nevertheless, he worked out an awesome deal with *Vogue*, which in 1998 published an article titled "Smile! How to Buy Cover Girl Teeth." It should have been titled "Smile! How to Get Cover Girl Teeth for Free in Exchange for Writing a Glowing Profile of a Dentist in *Vogue*." In exchange for the profile ("A close friend I hadn't seen in months told me I looked so great so many times I was embarrassed"), the *Vogue* writer received $5,000 worth of dental repairs and veneers, which she did not disclose in the *Vogue* piece. And the piece failed to mention that Rosenthal had ever been suspended from practicing.[3]

Rosenthal told the *New York Times* in 1999 that he had been disciplined for misusing prescription forms to obtain sleeping and diet pills but that another person had stolen the forms and used them in his name.[4]

A few months after our interview, Rosenthal was sued for $20 million by a former associate dentist, Dr. Peter Rinaldi, who claimed that Rosenthal promised upon his hiring that he would make him a partner in the business within three years. Rinaldi's suit also claimed that Rosenthal accepted furs and jewelry for his wife in exchange for work. Rosenthal fired Rinaldi, and Rinaldi filed his suit.[5]

The lawsuit brought by Rinaldi was eventually dismissed.

Ellen Fein, coauthor of the bestselling book *The Rules*, also filed a highly publicized complaint against Rosenthal. Fein said in the complaint that Rosenthal had given her "gigantic" teeth that drove her husband away and ruined her health. "I wake up every single morning with teeth and jaw pain. . . . I also needed an immediate gum graft . . . [and] a root canal," she continued. "My marriage disintegrated—of course there were other issues—but all the complications that came from the procedure were the things that led to divorce."[6] The complaint was settled.

Then, a former patient of Rosenthal's set up a Web site, Baddentist.com, that serves up all sorts of sordid details about the dentist, his practice, and his personal life. Rosenthal retaliated: he offered money to construction workers if they would throw dirt on a woman who was distributing Baddentist.com flyers outside his office, according to the *New York Post.*[7]

The former patient founded the site to warn other patients about Rosenthal. He would give me only his first name—David—because he had a new dentist and didn't want the dentist to stop treating him for fear of bad publicity. David started the site because Rosenthal, he told me,

> ground three of my normal, healthy teeth into tiny stubs after explicitly promising not to do so, after I came to him to replace a cracked bridge I had from a childhood accident. Five other people have reported to Baddentist.com that he did exactly the same thing to them. In my case, this led to eight months of TMJ treatment and two years of braces. When I asked him to forward my records so I could seek alternate treatment, his office substituted someone else's records instead. When I pointed this out, and explained that I needed them for my treatment, his office told me that my records were "lost" and that they would not look for them. . . . I can understand a dentist making a mistake, or even being aggressive about marketing himself. But destroying part of my body, and then destroying records that I needed for my treatment in order to cover it up, while simultaneously threatening to retaliate if I ever told anyone what he did to me, all seemed like a little too much.
>
> So, I decided I would make people aware quite simply of what a lousy and dishonest dentist he is. I created the Web site, not a particularly time-consuming activity, and have added items to it over time as people have

come forward and shared similar experiences with me. At this point, the Web site doesn't really require any time or energy at all to maintain. It's no work to just leave it up. Rather, it would require work to take the site down. It is simply my hope that it might help others make a better choice in a dental practitioner, and not make the mistake I did. I know that the vast majority of successful dentists are honest and hardworking. But, clearly, there really isn't any adequate system in place to sort out those dentists from the ones who are successful only because they engage in dishonesty and deceptive marketing.

In many ways, I could sympathize with Dr. Rosenthal. It would be terribly unfair to target a doctor whose treatment had been appropriate. Rosenthal wrote to me in an e-mail: "in general, it is the nightmare of every high-profile doctor, dentist, lawyer, other professional, or celebrity to have someone with a lot of time on his hands, and apparently some money, stalk him/her or his/her family."

The patient, David, said he had never stalked Rosenthal or his family, only that he simply wanted other patients to know about his experience with Rosenthal.

In the meantime, Rosenthal has been working hard on his own site, aboutbaddentist.com, the first line of which reads, "Dr. Rosenthal is a good dentist!" At the top, he declares that his prices are indeed higher, but there is a reason for this: "Larry Rosenthal has a lot of celebrity friends. He is the most expensive dentist, and that's how you can tell that he is the best. The best always costs the most."

Toward the bottom of the site, however, he appears to have adopted a policy of dental glasnost, declaring that indeed some of the charges on baddentist.com are true, and worse. He reports that he had indeed lost a jury trial for medical malpractice and was ordered to pay $600,000 in damages, and that he settled other malpractice cases, and that he is currently (as of April 2006) dealing with another malpractice case. He writes that he has previously "lied under oath, falsely stating that his license was suspended because someone had stolen it and used it to obtain diet pills, which Dr. Rosenthal also falsely stated to the *New York Times*. Dr. Rosenthal admits that he personally wrote improper drug prescriptions for Quaaludes and other drugs, and that he illegally purchased and dispensed cocaine and other drugs, and this is the actual reason why Dr. Rosenthal's license was suspended." The mea culpa continues. "Dr. Rosenthal has also previously lied, including lying under oath, about baddentist.com and its creator."[8]

Since I met Dr. Rosenthal, he has by my count cycled through at least two more public relations firms. Snyder and he have long since parted ways. When I spoke to his new publicist and explained the project I was working on, she told me I had to come in to the office and meet Rosenthal. I would absolutely adore him, she said. "He is the best dentist in New York, despite what everyone says," she exulted. "And I'm not saying that just because he's paying me to."

Eleven

My Love Affair with Dr. Michelle

am not obsessed with the way I look.

Let me clarify. By "obsessed," I mean someone who stares at every pore of her face every hour of the day, who cannot leave the house in sweatpants, who is paralyzed by the fear that the world will find her unattractive, reject her, isolate her.

I'm not anorexic or bulimic. I haven't had my breasts lifted or pumped up. I am not the kind of woman who sits in front of the mirror for hours scrutinizing her flaws, pushing her nose this way and that, or smoothing her cheeks upward to see what she would look like with a face-lift.

I am not obsessed—at least not in the fevered way that some women are. I read with fascination—with satisfaction, really—the books and articles by women who suffer from serious body dysmorphic disorder and who have spent hundreds of thousands of dollars on cosmetic surgery, bankrupted their families, alienated their spouses. I marvel at their levels of concentration and their abilities to find themselves and their bodies so fascinating and worthy of contemplation and investment. It is hard to watch the talk shows on which, say, a twenty-eight-year-old woman has transformed herself after twenty-six surgeries into a plastic goggle-eyed doll with cartoonishly inflated lips and postapocalypse-white teeth and not feel a small measure of satisfaction that, no, that was not me—I could never be that obsessed.

I don't have body dysmorphic disorder, which is defined by the American Psychiatric Association's DSM-IV as "a preoccupation with a slight or imagined defect in appearance that causes significant distress or functional impairment and that cannot be accounted for by another mental disorder." I'm not obsessed with my weight. I don't have the restraint of anorexics or the physical derring-do of bulimics. Making oneself vomit in the quest for a slender figure is something that runs so counter to human nature I have to admit I'm too much of a human animal, dedicated to my survival, to even attempt it. Obsessed? Not me.

What I do is what we refer to in New York as maintenance. I am not preoccupied beyond therapeutic reach or common sense; I maintain. There are degrees of maintenance. In a recent issue of *O*, the writer and director Nora Ephron published a four-thousand-word essay about her own maintenance habits. She spends more on highlights and hair color each year than she spent on her first automobile. She has spent $20,000 on her teeth. She spends eighty hours a year having her hair blow-dried. She takes a taxi across town to have a woman shape her eyebrows. Her maintenance schedule takes up at least eight hours a week. Maintenance, as she defines it, is "what they mean when they say that 'After a certain point, it's just patch, patch, patch.' Maintenance is what you have to do just so you can walk out the door knowing that if you go to the market and bump into a guy who once rejected you, you won't have to hide behind a stack of canned food."[1] In another feature in the same issue, the *O* editors asked women to detail their own maintenance schedules. One Manhattan woman, Nichole Vowteras, forty-nine, outlined a plan that included in part: a haircut every six weeks (for an annual total of $4,800), craniosacral massage once a week ($8,320 a year), and

Botox ($3,000 for the year), for a total financial outlay of $66,591.[2] It sounds excessive, but on the Upper East Side of New York City, the body and the face are considered to be something like a garden, or an expensive winter coat. They are to be tended and cleaned, cared for every day in the hope that the buds will remain dewy or the shoulders crisp.

It is difficult to imagine a tribe of human beings so narcissistic, so self-involved, that all they do, most of the day, every day of the year, is take care of their personal appearance. But that is exactly what a certain type of woman in New York City does. And it's not narcissism—nor is it vanity, frivolousness, or low self-esteem. It's become a way of life, part health routine, part beauty regimen, part political philosophy.

Nowhere is that more evident than in certain American social sets, where it is a given that one will undergo some sort of major procedure every year and monitor the subtle ravages of time on a daily basis. In New York, the former beauty queen wife of a business mogul has a photographer take pictures of her nude body once a year so that she can scrutinize herself for flaws to be corrected at the hands of her surgeon. Women at swanky restaurants like Swifty's and Michael's who ten years ago wouldn't have been caught dead publicly debating the merits of a face-lift now toss around clinical terms like *nasolabial fold*, *botulinum toxin A*, and *short-scar face-lift* with the élan and enthusiasm of surgeons.

No one in New York helps more people seem to be something new than Dr. Patricia Wexler, the dermatologist who has treated Sean "Diddy" Combs, socialite designer Tory Burch, Vera Wang, Ellen Barkin, Donna Karan, Blythe Danner, Barbra Streisand, and practically every model in New York City. In 1998, when I first met Dr. Pat, her status as a guru was already assured. Barkin told me that she spoke to Dr. Pat at least once a week for advice on what procedures to try next. Dr. Pat was so thorough, so accomplished, so friendly, so affable, so trustworthy, in fact, that Ellen Barkin, movie star, considered Dr. Pat her primary physician. Even then, like many other dermatologists, Dr. Pat was picking up a lot of procedures from the field of cosmetic surgery, like liposuction.

By 2005, Dr. Pat was a bona fide celebrity on her own. In the fall, the designer Carolina Herrera hosted a party for Dr. Pat's new skin care line. Calvin and Kelly Klein showed up; so did Christie Brinkley. At the end of the party, everyone was clamoring for the goodie bag, which included a full set of Dr. Pat's new products. As a famous divorcée of some social status left the party, she delivered a hissing order to an assistant inside the velvet rope: "I need two, can you get me two, I need two, can you get me two," as if she were asking to buy crack, not asking for an extra goodie bag.

Dr. Pat believes that New York women in the maintenance game think of dermatology and cosmetic surgery much the way they think about a new accessory. "It's like the new pair of shoes, the new handbag," she said. "They've got to have it or they'll be out of the loop. They won't have their Manolos. That's how they treat a lot of these procedures." What draws many women to the newest and ever more expensive treatments is the same competitive consumerism that drives them to get into hair-grabbing fist fights at the Dolce & Gabbana semiannual sample sale. Admitting you've had the latest wrinkle filler is no longer a mark of shame; on the contrary, it is a status symbol in the mind of the twenty-first-century consumer who believes that self-maintenance and an abiding respect for personal aesthetics are deeply moral obligations, to be conducted with militaristic precision: Survey the landscape. Find the enemy. Attack.

In beauty—as in politics or wealth or social ritual—all is relative. I am 5'11" and normally weigh about 148 pounds. In Los Angeles, this means that I am fat, repulsive, and cannot find a pair of blue jeans to fit me in any of the tony boutiques. If I stop in at Fred Segal, the chic celebrity haunt in Beverly Hills, I'm ushered politely away from the Hudson "supermodel" blue jeans toward the sweatpants and dresses made in stretchy fabrics or the shoe department. (No matter how fat you are, shoes usually fit.) The women who shop there have bottoms that are no bigger than mine was in the first grade. In New York City, I'm considered a touch on the pudgy side but acceptable, and my stylish, unusual height makes up for it. In Wisconsin, on the other hand, I see relatives who think I'm not only a touch short but on some kind of sicko starvation diet.

But I'm not a sicko. I'm not obsessed. In my passion for maintenance, for preserving the outer fleshy envelope in its best shape, I'm simply *relatively* obsessed. There are lots of women with worse problems than mine. (Although this is beginning to sound familiar: as with all addictions, those who are addicted are always looking over their shoulders, pointing out someone else who has a worse habit.) Unlike one of my friends, I don't carry the phone number of Sharon Osbourne's plastic surgeon in my wallet in case I happen to move to California. I'm not like those women I know in Greenwich who have liposuction every year. (Greenwich, Connecticut, once had a reputation as a terribly Waspy and restrained place, but it is in truth one of the more decadent communities in the entire country.)

I hadn't ever given too much attention to my looks before beginning to write articles for the *New York Times* about Botox and cosmetic surgery. After a while, submerged in the universe of the looks-obsessed, I began to wonder how a few small physical adjustments might help. Over the course of the last ten years, I have developed a habit that some women in less vain parts of the country might find offensive and certainly a serious signal that I am, indeed, obsessed. In other parts of the country, however, some women might look down their noses at me and chortle at how hopelessly frumpy and untended I look. What, no hair extensions? No boob job? No capped teeth? Is she some sort of troglodyte? And although I never believed I was addicted to the singular process offered by practitioners of cosmetic surgery—the skin peels and shots, the expensive creams and procedures, the lipo and the computer imaging systems that show you the You you ought to be, not the You you currently are—it would take an experience that brought me to the clichéd yet desperate station at which all addicts must arrive to see my obsession clearly: rock bottom. I arrived at this place on a dark January night and saw that my vanity had deprived me of my humanity, that I was, in fact, obsessed beyond the normal boundaries. I was a junkie with a problem.

In a city like New York, people like to talk about their addictive personalities, as if having an addictive personality were a mark of achievement. Speaking of one's addictive tendencies removes a person to an elite group of movers and shakers, people who matter, people with intense feelings and passions, with problems that are more complex and lofty than merely the quotidian. Branding oneself an addictive personality is also a way of proving that one is neurotic enough—in a comfortable, tolerable way—to be accepted into the city that is the celebratory kingdom, the great toga party, of neurosis. And so people boast of their quasi-addictions to things like their BlackBerry, to chocolate, to yoga: *I am totally addicted to my spinning class. I am totally addicted to Tasti D-Lite. I am totally addicted to* The Sopranos.

Then there are people who do develop serious addictions to alcohol and drugs. The kingdom of neurosis is also the kingdom of jumbo martinis and delivery drugs, cocaine and pot and painkillers that come to your doorstep via friendly messenger.

I'm not an addictive personality in either of those senses. I can pick up a cigarette and smoke half of it, put it down, and not think of a cigarette for six months. I can take booze or leave it (although I usually take it). The one time I tried cocaine it put me to sleep. After a few episodes of pot smoking, which I didn't really like, I gave it up after I began to notice words *(minuscule, meticulous)* disappearing from my vocabulary.

(There was one exception. A personal trainer once gave me a Vicodin because my neck hurt. At home that night, I slugged it back with a glass of white wine. A half hour later, my body felt as if it were filled with warm honey. The air in my musty New York

City apartment on an air shaft was magically sweet and rich-smelling. The television emitted a warm, roseate light. I found intense pleasure and intellectual stimulation in an episode of *Everybody Loves Raymond*. In the morning, I vowed never to take a recreational Vicodin again.)

And then when I was twenty-eight I met Dr. Michelle Copeland, a plastic surgeon, at a party on Long Island. A lawyer friend introduced us. "She's fantastic," he said, pulling me aside. "Look at my skin and see how great it is. She's the reason." I began seeing Copeland every two or three months, not for anything major, just some dermatological treatments. And if someone as serious as this lawyer was doing it—he had argued cases before the Supreme Court of the United States!—I should be, too. This was just a part of physical maintenance, like going to the doctor for a checkup or having your car tuned.

Like other patients, I began to refer to her as Dr. Michelle.

My relationship with Dr. Michelle—my reliance on her—very slowly deepened into something that resembled addiction. We had an established routine: Come into the office and put on a little EMLA cream, a topical lidocaine solution that numbs the skin. Put on a robe and go into room number one, where Dr. Michelle would go over my face with a microdermabrasion tool, a fine sandblaster that sprays tiny crystals across the face, simultaneously abrading and suctioning off the dead skin cells. Perusing my face, she might find a couple of red veins or an area of redness to zap with an intense pulsed-light laser, which cauterizes veins and wounds the skin, stimulating the production of new collagen. There might be milia, hard nodules of fat and protein, to be excised. She would then slather my face with a black goo, which she zapped off with another laser. A nurse would clean me up and occasionally slather on more goo—this time, a clear coupling gel—for another laser, again to restore collagen to the underlying structures of my face. Dr. Michelle would run it over my face, each wave of light snapping like an elastic band against my skin.

We would think up other things to do. My upper lip might be

looking a little thin. So over the years we tried two or three things to plump it up: nothing trashy looking—subtle, subtle. We tried collagen derived from cadavers. The effect was good, but it disappeared in about two weeks. Ditto with the collagen derived from fetal foreskin cells. I wanted to try a form of hyaluronic acid available in Europe called Juvederm, because Dr. Michelle seemed enthusiastic about it. I paid my friend Nancy $150 to buy me a tube while she was on vacation in Italy. (Hyaluronic acid is used in eye surgery and to treat joint pain in athletes.). She brought it back in a paper envelope from an Italian pharmacy. I enlisted a dermatologist to inject me with it in a few places—Dr. Michelle's enthusiasm waned once she saw me clutching a travel-worn paper bag—and the effect was good. It lasted a few months.

I got Botox at least twice a year in the corners of my eyes, where crow's feet form, in the wrinkles across the top of my forehead, in the wrinkles between my eyebrows.

Dr. Michelle was always cautious and prudent.

"Can't we use it here?" I asked her, pointing to the rings that are a natural part of the skin of the neck.

"Don't be crazy," Dr. Michelle said.

The visits could last as long as two hours. After the entire process was over, I would pay the bill—often somewhere around $1,800—leave her office, occasionally clutching a blue ice pack to my lip or my forehead, and stagger down Fifth Avenue hoping no one saw me and wondering: was it wrong to pay my mortgage late so I could get some Botox?

The fundamental paradox of this kind of addiction, if one can call it that, is that I was involved in a process of self-improvement. Wasn't addiction something that was bad for you, that ran you into the ground and trampled your body or your spirit? Certainly, classic addiction—smoking, drinking, taking pills, and the whole panoply of other destructive personal habits—would make you wrinklier. Wasn't Auden addicted to tobacco and alcohol, and look at his skin, crosshatched in those entrancingly deep lines. While I, for one, was becoming smoother by the day. Even people who were addicted to healthy activities like exercise—running, aerobics—eventually got injuries that indicated it was time to slow down.

I ran through the questions I remembered from various sources about addiction. Common symptoms include things like participating in addictive behaviors more often than you intend. Excessive time spent seeking the addictive object. Pursuing and fulfilling the addiction at inappropriate times. Giving up other things in life to pursue your addiction. Of these, I could check only one, the last: I had given up buying clothes. My salary went into the mortgage on my apartment, taxicabs, and my Botox fund.

But the other categories didn't apply.

One afternoon, I was flipping through magazines at work and came across the hundredth article about liposuction I had read in *Allure* and *Vogue* and *Elle*, and before I even read it, a little bell went off in my head. It was the same bell that went off when I decided to paraglide off a 10,000-foot mountain in southern Idaho, the same bell that sounded when I decided to get married. It was the pinging, tonic sensation that accompanied the possibility of some mind-opening, life-changing experience, a hopeful voice that gave me encouraging pep talks every once in a while: *I can run the New York City Marathon! I can jump off that rock face with nothing but parachute silk and some strings on my back! I can be legally bound to one person for life. I can do it!*

This time, it said something different, and perhaps less profound: *I can get liposuction!*

I called Dr. Michelle and scheduled the consultation. I had run the marathon, after all. I had trained for years, eaten right, done ten thousand leg lifts—and I still had those two little annoying jiggling pouches of fat on my thighs, which the beauty industry appropriately yet repugnantly refers to as "saddlebags," as if the bearer were some sort of pack mule.

In the parlance of addiction, I was moving on to the serious junk. The Botox, the collagen, the facial peels—that was kids' stuff, comparable to smoking cigarettes in the back alley with the bad crowd from school. This was big: surgery. Anesthesia. I was moving into a shooting gallery downtown, renouncing my parents, and selling my children for crack.

Besides that, it was foolish and vain. Come on: I was a reporter for the *New York Times*. I was smart. I knew what a diluted stock was. I had been on *Nightline*. I had flown on George Bush's campaign plane. (He forgot my name and patted me on the head, greeting me with the phrase, "Hey, *New York Times*." It was repulsive but strangely endearing at the same time.) I had covered the World Economic Forum. People watched CNN and Bill O'Reilly and occasionally heard my opinions. And by the way, O'Reilly needed teeth whitening, Botox, and a thorough microdermabrasion session. Up close, he looked like Darth Vader.

In my universe, no one who was a serious person relied on his or her looks in any way. The life of the mind was supposed to mean a renunciation of the body. I was a member of a level-headed, grave group of professional journalists who collectively gravitated toward one of two ideals. The men, with a few athletic exceptions, were generally stoop-shouldered and slightly paunchy, their skin tinted an even gray tone from the fluorescent lights of the newsroom. The women, with two or three glamorous exceptions, tended toward the slightly unraveled. It was a perfectly attractive but just slightly harried look—pure New York intellectual. A paunchy stomach spoke proudly of the hours spent in research and writing, not out playing ice hockey or running in the park. A head of wild curly hair and a patched sweater said that the bearer had been so immersed in work she had no time to run a brush through her hair or go shopping—a waste of time, indulgent frippery. We were, as a group, exempted from the colloquial demands of the flesh and of the vanity it inevitably demanded.

"Do you really think you need to do this?" my soon-to-be husband asked.

I found myself saying something unthinkable.

"I just think it will make me look better," I said. "And I think I will feel better about myself."

Even as it came out of my mouth, the explanation echoed queasily in my ears, damning, the same empty justification I had read in a dozen women's magazines and dismissed as a load of simpleton psychobabble. *I'll feel better about myself. I just want to feel better about Me.* On an intellectual level, I knew that removing sixteen ounces of fat should not make anyone feel better about herself. The self is the soul, the accumulation of ideas and intellect and spirituality and experience and beliefs. It is what goes on beneath the muck and sinew and skin on the outside.

But on an emotional level, the draw was powerful, ineluctable, visceral, inexplicable: I just wanted it, like a child wants a toy in the window. I wanted to step off the cliff and try something extreme. Maybe there was some magic in it. Maybe it was as good as the women in all those testimonial articles claimed. Maybe, the hopeful little voice suggested, it would change my life.

And I was curious: I just wanted to try it.

Because maybe if it was good, I would do it again.

Which would be worse: To be dead or to be dead and have everyone know you died because you were vain and wanted to look great in a bikini?

I had never had surgery of any kind, had never been under anesthesia, and as the day of the procedure arrived I felt apprehensive. Thoreau's advice to be wary of any enterprise that required new clothes kept running through my brain, slightly modified: beware of any enterprise that requires you to not eat or drink after midnight. Suddenly, the whole venture seemed foolhardy and wasteful. If I died on the operating table, not only would I be dead but everyone would know I died because I was having fat suctioned off my thighs and rear. I had to have a sip of water in the morning, and I wondered if I would drown in my own vomit later. *Mama Cass, Jimi Hendrix, Alex Kuczynski . . .*

Liposuction, curiously enough, would not have evolved without the tools of abortion. In 1976, women in Paris began to buzz about Yves-Gérard Illouz, who had developed a method for removing deposits of fat without leaving a scar. Prior to the 1970s, surgeons—such as the famed Dr. Ivo Pitanguy of Brazil—would use a scalpel to make an incision and cut out the deposit. This, understandably, left a scar. Another European surgeon used a tool with a blunt blade that chipped away at fat, but it left a scar, too, and caused other complications. Illouz decided to try gynecological instruments, specifically the cannula used to perform suction abortions. (Surgeons suggested it was his familiarity with performing abortions that led to the discovery.) His technique was picked up by plastic surgeons first in Beverly Hills and then in Las Vegas.

Dr. Michelle operates out of her own offices. She has a full operating theater, staffed with anesthesiologists and nurses. She is certified by the American Board of Plastic and Reconstructive Surgery. She is a fellow of the American College of Surgeons and a member of the American Society for Aesthetic Plastic Surgery and the American Society for Plastic and Reconstructive Surgery. She is assistant professor of surgery at the Mount Sinai School of Medicine. She is an attending surgeon at the Mount Sinai Medical Center and Manhattan Eye, Ear & Throat Hospital. Her husband is one of the best cardiologists in New York. If anything went wrong, I would be taken care of.

The nurse instructed me to lie facedown on the table, which had been configured to accommodate this position. At first, I was confused: a patient entering surgery, etherized upon a table, brought to mind cinematic images of me in a supine position on a hospital bed, a mask over my nose and mouth, wiggling my fingers good-bye to my family like Debra Winger in *Terms of Endearment*. But this was cosmetic surgery: this was practical. I was having fat sucked out of my rear, so why would I be lying in any other position than facedown with my bottom, the actual work site, sticking into the air?

The anesthesiologist couldn't find a vein in my arm and poked several times at my forearm. It made me nervous. Queasy and sweating, I was about to leap up from the table and announce that I was no longer interested when she sank her needle into some deep bloody conduit and it found its place. Count backwards from ten, she said.

Ten, nine. I fought the sensation of being pulled into a churning, cold black ocean. I tried to open my mouth to scream, but the mouth—for suddenly, it no longer belonged to me—wouldn't open.

General anesthesia works by altering the flow of sodium molecules into nerve cells, or neurons, through the cell membrane. The drug does not appear to bind to any receptors on the cell surface and does not seem to affect the release of the neurotransmitters that transmit nerve impulses from the nerve cells, and its exact mechanism is not known to doctors. That is frightening enough. They do know, however, that when the sodium molecules do not get into the neurons, nerve impulses are not generated and the brain becomes unconscious. It becomes a vegetable floating in its warm bath of brain fluid. It might as well be a rutabaga in a stew. Under anesthesia, the brain does not store memories, it does not register pain, and it does not control involuntary reflexes. While doctors often compare the experience to a deep sleep to assuage patients' fears, it is to sleep what a lapping wave at sunset is to a tsunami. In sleep, some parts of the brain speed up while others slow down. Under anesthesia, the loss of consciousness is widespread, affecting the entire central nervous system. Everything slows to a grinding halt.

Two hours later, I awoke to a fog. The anesthesia hangover is dense, and I was not prepared for its suffocating incapacitation. When I tried to speak, my mouth produced a wretched slur. My body was reluctant to move and felt foreign, apart from me, the arms and legs meaty, floppy appendages that belonged to another person but had somehow been attached to my own body.

The nurses were bundling me into a wheelchair. A wheelchair meant moving, and rolling, and transportation, and I couldn't even speak, so how did they expect me to be mobile? I thought of Jean-Dominique Bauby, the French magazine editor who after a stroke found himself afflicted with the rare condition called locked-in syndrome: his mind was intact, but he had lost virtually all physical control and was able to move only his left eyelid. Unable to write or speak or move, he dictated his memoir, *The Diving Bell and the Butterfly*, to an assistant who recited a frequency-ordered alphabet until Bauby blinked his eyelid to signal the letter he wanted. I was stupefied. He had had a stroke; I, on the other hand, had willingly turned my brain into some sort of biochemical slurry in the name of beauty—no, not even beauty. In the name of having a smaller ass.

A friend bundled me into a car on Fifth Avenue and brought me home. As I drifted off to sleep, I talked myself out of panic: *My brain will recover. My brain will recover. My brain will recover.* And if it wasn't going to, panicking would not help the situation. *Breathe in, breathe out. One-nostril breathing. Do not panic.*

In the morning, my head was clearer but still fogged. It would take about a week to feel fully restored. I got out of bed and gamboled to the mirror: my lower body was swaddled in a black undergarment, something resembling extremely tight nylon bike shorts, but with the strategic areas cut out for the bodily functions. Purple and green bruises spread beyond its edges. I looked as if I had been in a terrible car accident.

Apart from the dull pain of the healing process, for which I took Percocet and Tylenol No. 3 for three or four days, what was most disturbing was the incarceration imposed by the garment, which I was not to remove for two weeks lest my thighs heal unevenly. The garment was made of itchy, hot material, and its edges dug into my skin, leaving irritated welts. It was my torturer, day and night. It fenced me in, kept my body in check, restricted my movement. At night I had dreams that someone was wrapping cellophane around my head and I was suffocating. During the day I went to work, wearing billowy skirts, sure that everyone was looking at me strangely. Cosmetic surgery traitor!

I was, for several weeks, overwhelmed by a deep sense of shame. I couldn't believe how much I had willingly hurt myself. I begged my fiancé (now my husband) to reprimand me if I ever thought of doing something so stupid again. It wasn't worth it: the fear of some terrible edema choking off the blood flow to my legs, the painful constriction of the bandage, the lingering fog, the moral shame in knowing that if I had spent eight weeks eating salad greens and running twenty miles a day all of this would have been taken care of by nature, the shame in wasting money that could have been used for something better. I had spent $6,000—about the annual salary of the average Hungarian, Mexican, or Korean—to correct a minor imperfection of my body, a flaw so trivial that ultimately no one, not even my fiancé, would ever notice a difference.

After two weeks, I was allowed to take off the garment. I tossed it in the garbage at Dr. Michelle's office, and she seemed surprised. "What if you want to use it again?" she asked. Again? Not in a million years.

After a few weeks, the bruising subsided. The swelling was gone. The memory of the self-torture, too, had vanished. All of my vows of surgical chastity evaporated as I put on a bikini and walked out to sit next to our swimming pool. The only evidence of the recent month's physical warfare was two freckle-sized scars on my outer flanks, the former incisions through which Dr. Michelle had withdrawn the fat. And only a pro would know what those were.

I lay facedown on a lawn chair and breathed in the sweet smells of the day. The sun beamed powerful, healing jets of warmth onto my back. My young stepson-to-be was playing nearby with a friend. I felt a shadow pool on the backs of my legs.

"Hi," a small voice said. I turned around, and it was the friend of my fiancé's son. A boy of about eight or nine, he was the son of a fashion model. He was kind of a troublemaker, but I liked him.

"Hi," I replied.

He screwed up his face, trying to blunt a smile. "Did you have fat cut off your butt?" he asked.

Excuse me?

"Did you have fat cut off your butt," he said, exasperated. "You have the dots, and my mommy has some, and her friends have some, and she told me that when ladies have those dots that means they had fat cut off their butts."

I was shocked. At the depravity of a society where eight-year-old boys know how to tell who has had liposuction and who has not. At the fact that he felt the freedom to ask. At the fact that he knew (the knowing, wink-wink smile) but was asking just to let me know that he knew. At the fact that models get liposuction. He probably wanted to show off how much he knew. I wondered: At the beach, could he tell which mommy's breasts were real and which were fake? Could he tell who had had liposuction under her chin? A nose job? Whose daddy had a face-lift and hair transplant?

"No, I did not have fat cut off my butt," I said as I stood up, making harumphing noises and gathering my towel around my waist. I marched back to the house, fuming. I had lied. I was mad at an eight-year-old for finding me out. But he had me busted: I was now the proud owner of an ass that didn't rightfully belong to me.

X X X

When I was twenty-five, I wrote a story for the *New York Observer* about the stretch of Park Avenue known as Plastic Surgery Row. Part of my research had been to ask each doctor what he or she would do to me if given free range. No one said liposuction. All of them said that I could probably use a little work on my upper eyelids. They were puffy, and one of them was puffier than the other, which—especially when I was tired—caused me to resemble Bill the Cat.

When I was twenty-nine, I went on a date with a plastic surgeon. An older friend of mine, who had had him do her face-lift, set us up. He was smart and seemed nice, and with his cap of wheat blond hair, his rosebud lips, and his cornflower blue eyes, he embodied a kind of Middle West Aryan perfection that is a curiosity in New York. I told my mother I was going out on a date with a plastic surgeon, and she said, "I would love to have a son-in-law who could give me a discount on a good face-lift." We drove around Manhattan in his convertible, sang Cole Porter songs, went to a movie. In the hallway of the theater, walking past the posters for the coming attractions, he pointed out which stars had had bad work.

He pointed to an actor who was starring in a thriller about a man who hires someone to kill his wife. The woman who played his wife was about half his age. "The worst face-lift I have ever seen," the surgeon pronounced. The actor's eyes were as wide and round as those of a Japanese anime cartoon character. His cheeks pulled back unnaturally. Later, I met the actor in the flesh. His eye sockets were still weirdly devoid of flesh, but his cheeks had relaxed.

The surgeon drove me home and he parked his car in front of my building. We talked. At one point, he reached over to touch my cheek.

"We would have a beautiful child together," he said. Golly! I felt goofy: Cole Porter, children. My thirtieth birthday loomed. I could *like* this guy. Then his gaze suddenly shifted from one of romantic attachment to one of clinical scrutiny. His hand dropped.

"But we both have such puffy upper eyelids," he remarked, straightening up and putting the key back into the ignition. "The kid would need a prophylactic bilateral upper bleph before kindergarten."

A what?

A bilateral upper blepharoplasty, he explained—a preventative procedure to remove the fat from both upper eyelids, so the kid wouldn't grow up with puffy ones like ours.

He wasn't kidding. It was our last date. The next time I saw him he was presenting a new face-lift technique on a cadaver at a plastic surgery conference.

During the years after the liposuction adventure, I visited Dr. Michelle for a number of dermatological treatments: Botox, collagen, the lasers, the goo. She introduced a line of expensive unguents and gels, which I bought. Sometimes, the bill was $1,500. Sometimes, it was $3,300. Money that should have been flowing into my savings account was flowing into my face. And my face looked good. My seriously beautiful cousin who lived in Beverly Hills told me I looked younger than I had when I was twenty. As the commercial says: Priceless.

And again I heard the little bell. Why not make another adjustment? It was time to do my eyelids. They were puffy. They looked as if I stayed up late every night drinking red wine. On the one hand, their habit of settling halfway down the mast gave me a languid, Charlotte-Rampling-in-the-bedroom look. Many evolutionary biologists consider bedroom eyes—the eyelids low-slung—the ultimate in sensuality. During the last stages of sexual encounter, the muscles holding the upper eyelids in place often let go, so someone who has permanent bedroom eyes may have the look of someone on the perpetual edge of orgasm.

That might not be such a good thing. And besides, they made me look less like I was on the precipice of orgasm than on the precipice of a serious hangover.

"You've got a Kathleen Turner thing going," Dr. Michelle said. "Do what you want, but I personally think you would look better if your eyes opened up a little more." She took some photographs of my eyes and on her computer used a mouse to open up my eyes. "They will look bigger and bluer," she said. "You'll see."

Jesus. But my eyes? The eyes are the center of our identity. The word *pupil* originates from the Latin for "little doll," referring to the tiny figure you see—yourself—when you look into the reflection in another person's eyes.[3] In Islam, the spiritual core of a believer is called "the eye of the heart." In his essay "Nature," Emerson celebrates the eye as the thing that most potently presents our identity and brings us closest to God: "Standing on the bare ground, my head bathed by the blithe air, and uplifted into infinite space, all mean egotism vanishes. I become a transparent eyeball, I am nothing; I see all; the currents of the Universal Being circulate through me; I am part or particle of God." Proust wrote in *Remembrance of Things Past* of a woman whose eyes "shone like the transparent wings of a sky-blue butterfly" and called the eyes "those features in which the flesh becomes a mirror and gives us the illusion that it allows us, more than through the other parts of the body, to approach the soul."

Eyes are among the most easily identifiable feature on the human face, the one thing that, if hidden, can fully obscure a person's identity. The quickest camouflage is a pair of sunglasses. Eyes are a part of language in a way that no other part of the body is. We see things with new eyes. When we agree, we see eye to eye.

We eye things we covet. We keep an eye on our possessions. Certain cultures speak of the "evil eye." Eyes provide, or prevent, intimacy; on the subway, we avoid strangers by averting our eyes. To flash open our eyes is an invitation, an unveiling of the self. Those who won't or can't look into another's eyes cannot understand the subtleties of human expression and feeling. Psychological researchers note that autistic people, who are often impaired in perceiving emotions and the psychological states of other people, are often unable to look directly into the eyes of another person. The eyes reveal our intentions and provide human cues. When we look at the eyes of another and see them looking off in another direction, we instinctively follow their gaze.

Beyond all the power and portent of the eyes themselves, my eyes were so, well, *me*. The multiple eyes you see on the cover of this book are mine before I had the procedure: almond shaped and slightly slanted, they crinkled a certain way, they closed a certain way, they expressed skepticism and joy a certain way. If even the tiniest amount of fat were removed from my eyelid, would they look the same? Would people see me or a different person? Would my soul appear differently to people?

"No one will notice anything is different," Dr. Michelle said. "They will just notice that your eyes are more blue."

But what about my age? I was only in my early thirties. Wasn't this kind of serious surgery designed for old ladies? I was haunted by the face of a woman friend of mine in her fifties. A refined and petite beauty, a woman of serious professional accomplishment, she had had what I would describe as a bad, or perhaps extreme, face-lift. I was at a Christmas party, and a head with brown hair that was vaguely recognizable popped up out of the crowd. But the face before me, croaking out my name, was a mask that only dimly resembled the face of my friend.

"Hi, Alex," the meat puppet that used to be my friend said.

The mouth of this creature worked itself open, rather than its lips simply parting and speaking. The skin between the nose and the ears was pulled so tight it actually looked painful. Her eyes seemed stretched, as if they had been imprinted on Silly Putty and savagely pulled outwards.

Her face was an illustration of the desperate parody that bad cosmetic surgery can make of human life. Although it attempts to relax our faces into the silhouettes they held in our youth, sometimes youth and the reclamation of life are the last things such surgery evokes. In her case, the new visage spoke of the opposite: with the skin so visibly manipulated, it showed off her mortality, highlighted the fact that human beings are mere skin casings for something—a spirit, a soul, a mind—until they shred apart. Her face was a visible rendering of death, palpable and close.

Her companion, a gruff, broadly built man with an equally bluff ego, was standing by the bar, chatting up every woman in her twenties and thirties who came up for a drink. I couldn't bear it: here she was, a caricatured mask, a grotesquerie of youth, a product of willing self-mutilation. And ten feet away was her boyfriend, who didn't even have the decency to respond to her ritual scarring by not flirting with every twenty-five-year-old who walked by. Even the ugly ones. He wanted one thing: *youth*. My stomach lurched.

"Oh. Hi!" I screeched in a high singsong, trying desperately to camouflage my shock. My mouth was open, and I closed it. My social antennae vibrated mightily, and the next words tumbled out, as false as anything I have ever said in my life, as enormous a lie as I have ever told: "Wow. You look great. What have you been doing?"

I hoped that she would think I was convinced.

The host of the party came up behind her and started making *snip-snip* motions with his fingers, as she continued to smile her innocent, rubbery smile.

"Excuse me," I said, and went straight for the bar.

Her experience frightened me. But Dr. Michelle showed me pictures of women in their thirties whose eyes she had done. On one screen, their eyes looked like mine, the eyes of someone who had worked hard late at night and partied late at night, who had stayed up studying for exams and stayed up late writing articles on deadline. Their eyes were tense and old looking, shrouded in delicate folds of hanging skin. In these pictures, I saw women who looked like me: professional, unsilly women who were just doing something very subtle. On the next screen, their eyes were open, wide, bright, but still retained their original shape. In fact, I was convinced, you could see more of their soul.

I thought about it overnight. Unable to quiet the little bell, the next day I signed up for the surgery.

X   X   X

On a Thursday morning, I arrived at Dr. Michelle's office. The surgery and recovery were dramatically smooth this time, from the beginning. I was prepared for the aggressive anesthesiologist from the previous surgery, the one who had poked me until I turned green. But a different anesthesiologist was in residence that day, a relaxed and jovial bearded man, and he joked about how the anesthetic process would make me feel as if I were drinking margaritas.

"Would you like salt or no salt?" he asked. His beard gave him a kind of fuzzy, bearish warmth.

"Rocks, no salt," I said. This time, going under didn't feel like being submerged beneath ocean waves against my will. I didn't struggle. Smiling, I slid into a warm bath and was out. It would be an ideal way to die, I thought at the time: ignorance is bliss.

Dr. Michelle scooped a tiny dropperful of fat out of each of my upper eyelids and sewed them each back up with one long black stitch. The process took less than an hour. The effects of the anesthesia on my acuity seemed less intense than they had before. Had my body somehow developed a tolerance to anesthesia? Was I getting used to it? Or had it been more efficiently administered? Or, simply because I had been out for a shorter period of time, did it affect my body and brain less intensely? I don't know the answer.

On Sunday night, my father came over for a drink. I wore eyeglasses. He noticed nothing. The next morning I had the stitches taken out and went to work with makeup on. A week after the surgery, my eyes looked the same, just slightly more open and aware-seeming. The changes were so subtle no one noticed that I had done anything. A couple of people asked me if I had lost weight or if I was wearing colored contact lenses, because my eyes seemed so blue. My sister asked if I had had a nose job. There was no pain in the recovery, unlike in the liposuction experience: there had been none of that gargantuan violence done to the body, just two stitches, one over each eye.

After about a month, I realized what a miracle had taken place. It felt like I had cheated on something but wouldn't ever get in trouble. There would be no more pictures of me in which I looked half asleep. My eyes were bright. It reminded me of the first time I had gone running in Central Park wearing contact lenses. After years of wearing eyeglasses, I could see everything: the colors seemed so fresh and vibrant. My eyeballs could dip up and down, to the side and forward in any angle, and everything was visible. It took me about six months to stop feeling giddy every time I wore them.

This was going well. I began to think perhaps I should start saving up for something else down the road. I began to look around at my body in a more critical, almost geographical way.

I thought of the acquaintance of mine, the former beauty queen, who has a photographer take a clinical set of pictures of her nude body every year so that she can look at them and decide what needs to be done next. What could I do next? What about some more liposuction? What about having a washboard stomach? What about a fantastic nipped-in waist? Why were my upper arms always just a little too fleshy, even when I was at my lowest weight? What about that? Was I getting something resembling a bulb on the tip of my nose?

At the time, it seemed almost like common sense. Most plastic surgeons like to talk about the benefits of doing work earlier rather than later. When the skin is young it snaps back faster and heals better, they say. Better to do lots of little procedures along the way than having the whole shebang retooled when you're fifty-five. People notice less when you're younger. Plus, when you're younger, you're in the feeder system. You get our mailings and brochures. You think more often about the things you can do.

So. Back to me. Why not have a prophylactic nose job?

I go to our neighborhood Italian restaurant to meet my husband for dinner. One of the waiters comes over and in loud, Italian-accented bluster says, "You look fantastic, Mrs.! My goodness! Have you been to a spa? Maybe a little plastic surgery?" He follows his sentence with an explosive guffaw, until he sees my face: my eyes are popped wide in surprise and my mouth is open. He realizes his joke is not a joke.

"Ha, ha, ha," I say, issuing a staccato choking noise that I hope sounds like laughter. "What a funny joke."

"Yes, a joke!" he returns brightly. "A funny, funny joke! Would you like to hear the specials?"

At the wedding of another cousin, I take a picture of my mother. Later, using Adobe Photoshop, I trim down her nose a little and remove some wrinkles.

"Mom, I think you would do great with some intense pulsed-light laser therapy," I instruct her with the air of a sage, shuttling back and forth between my before and after pictures of her. And then the pantomime of Dr. Michelle: "And we ought to seriously think about doing your nose."

She stares at me with a look of disdain I have never seen on her face.

"You have got to be kidding me," she says.

Someone sends me the first season of *Sex and the City* on DVD. As the first episode opens, I notice the most astounding thing: Sarah Jessica Parker has wrinkles. She is as wrinkled as a shar-pei in the first episode, but by the third—through the seventh—season, she has no wrinkles in her forehead, around her eyes, or around her mouth. She has pulled a Doris Day, of whom Oscar Levant remarked that he knew her before she was a virgin. We knew Sarah Jessica Parker when she had wrinkles.

At my husband's high school reunion in New Hampshire, the woman at the TGI Friday's asks me for my ID when I order a glass of white wine.

"Oh, do we have drink tickets or get discounts or something?" I ask.

"No, I need to see your driver's license," she says, leaning toward me, her hand curled in a no-nonsense, gimme-gimme gesture. I hand her my driver's license. She looks at it and squints back at me. "Really?" she asks.

The legal drinking age in New Hampshire is twenty-one. I have been carded at age thirty-six.

There are those that argue that there is something fundamentally unfair about the regime of cosmetic surgery and medical beautification: it allows the haves to trump the have-nots in yet another forum. It used to be that beauty was the province of the genetically lucky; that is no longer true. Those with enough disposable income and time can pay for the full lips of a teenager and the smooth eyelids of a twenty-year-old, while those who don't have money and time are relegated to the unfortunate, unkempt masses. They are resigned to a life of dealing with aging and all of its external indignities.

Aging is a part of the human condition, just as depression and anxiety are, and critics argue that we ought to live with those things if we are to be considered faithful to the human condition. Cosmetic surgery is a luxury, motivated by pleasure, not by the need to end suffering. Medicine and technology should not intervene to change appearances, nor should surgery be used to fulfill a desire to adhere to fashion. Kathryn Pauly Morgan, a feminist philosopher, has even proposed using the technology of cosmetic surgery to make oneself ugly and starting up a "Ms. Ugly Canada/America/Universe/Cosmos" contest. Morgan suggests "bleaching one's hair white and applying wrinkle-inducing 'wrinkle creams,' having one's face and breasts surgically pulled down (rather than lifted), and having wrinkles sewn and carved into one's skin."[4]

A "Ms. Ugly" pageant could be one form of revolt. A second would involve protest. Morgan proposes that anti–cosmetic surgery activists could erect a fantastical set of "Beauty Body Boutiques"—"Here one could advertise and sell a whole range of bodily contours; a variety of metric containers of freeze-dried fat cells for fat implantation and transplant; 'body configuration' software for computers"; and an array of false breasts in different sizes for shoppers to peruse and of false penises, so men could determine for themselves the size of the penile implants they would like to have. Her point, in 1991, was that such boutiques don't exist and that, if they did, we would find the commodification of cosmetic surgery and of our bodies so disturbing and ghoulish we would be turned off the prospect forever.

But in 2006, such boutiques do exist, in the form of so-called medi-spas, medical offices and surgery boutiques such as Rodeo

Drive Plastic Surgery, found in a mall in Beverly Hills. Bodily contours are advertised and sold through the Yellow Pages. Fat cells are harvested and retransplanted into the body. Computer software helps sell us images of beauty and convinces us to have surgeons cut into our faces. Morgan's dystopia has become our utopia.

Not all patients who sign up for cosmetic surgery are seeking standard beautification procedures. Dr. Bruce Nadler, a surgeon in New York whose clientele includes many members of the body-building crowd, told me that one of his patients, a former Navy SEAL, "was ashamed in the locker room because all his buddies have these battle scars." "Shark bites, knife scars, injuries. You know, marks of war." The retired warrior decided that he needed something to spice up his torso: a bullet wound.

"We had several conversations about it," Dr. Nadler said. "What size bullet might he have been shot with? Would there be an exit wound?" Dr. Nadler set to work finding the right instruments to fake the bullet entry and exit. "He's incredibly happy now," Dr. Nadler said. "He gets to show off his stripes." And Dr. Nadler, whose neck bulges with the muscles of the physically obsessed, told me he was looking forward to the next stream of clientele who might choose such a tough-guy procedure: "the rappers."

As heartily as critics of cosmetic surgery choose to agitate against it, one can counterargue that they are mere Luddites, unwilling to see the benefits of technology. If medicine is able to address suffering, does it matter what the origin of the suffering is? Why shouldn't medicine move beyond simply addressing issues of pain and illness into the realm of giving pleasure?

American culture very deeply ingrains in us—in women and increasingly in men—a norm of what is considered attractive, no matter how hard we agitate against it. Our cultural bedrock is rooted in vanity and self-invention, and we will embrace any new techniques if they promise us thicker heads of hair, bigger breasts, or straight teeth. Breast implants have become so common they've caused the average bra size to go up a full size in the last fifteen years.

Because women have for so long been judged by their appearance, that judgment still affects our moral assessment of their character. It is still important for a woman to be good-looking, because in being good-looking she will be defined as good. Women who deviate from the template—whether that template is New York soignée, Beverly Hills extravagant, Miami flamboyant—fail to live up to the standards we are taught by *Star* magazine to believe are acceptable, the norm.

In that respect, I hate cosmetic surgery. I loathe the idea that I am required to fit into a model. On the other hand, I won't be accepted by a culture that embraces beauty until I look like someone who belongs inside it. And I can't subvert what I can't get access to. It's as if the cosmetic beautification process was just a way to assure other people—the pampered, the well-to-do, the glamorous—that you're with the program and you're not going to upset their apple cart. A hideous thought.

A writer I respect published a piece in the *New York Times Magazine* about young women who flock to Botox in their teens and twenties. I read the essay, hoping for some insight into my own obsession. "Only a fuddy-duddy feminist might warn that, if they never allow themselves to frown, they will turn into puppet-faced Stepford Wives," she wrote. "There is, however, the risk that their desire to cheat time will become an all-consuming passion. Running to doctors whenever normal aging signs appear, they might forgo the benefits to be gained from the accrual of experience. It is only through time that they can achieve mastery at work, deepen relationships with friends, build families of their own. This is called life, and sometimes it produces a furrow or two. But it is worth it."[5]

She did not sound convincing at all. Why wouldn't I be able to have deep friendships if I got Botox? I tossed the magazine.

X
X X

n January of 2004, I decided to try a new product, Restylane. For several years, surgeons and dermatologists in New York had been using it even though it had not yet been approved for any human use by the Food and Drug Administration. Doctors simply bucked FDA restrictions and had the drug shipped from abroad.

Restylane is a commercial name for a synthetic form of hyaluronic acid, a mucuslike substance that occurs naturally in human joints and skin. According to Q-Med, the company that makes Restylane and its counterparts, Perlane and Restylane Fine Lines, patients do not need to be pretested for allergic reactions because the drugs are synthetic, unlike collagen, which is often derived from bovine or porcine sources, or other collagenlike fillers, some of which are derived from human cadavers. Traditional hyaluronic acid is derived from what is called avian sources, the combs of roosters. I wanted to have some of the new synthetic form injected into my nasolabial folds and maybe my upper lip.

"Nobody will say they are using it, but believe me, there are lots of little moles bringing it into the country," Dr. Patricia Wexler told me before it was approved. "You go to your doctor and they will go to the cabinet and unlock it and tell you not to tell anyone. Nobody is going to admit to it."

As so often in the world of cosmetic enhancement, it was doubtful that any government agency was going to go after doctors using Restylane. Those who had the drug mailed to them from overseas would otherwise have put themselves at risk for malpractice suits, professional rebuke, and, in extreme circumstances, revocation of their medical licenses. But enforcement was extremely unlikely for several reasons. In theory, in New York, the State Department of Health could reprimand a doctor or, at the remote edges of possibility, act to suspend his or her medical license, according to Kristine Smith, a department spokeswoman, but in practice the likelihood is remote. "It is not just a matter of someone saying, 'Hey, I heard this doctor is using a medicine not approved by the FDA,'" Smith explained to me. "Can we prove the doctor was negligent or incompetent? Would other experts in the field consider the care to be substandard?"

Not only was it difficult to prove that a doctor was giving substandard care, there was some foot dragging on the part of government agencies to heed the complaints of patients who requested illegal beautifying procedures. It was, one state health department official (from a state other than New York) told me, the equivalent of a jury's finding a rapist not guilty because the victim dressed seductively and got drunk. In other words, she asked for it. Doctors were also annoyed at the FDA's slow approval time. "The FDA in this case is being a bit overcautious, because Restylane has been used in so many countries and so many good places like Canada," Dr. Rod J. Rohrich, who at the time was the president of the American Society of Plastic Surgeons, told me. Restylane was not entirely free of complications. Dr. Trevor Born, a plastic surgeon in Toronto, registered some adverse reactions. "There have been reactions, such as patients who develop draining cysts," he told me. "But in the three thousand I have treated, I had one patient who had some redness for about three weeks and that was it."

In the press release announcing FDA approval of Restylane, it was described as for use in the "correction of moderate to severe facial wrinkles and folds, such as nasolabial folds." And that's it. The most commonly reported adverse events were redness and swelling, which typically occurred at the injection site and were transient and moderate. In countries other than the United States, Restylane was also approved to enhance the appearance and fullness of lips, although the safety of Restylane for the amplification of lips had not been established in controlled clinical studies submitted to the FDA.

According to literature from Q-Med, "It is produced biotechnologically by natural fermentation in a sterile laboratory environment. This significantly diminishes the risk of transmitting diseases between species or of eliciting allergic reactions in patients who are sensitive to common foods, such as beef, chicken and eggs. [It] has been extensively researched for over a decade and proven to be safe and effective."

It sounded fantastic. I made an appointment with Dr. Michelle, far in advance. Her schedule was now booked up solid with surgery and skin care, and I had established the habit of calling three weeks ahead to get a time slot. An appointment with her took precedence over all other events.

And then my friend Jerry Nachman died.

The first time I saw him, he was reclining on the porch of a friend's house on Shelter Island, New York. He was wearing a bathing suit. He was short and rotund, and his skin was plastered with nicotine patches. In various places, skin tags—excess skin that grows off into rootlike, waving flesh anenome—sprouted from his body. He chewed on a wet cigar. He was almost entirely bald. He had moles on his face and speckling his body. He was a friend of my then boyfriend, and we became close.

He had been the editor of the *New York Post* when Marla Maples and Donald Trump began their affair. "Best Sex I Ever Had," said the cover of the *Post*, and Jerry loved to joke that it was the ultimate libel-proof headline. "He could never sue us," Jerry would say. "He would have to prove that he wasn't the best sex she had ever had, and what man would do that?"

He wrote for *Politically Incorrect* and told people that his one distinction there was that not one of his jokes got on the air in two years. Then he became editor of MSNBC and had a nightly talk show. For many years, when I was part of a reporting team that covered the media industry for the *New York Times*, he was a daily phone call, someone I counted on for perspective, for good judgment, and often for a great opening paragraph. At night, he and I and a group of other regulars would converge at Elaine's to hash out the events of the day. He had been married to a patrician blond beauty, but they had divorced. He was, by far, one of the most physically unattractive people I have ever known. He was proud of his ugliness, and with good humor, not defensive humor, he made it a badge of honor.

In January of 2003 he announced that he had a malignancy in his gall bladder. The last time I saw him was in late 2003 on his

MSNBC talk show, *Nachman*. He was on the set in New Jersey, and I was at a remote studio in New York because I didn't have time to get there. He told me he was feeling great and we went on the air. We discussed the closing of Rosie O'Donnell's magazine, *Rosie*. At the end of our talk, during which I criticized O'Donnell's brusque attitude, Jerry said, "So here's a question, since you said that Rosie is not nice. You know me very well. Am I nice?"

I replied, "You're an extremely nice and wonderful man. You're probably much nicer than she is. And you probably don't have as many chips on your shoulder as she does."

He closed with, "Not me. Alex Kuczynski, thanks for talking with us." We chatted for a few seconds longer, and he made me promise to come out to New Jersey to have dinner with him.

"Really, Alex, it's civilized out here," he said.

"I promise," I said.

Three months later, I was at home alone. My husband was away. It was one of those bleak January nights, a cold, dark winter evening when spring and warmth seem painfully, achingly far away. I would do some stretching exercises and watch the evening news. I turned on the television. Jerry was dead.

The funeral was scheduled for two days later. I flipped through my date book to find out what I would have to cancel to make it. And there it was: my appointment with Dr. Michelle. My heart did a little turn. Then something happened. I decided I could make it. I would just do both.

After the funeral, there would be a gathering at Elaine's, and a few of us were asked to make some remarks. But I could squeeze in a microdermabrasion-and-Restylane session in between the two. After all, it would take a couple hundred disorganized, taxicab-hailing mourners at least an hour to leave the congregation on the Upper West Side and make it all the way to Elaine's on the Upper East Side. And my skin always glowed after a microdermabrasion treatment.

I went to Jerry's funeral. After it ended, I sprang to life and jumped into a car I had hired for the occasion to streamline my plan. Elaine Kaufman, the owner of Elaine's, needed a ride, so I had the driver drop me at Dr. Michelle's and take her to the restaurant. Then he would meet me back at the doctor's office. I would pull off the plan with the efficiency of a military operation.

I barreled forward. I did not stop to think through the various potential outcomes. If I had, I might have gone through the checklist of the common symptoms of addiction: Participating in addictive behaviors more often than you intend. Excessive time spent seeking the addictive thing. Giving up other things in life to pursue your addiction. Pursuing and fulfilling the addiction at inappropriate times.

Pursuing and fulfilling the addiction at inappropriate times.

If there was ever an inappropriate time to fulfill my addiction, it was right before I was supposed to honor the memory of a close, recently deceased friend.

I explained to Dr. Michelle that I was in a hurry and pressed her to give me the Restylane. She put some numbing cream on and injected a small amount into my nasolabial folds. Restylane is a viscous substance, and so she would inject in drops and then massage them through the skin until they coalesced together and achieved the correct effect. She asked me if I was ready to do my upper lip.

"We'll just use a little," she said.

The lip is an extremely sensitive area. I hummed opera, loud, to take my mind off the pain of the injection and the pain of her massaging the gel into place. Jesus, I said, after she was done. That hurt. The nurse gave me ice packs and counseled me to rest with the ice for twenty minutes. Then I would be free to go.

But something was wrong. After ten minutes, the ice packs, which should have settled down onto my face as any swelling decreased, had actually risen high off my face. I pulled them off and went to the mirror.

I thought at first that I was hallucinating. There was a large mass under my nose. I looked closer, widening my eyes to make sure that what I was seeing was real. It was my lip. It was enormous, a cartoon upper lip bigger than any I had seen, even in the worst plastic surgery disaster photographs.

I opened the door to the hallway and made a mewling noise. Because my lips didn't meet, I couldn't make understandable human noises. The nurse rounded the corner. She was new, unseasoned, and her reaction was not helpful.

"Oh my God, oh my God, I've never seen anything like it!" she said with a yelp, tossing her metal tray into the air and scurrying away to get Dr. Michelle.

I lay there for another three hours with ice packs. While my friends were gathered toasting Jerry twenty blocks away, Dr. Michelle was using a small spatula to apply gobs of steroid cream to my upper lip, which had swollen to the size of a large yam. With my lip so grotesquely swollen, I was unable to speak and could only push out semirecognizable sounds using my upper teeth and lower lip. I was terrified that my lip was damaged forever, horrified that I had insulted Jerry so soundly. I had chosen to keep the idiotic appointment—my upper lip never needed filling anyway!—instead of making sure I would be available to mourn Jerry with all of our friends.

Dr. Michelle called my pharmacy and had them send a prescription for steroids, both cream and pills, to my apartment. The nurse helped me out to the car and driver, who had been waiting for three hours to take me to Elaine's. I couldn't go to Elaine's. I couldn't speak. I looked like a freak.

The driver took me home. I clutched a sweater over my face so the doorman wouldn't see what had happened. I was deeply relieved my husband was traveling: as understanding as he can be, this was a visual memory I didn't want imprinted in his brain.

At home, I examined my lip and popped several of the steroid pills (as directed) with a mug of vodka as a chaser (not directed). I wandered around my apartment, sobbing, my lip jutting out. I tried to see the comic side of my misadventure, whirling theatrically around my apartment, pretending I was Goldie Hawn in *The First Wives Club*. Of course, the author of the book upon which the movie was based, Olivia Goldsmith, had died the week before at Manhattan Eye, Ear & Throat Hospital, so this was perhaps not the best comic choice.

The phone rang all evening long, but I didn't pick it up. I couldn't speak because my lip was so swollen, and I couldn't speak because I was loaded. There was nothing to do but sit on the bathroom floor with my mug full of vodka—I don't know if I chose the one that said "Happy 29th Birthday—Again!" on purpose or not—and weep. At eleven o'clock, I staggered to the television set to watch the local news coverage of Jerry's funeral.

It took about five days for my lip to return to normal. I called my editors and said I had to work at home for personal reasons. Two weeks after the Restylane, the skin on my upper lip, which had been stretched to beyond capacity for so long, sheared off in thin papery strips.

Jerry, who was always a straight shooter, would have read me the riot act. He would have called me an asshole. And if Jerry would have called me an asshole, that meant I had done something terribly wrong.

There was no greater wake-up call. I began to taper off my visits to Dr. Michelle Copeland.

x x x

A year later, I am at a conference of the International Society of Aesthetic Plastic Surgery in Houston. I stop at the Q-Med booth, and the young Swedish man there and I have a long discussion about Restylane.

"I tried it in my lip once," I tell him. It's helpful at plastic surgery conferences to offer up what you've done: the doctors and pharmaceutical reps then don't feel that you are a confrontational reporter hoping to root out the evils of vanity. By telling them you've tried Botox or lipo, you are saying that you're one of them. You understand. You've been converted.

"How was it?" he asked, a flash of concern crossing his face.

I tell him.

"Well, you shouldn't use it in your lip without being on steroids first," he said. "You have sensitive skin. Of course you would have had that reaction. I would never use it in my lips."

I have now sworn off the big stuff. It's been a year since I've had Botox, two years since my last tango with collagen. I gave up on Restylane after that first fling. Barring any need for reconstructive surgery, I will never have implants put inside my body, not cheek or calf or breast. I haven't done a thing to my lips. Curiously, I am not worried about aging, per se. I like aging: I get smarter every year. What I do worry about is getting old, about getting that tired look that marks the faces of people who haven't done what they want to do with their lives, people who shrink from life. Most amazing of all, I noticed the other day that my upper eyelids are getting that puffy, lopsided look again. It was a eureka moment. No matter how much money you spend, or how much plastic surgery you have, or how many dermatologist visits you schedule, inevitably, time's winged chariot will catch up to you and march all over your face.

Twelve

The Fatal Quest
for Beauty

I n the course of little more than a year, three women died in New York City during or immediately after cosmetic surgery.

When Susan Malitz, a fifty-six-year-old Connecticut woman, was admitted to Manhattan Eye, Ear & Throat Hospital for a routine face-lift on February 16, 2004, the mood of the hospital staff and the patients was one of mindful caution. Just one month before, the novelist Olivia Goldsmith, fifty-four, had died after going into cardiac arrest during cosmetic surgery there. But Malitz, whose husband is a urologist, was confident enough to proceed. She had been reassured by friends and hospital staff, and, after all, she would be under the care of Dr. Sherrell J. Aston, the highly regarded chairman of the hospital's plastic surgery department, and Dr. Gary Mellen, an anesthesiologist with an excellent record in patient safety.[1]

It seemed a statistical impossibility that anything could go wrong, plastic surgeons on the hospital's staff said at the time, that lightning could strike twice in the same spot. Yet, horribly, it did. Malitz, under sedation, was given an injection of lidocaine—a local anesthetic—combined with epinephrine, to prepare her for surgery. A half hour later, her heart began to race—as fast as 240 beats a minute. She went into cardiac arrest. Though doctors worked frantically to resuscitate her, ninety-two minutes later she died.

The two deaths were terrible tragedies for the families of Goldsmith and Malitz, to be sure. Goldsmith was working on a new book, and her mother and sister were very close to her. Malitz had a twenty-one-year-old daughter and an adoring husband. And the deaths cast a grave pall over one of the country's most prestigious hospitals—a forerunner in research and training and a magnet for well-heeled patients from around the country—as well as over the business of cosmetic surgery, which had developed a reputation as low risk and almost carefree. There was a belief that people with enough money and common sense would surely avoid the risks of the poor and less educated, who were forced to go to surgery mills in questionable neighborhoods for their face-lifts. The city's well-to-do were gripped by the kind of arrogance that comes with youth or moderate wealth. They were convinced that they were immune to danger. Weren't Goldsmith and Malitz being treated at one of the world's finest cosmetic surgery facilities on the planet? Malitz's doctor was the chief plastic surgeon, a man with an impeccable personal and professional reputation.

Dr. Aston was without blame in the death of Mrs. Malitz. Reports about her death and Ms. Goldsmith's from the New York State Department of Health, as well as autopsy reports concerning both women from the medical examiner's office, documented the final moments, minute-by-harrowing minute, of the two women's lives. They also raised questions about the actions of doctors and the procedures followed by the hospital, especially those concerned with anesthesia practices.

Manhattan Eye, Ear & Throat, believed to be one of the safest hospitals in the country, was later charged with "egregious violations" by the health department and fined $20,000, a first in the hospital's history, according to a hospital spokeswoman.

Patients instantly became more curious about risks and more demanding of their doctors. Dr. Robert C. Silich, a plastic surgeon at New York–Presbyterian Hospital, described the impact on his practice as enormous. "I've not had one patient not mention it to me," he told my colleague Warren St. John at the time, referring to the two deaths. "I'm finding that more people want to be done in the office because they think it's more controlled" than a hospital environment, he said. "There won't be any residents around—it will just be me, and I won't have patients in another room." Although this did not happen in the Malitz case, sometimes busy plastic surgeons in New York, Los Angeles, and elsewhere doing elective cosmetic work in hospitals keep a number of patients on operating tables at once and dole out varying amounts of actual surgical work to residents and fellows, or surgeons in training. The chief surgeon can then limit his time with each patient, overseeing the entire operation at ten-minute intervals while checking in on other patients. The practice is efficient from the point of view of the surgeon; it is not efficient in that patients are exposed to risks by people less thoroughly trained than the doctors they believed would be overseeing every minute of their surgery.

For the doctors at Manhattan Eye, Ear & Throat, the deaths resulted in unwelcome scrutiny. As head of plastic surgery, Aston, who built a prestigious practice catering to the vanities of Park Avenue society, enjoyed unquestioned leadership. He has operated on a member of my family and I can say from personal experience he was an exceptional doctor, caring and involved, who produced marvelous results. After the deaths, he was forced to engage in countless conversations and interviews with investigators and helped to coordinate the hospital's plan of correction, a comprehensive strategy for state investigators on how the hospital intends to change the way it does business.

The hospital's corrective measures after the two deaths caused a controversy of their own. Doctors were told they must give patients under general anesthesia additional breathing help, usually a breathing tube. Doctors at the hospital thought this practice excessive. According to Dr. James E. Cottrell, the former president of the American Society of Anesthesiologists and the chairman of anesthesia at Downstate Medical Center in Brooklyn, there are problems with using a breathing tube, including possible damage to the teeth, throat, and vocal cords, nausea, and lengthened recovery time.

"It is a big mistake for the hospital to dictate anesthesia, because the hospital is not qualified to dictate anesthesia," Cottrell said. "The hospital is not in the business of practicing medicine. The doctors are."

Anesthesia is not without risk but is certainly safer than it was thirty years ago, when one patient in 5,000 died from complications from the powerful drugs. The mortality rate has dropped to less than one death in 250,000 patients.

The investigation by the state health department was completed by the end of April 2004. It identified ten violations at the hospital, and each one drew a fine of $2,000, the maximum under state law. Ann Silverman, the hospital spokeswoman, told me that it was the first time in memory that the hospital had been fined. The health department cited the hospital with failure to do thorough preoperative work on Goldsmith, failure to monitor the vital signs of both patients, poor communication, delays in responding to emergencies, and failure to ensure that safety equipment was working properly.

In the case of Malitz, investigators focused on how much lidocaine she received. The health department found that her first dose significantly exceeded the maximum *PDR* recommended amount. Perhaps the most disturbing finding came in a highly disputed medical examiner's report, which noted a small hole in Malitz's larynx consistent with a needle puncture from a syringe that would have been used to inject lidocaine. (Her doctors deny this.) Some doctors and toxicologists speculated that if a large amount of lidocaine was mistakenly injected into the windpipe, rather than simply into the fatty tissue in the neck, it might have been taken up rapidly into Malitz's bloodstream through her lungs, where it could have been systemically absorbed, thus reaching a toxic dose quickly.

In the end, the medical examiner found that Malitz had four times as much lidocaine in her bloodstream as it would take to kill her, though much of it might have come during the frantic attempts to resuscitate her. (Lidocaine can be used to steady an irregular heartbeat.)

The report also indicated that the lidocaine injection was administered not by Mellen, the anesthesiologist, or by Aston, the surgeon. Instead, it was administered by a fellow in the plastic surgery training program at the hospital, according to doctors familiar with the case. It is not unusual for fellows to give injections of this nature, Silverman, the hospital spokeswoman, said. "Plastic surgery fellows are completely trained surgeons who have independent operating privileges," she said.

The amount of lidocaine injected as local anesthesia exceeded the maximum recommended dose, according to the New York State Department of Health report. Malitz received an injection of 200 ml of lidocaine 0.5%, which is the equivalent of about 20 mg/kg; the recommended maximum dose is 7 mg/kg. Surgical personnel also failed to note that she was hypoventilating. It is worth noting that Malitz suffered from myasthenia gravis, a neuromuscular disease characterized by weakness in the voluntary muscles of the body, as defined by the National Institute of Neurological Disorders and Stroke.[2] Researchers have reported that while most myasthenia gravis patients undergo anesthesia without complication there are some cautions regarding the use of muscle relaxant drugs, which are often used during insertion of an endotracheal tube. Local anesthetic drugs such as lidocaine, which Malitz received, have muscle relaxant properties that may cause weakness in a patient with myasthenia gravis.

Goldsmith's death was a story of terrible New York irony. Most famous for her novel *The First Wives Club*, in which she exhorted women, Ivana Trump–style, not to get mad but to get everything, Goldsmith was a symbol of the middle-aged fear of aging. In the novel, the scorned first wives of middle-aged husbands act out revenge plots against the men, who have left them for younger women. The novel—and the 1996 movie—tapped into a mother lode of female anger: women were angry at men for leaving, and they were angry at men for getting the long end of the age stick. Men, it turned out, were allowed to age and to get gray hair and to sag, and still enjoy the company of younger mates. Women were not. But the book and the movie reversed that belief: women could get older and still enjoy their lives to the wicked fullest. And yet here was Goldsmith, dying in middle age while trying to do the thing she had preached against: look like a younger, second wife.

In her case, the state health department's report concluded that her surgeon, Dr. Norman Pastorek, did not sufficiently question Goldsmith about her medical history, which it considered "significant." She may have been taking antidepressants, serious medications that can conflict with anesthetic agents, and failed to tell her doctor about them.

Goldsmith entered Manhattan Eye, Ear & Throat on January 7, 2004, for a chin tuck. Pastorek's practice has focused on plastic surgery for the last twenty-five years, although he is certified by the American Board of Otolaryngology, the specialty of ear, nose, and throat doctors. I reached him soon after the report was issued. "It's really hard to talk about," he said, adding that Goldsmith had been a close friend. "I really loved that woman."

As Goldsmith's procedure began, a nurse anesthetist proceeded to put her under. Something went wrong. There was a drape cloth covering Goldsmith's chest, so the nurse anesthetist couldn't see if Goldsmith's chest was rising and falling with each breath. Nor did the nurse anesthetist use a stethoscope to see if

Goldsmith's breathing was regular and steady. Both failures were violations of the state's code of health standards.

It is common practice for nurse anesthetists to administer anesthesia. Of all the anesthesia given to patients each year, 65 percent is delivered by certified registered nurse anesthetists, nurses with a graduate degree in anesthesia, or CRNAs.[3] Medicare recognizes their qualifications and reimburses them for their services. In recent years, the increase in cosmetic surgical procedures has made the nurse anesthetists a powerful force. With so many procedures taking place, there simply haven't been enough anesthesiologists to handle the workload, they argue. Their lobbying work is similar to that of the California dentists who want the same rights as plastic surgeons.

It has been left up to the states to decide the law in these cases. So far, twelve states have made it legal for a nurse anesthetist to practice without being supervised by an anesthesiologist.[4]

In the case of Goldsmith, a few minutes after the nurse anesthetist administered anesthesia, she was no longer taking in sufficient oxygen, a condition known as hypoventilation. "Instead of addressing the hypoventilation," the health department reported, she was given Fentanyl, a strong narcotic—a depressant, for a patient who was having trouble breathing. Goldsmith's heart slowed to an abnormal pace. She suffered cardiac arrest, according to the office of the chief medical examiner, went into a coma, and was taken to Lenox Hill Hospital. She died on January 15.

Little more than a year later, Kathleen Kelly Cregan, the Irish woman who flew to New York for a secret face-lift and nose job, died. Thomas Moore, the malpractice lawyer who is representing Malitz's family, is representing the family of Cregan as well. He argues that his patient was "abandoned" by her physician, Dr. Michael Evan Sachs, and that she was not moved to a hospital soon enough after she started complaining of breathing problems. "I will argue that there was a series of failures in surgical care that led to Kay's death, amounting to gross neglect," he said in early 2006. "I will contend that this doctor basically ran out on his patient, that he left her to nursing staff and didn't oversee her recovery properly. There was a period of at least two hours where Kay was indicating respiratory problems and should have received emergency medical care."[5] As of spring 2006, Moore expects that both the Cregan and Malitz cases will go to trial or be settled within the year. As part of the discovery process, he is without a doubt trying to determine if the autopsy report concerning Malitz was not accurate, as sources closely involved in her case have contended.

Cregan was lured to her death by one of the most-sued doctors in the country, with a jaw-dropping record of thirty-three settled malpractice suits since 1995. In 2004, the year before Cregan's death, the New York State Department of Health banned Sachs—an ear, nose, and throat doctor by training—from performing complex nasal surgeries without supervision by another surgeon. He had courted fame by giving frequent interviews to magazines like *Elle*, *Cosmopolitan*, and *W* and, in 1993, scored an appearance on *Oprah* to talk about his work doing revisional rhinoplasty—or fixing botched nose jobs. But as he became more famous, he attracted more lawsuits. In 2000, the New York *Daily News* put Sachs on a list of the most-sued doctors in New York.[6] Soon after, the state began an investigation of him for performing sixteen surgeries on the same patient. It was this investigation that led to the state's prohibiting Sachs from performing any nose procedures that required two or more surgeries unless he was supervised by another surgeon.[7]

With his reputation on shaky ground in New York and the United States in general, Sachs decided to attract patients from abroad. In 2002, he focused on Ireland, a potential gold mine for American plastic surgeons. The economy was robust, Irish citizens perceived American doctors as better trained than Irish ones, and the traditional, stoic religious culture was just beginning to yield to the vanity-driven appeal of cosmetic plastic surgery. He had already had some success in England, making a name for himself by operating on an English couple, Maureen and Neil Ingram, for a BBC program called "Naked: 18 Till I Die." A spread in the *Mirror*, a London tabloid, reported that Maureen Ingram thought she looked dramatically younger. "Almost overnight fifteen years were wiped away," she said after having a face-lift at Sachs's office in New York.[8]

Sachs was content to tout his superiority over Irish surgeons. He told the *Irish Examiner* that most plastic surgeons in Ireland "wouldn't be allowed to practice for five minutes in New York."[9] And he was quick to play up his own credentials at the expense of accuracy. In 2003, Sachs appeared on *Ireland AM*, the highest-rated Irish morning television show, where he was introduced as "chief of research and associate professor of facial plastic surgery at New York Eye and Ear." Though the titles were decades out of date, Sachs did not correct the record.

Cregan learned about Sachs from an article in a Sunday paper that described his transforming a woman through a face-lift. (He provided surgery; the woman provided free publicity in exchange. In the United States, professional medical organizations frown on this kind of tit-for-tat exchange. Even the doctors on *Extreme Makeover* are paid for their services.) Cregan visited his Web site to look at his credentials and was likely impressed. After all, it reports that he is surgical director of the Sachs Institute for Facial Plastic and Reconstructive Surgery.[10] There is only one member of the Sachs Institute, unfortunately, and that is Michael Sachs himself. She would have learned that he has a softer, artistic side, too: on the Web site, Sachs has put up some of his paintings and photographic artwork. One can learn that he has "always integrated various artistic endeavors in his life." And, of course, there is no information about any problems or prohibitions concerning his medical license.

Sachs lives in a town house on the Upper East Side of Manhattan. A week after Cregan's death, I walked up to see it. It is a gorgeous three-story Georgian brick house, with black wrought-iron gates out front and cheerful floral plantings. On the day of my visit, a man in a dark overcoat with a wire in his ear paced back and forth in front of the house, scrutinizing every person who walked down the block. It was the first and only time I have ever seen a surgeon apparently feel the need to employ a private thug for protection.

A lot of things can go wrong in cosmetic surgery. Anesthesia-related deaths and complications happen, and they don't always mean the practitioner has done something wrong. Sometimes, though, anesthesia is administered by someone who is not properly trained to handle the universe of complications. Some doctors are not plastic surgeons and are not properly trained or prepared for the delicacies of cosmetic surgery. Some lie about their credentials and present themselves as better prepared than they are. Some don't tell patients that they have been sued countless times, or the states they work in don't make it easy for patients to learn about the professional conduct of doctors. Some don't tell patients that they never finished their medical school education but that their state allows some medical professionals to practice cosmetic surgery.

Sometimes, everything goes wrong, as in the case of Julie Rubenzer, a thirty-eight-year-old woman who in the fall of 2003 underwent a breast augmentation in the Sarasota office of Dr. Kurt Dangl. Dangl had no operating privileges at any Florida hospital. He was accredited by the American Board of Cosmetic Surgery, which is not recognized by the American Board of Medical Specialties. The members of the American Board of Cosmetic Surgery are trained in other areas recognized by the American Board of Medical Specialties, such as otolaryngology or dermatology, but not in plastic surgery. Rubenzer suffered cardiac arrest during the surgery, for which she paid $3,000. A nurse—not a nurse anesthetist or an anesthesiologist—administered anesthesia. The nurse, Michelle Lynn Lawrence, was later charged with practicing without a license. Rubenzer's father, Don Ayer, said he met Lawrence in Sarasota while his daughter was in a coma.

"Dangl introduced her to us as his nurse," Ayer said. "Then we find out she's a secretary with no medical qualifications."[11]

During the procedure, staff members assisting with the operation, according to their testimony to investigators, observed that Dangl became "exasperated" and forbade anyone from resuscitating the patient for several minutes after her heart seized.[12] She lapsed into a coma. Rubenzer died three months later in a nursing home. Dangl's license was revoked—eighteen months later.

State health officials said Dangl's "gross malpractice" led to her death and revoked his license and sentenced him to one year of probation. He was also charged with employing the unlicensed nurse. The nurse pleaded no contest to unlicensed practice of a health-care professional and also received twelve months probation.[13]

In Seattle, David Scott Kelley went to the office of Dr. Thomas Laney for liposuction on his neck and surgery on his nose and chin. Laney is formally trained as an oral surgeon, not as a plastic surgeon; he never received medical school or fellowship training in plastic surgery, although his Web site boldly states that he has "certification in plastic and reconstructive surgery." He is not board certified in plastic surgery by the American Board of Plastic Surgery. His Web site also offers a link to the Capital One cosmetic surgery lending site, which offers loans for cosmetic surgery with interest rates of almost 24 percent. At that rate, you'd be better off borrowing from your local friendly mob boss.

Laney testified that he had learned to do breast augmentations, tummy tucks, and liposuction by going to weekend seminars in hotels around the country. The anesthesiologist he hired for Kelley's surgery, Dr. Robert Solomon, specialized in performing drug detox procedures in the basement of his house, which he had converted into a drug treatment clinic, and he had been investigated for a 1999 death in his clinic that resulted in a $1 million settlement.[14]

Kelley was awake and recovering when he complained of a swelling on his lower face; Laney assumed there was hemorrhaging but could not find the source of the bleeding. An hour into the second procedure, Kelley stopped breathing. Laney waited six minutes before beginning CPR.

Kelley died within hours. Before his death, Laney had been sued ten times in matters related to medical care, most of which dealt with cosmetic surgery complaints and none of which Kelley knew about. Laney had settled nine of those cases out of court, for sums totaling close to $1 million to patients who said the doctor had damaged their bodies with liposuction and ruined their noses, among other reasons. Because he settled out of court and there were no sanctions against him, consumers had no way of discovering anything about his checkered surgical past. In many states, such as Oregon and Louisiana, consumers do not have any right to information on complaints that close without the doctor's being sanctioned.[15]

There's a case in the news every week, it seems. Take the sad story of Alexander Baez, a former bodybuilder who wanted to reclaim the broad, firm chest of his youth and went to see Dr. Reinaldo Silvestre of Miami for pectoral implants. The doctor's office turned out to be in a travel agency, not a medical office. And the doctor turned out not to be a doctor at all. Baez ended up with women's breast implants. Silvestre had been preying on the immigrant community in Miami for several years without a medical license of any kind. He is now an international fugitive.[16]

Sandy Leach, fifty-five, wanted a face-lift. At the office of Dr. James Kilgore in Sacramento, a nurse anesthetist sedated her. Leach went into cardiac arrest and died. Her family claimed she was oversedated.[17]

In 2004, state health officials were forced to impose a three-month ban on combined tummy tucks and liposuction after eight patients having the combined procedure died in an eighteen-month period. During the same eighteen months, other patients were gravely injured. Mona Alley went to the Florida Center for Cosmetic Surgery for liposuction. The surgeon pierced her intestine by mistake, spreading waste throughout her abdominal cavity. The resulting infection, bedsores, and loss of circulation led to the amputation of both her legs.[18]

In New York in 2005, Glen Altman, an athletic, healthy seventy-four-year-old who took daily three-mile walks in Central Park, underwent an eye tuck at the office of Dr. John DiTredici, who bills himself as a "renowned Manhattan Plastic Surgeon" on his Web site, Manhattanplasticsurgery.com. Complications during anesthesia left Altman in a coma and according to her lawyer, her brain was starved of oxygen for more than five minutes. Altman's daughter has sued the surgeon and his anesthesiologist.[19] DiTredici claims on his Web site to be "board-certified in Plastic and Reconstructive Surgery." But he is not, according to the American Board of Medical Specialties, certified in any of the organization's specialties. The case is pending.

Ultimately, consumers must educate themselves. Always choose a surgeon who is board certified by the American Board of Plastic Surgery. Accept no other board. If a doctor claims to be a cosmetic surgeon, be assertive and ask what his or her qualifications are. Patients planning cosmetic surgery tend to be less assertive in dealing with doctors than they ought to be. First, the surgery is putatively about their vanity and so patients don't feel they have the right to fully question a doctor about his or her credentials. Often, they are women, who have been trained all their lives to not make waves, confronting mostly male doctors. Planning a surgical procedure is not a time to care about whether a doctor feels comfortable with you. Rather, it is a time for doctors to make *you* feel comfortable and at ease.

Do as much research on the doctor's medical background as your state allows. If you don't speak English well, find someone who does and have that person help you.

Go on chat rooms and discuss the doctor's reputation. Consumers can call the American Board of Medical Specialties, the umbrella organization for the twenty-four approved medical specialty boards in the United States, to find out if their surgeon is certified in plastic surgery or in any other field. The hotline is 866-ASK-ABMS. While that hotline does not offer access to medical disciplinary action against doctors, consumers can call the Federation of State Medical Boards at 817-868-4000 and ask for a contact at their state board. Many state boards, such as that of New York, have fairly thorough databases of disciplinary action available on the Web. (New York's site is http://w3.health.state.ny .us/opmc/factions.nsf/physiciansearch.) For a complete listing of state medical boards, go to the Web site of the National Practitioner Data Bank, http://www.npdb-hipdb.com/genpublic.html. The data bank supplies information on doctors to health insurance companies and other professional entities but does not give information on specific doctors to the public.

Avoid doctors you found through lavish advertising campaigns and doctors whose names you read over and over again in magazines and newspapers. They are paying too much for a public relations staff and have to earn that money back. Or they are spending too much time courting press on their own and not enough time studying the continually evolving practice of medicine. Be skeptical of doctors' Web sites. Distrust doctors who use the same procedure over and over again and produce patients who all look the same; distrust doctors who are too tan, or who have bad hair implants, or who look as if they were Michael Jackson's twin brother.

Avoid doctors who talk to you about their brilliant extracurricular careers in art or painting or photography or literature. If they were Dostoevsky or Rodin, well, they would be off writing and painting, not being distracted by their artistic genius while they sink a scalpel into your thigh.

Thirteen

The Breast

I n the end, it all comes down to sex.

We can tell ourselves that we are having cosmetic surgery to improve our self-esteem and self-confidence, but in a quiet moment, many of us would admit we are doing it because we want to be wanted—by our husbands, by our lovers. We want to be admired by the guy behind the coffee-shop counter whose eyes follow the young women on line in front of us. We want to be ogled, and envied, by other women. What else could provoke us to drain our resources, invite a surgeon to slice us open and insert a foreign object into our bodies, and then endure an excruciating recovery? From a face-lift that returns the tautness of youth to a liposuction that molds a girlish thigh out of a flank stippled in cottage-cheese-like fat, it's obvious that we are looking for more than youth and beauty and the look of fecundity: We are looking for love. And we will accept lust.

There is no part of the body that has been more fetishized as the most immediate object of lust in contemporary America than the female breast. Omnipresent, it lives in our imaginations as the most totemic and powerful symbol of femininity. From the earliest recorded notations in literature, women have tried to amp up their décolleté. In *Inventing Beauty: A History of the Innovations That Have Made Us Beautiful, New York Times* patent columnist Teresa Riordan describes how Hera attempted to fashion an early version of a push-up bra for herself, said in the *Iliad* to be adorned with "brooches of gold."[1] There are literary references to corsets as early as the late Middle Ages, according to Marilyn Yalom's *A History of the Breast.* The household accounts of a French royal household in 1387 list six corsets. In 1350, in Germany, the *Limburg Chronicle* reported that low necklines on women exposed half the breast and surely were inspiring sexual lasciviousness.[2] By the 1800s, fashionable women were forced into clothing that shaped them into cones meeting end to end, the waist tightly corseted so the poitrine billowed out over the top like a plate of pillowy ice cream. The Empire style in the early part of the twentieth century featured a long, lean shape with breasts perkily pointing out on top. Briefly, the breast was sidelined as a point of focal interest during the 1920s when the boyish flapper was in vogue and the breast measurements of the average Miss America contestant measured just 32 inches. But the bosom returned with a vengeance after World War II, as couture clothes began to feature a nipped-in waist flaring out to a broad skirt and voluptuous bosoms. On through the 1950s, an era of mammary madness, the breast was celebrated as a welcome part of Americana, as pure and simple as Mom and apple pie and Chevrolet, and brassieres suddenly became the most complex garment a woman would ever own.

Theories about why breasts exist and why they are so fascinating are in no short supply. In *The Naked Ape*, Desmond Morris speculates that humans have pillowy breasts that form cleavage because cleavage is supposed to provoke in the male an archaic memory of a presenting backside when humans used to mate chiefly in the same manner other primates do, from behind. In Greek mythology, breasts represent nourishment and power: it is

Hera's breast milk that spurted across the heavens to form the Milky Way. The Hindu goddess Lakshmi arose out of a sea of mother's milk and cut off her breast for the god Shiva to replace a missing flower from the bouquet she sent him every night. (He stopped her before she cut off the second.)

Somewhere along the way the raw sexual nature of a Venus of Willendorf—her figure an almost feral, animal evocation of the sexual, succulent, life-giving female body—was transformed into the somewhat less animalistic classical figure of Venus, who was herself transformed into Barbie.

Yes, Barbie. Despite brief American forays into feminism, in which we have been encouraged to believe that a woman's looks are not supposed to interfere with anyone's ideas about her worth, American women—no matter their intellectual mettle—are somehow still supposed to look like Barbie. The ideal in the plastic surgery hubs—California, New York, Florida, Texas—is a slender body, small waist, boyishly narrow hips, and tiny, athletic buttocks, topped off with large, ample, fatty breasts.

The ideal breast itself is a model straight out of adolescence: a firm, smooth globe, the perfect marriage of cone and sphere, topped with a tiny rosebud of a nipple, one that has not been marred and dimpled by the application of infants' suckling lips. It is, of course, rather unusual for a woman who is slender on the bottom half to have enough body fat to sustain large breasts on the top. Yet so many American women choose to emulate this ideal—and so many men appear to admire it—that it points to our ever-growing love for the artificial over the organic. If U.S. culture is embodied best by its embrace of the artificial—artificial smells, artificial tans, artificial foods—there is nothing on a woman's body that is more easily subject to artifice than the breast. Whether it's a push-up bra or implants, breasts can be manipulated in such a way that they become the centerpiece of a woman's person.

Breasts represent all that is powerful and sexual about womanhood to many women, whether they are feminists, or intellectuals, or strippers—and frankly, the boundary between the three has been blurred in recent years. Carolyn Latteier observes in her 1998 book, *Breasts: The Women's Perspective on an American Obsession*, that her small breasts made her feel as if she had failed to reach her potential not just as a woman but as a human being. "My discomfort with small breasts was more than cosmetic," she writes. "I felt the lack as a poverty of being, as if my very nature were somehow stark and bony."[3]

Others see the breast as a direct influence not on their self-esteem but on their economic potential. Cynthia Hess, an exotic dancer from Indiana also known as "Chesty Love" who sought to have her 56FF breast implants (which cost $2,088) declared a tax-deductible expense, explained her reasoning to *Newsweek*: "It was obvious that the size of your breasts was in direct proportion to the size of your salary." (A U.S. tax court judge allowed the deduction, ruling that the implants increased Hess's income and that the breasts were so large and cumbersome—about ten pounds each—that they made her appear "freakish" so that she couldn't possibly get any personal benefit from them.)

Breast augmentation is the second most common aesthetic surgery in the nation, after liposuction. In 2004, 334,052 women in the United States had their breasts "enhanced" for purely cosmetic reasons, up from 101,176 in 1997, an increase of 230 percent. Nearly three million American women have had augmentations since 1980. The average cup size they request is a "full C," but each year a larger percentage of women opt for jumbo implants. Nearly 10 percent choose double D.

Nearly a quarter of all breast augmentation surgeries are performed in Southern California. It's a whole different world in L.A. than in the rest of the country, says Brian Cox, a Pasadena plastic surgeon who has operated on many actresses. "In L.A. a lot of people see getting implants as a career move. They see it as a cost of doing business." Remember the scene in the movie *L.A. Story* when Steve Martin gropes Sarah Jessica Parker? He pauses and looks confused. "Your breasts feel weird," he says. "Oh," she replies. "That's because they're real."

As the size of implants and the frequency of breast enhancement procedures have increased, the average age for patients has fallen. In 2004, 4,211 female patients in the United States age eighteen and under chose the elective procedure. Increasing numbers of parents are giving implants as a gift, including as a graduation present. On Long Island, Lulu Diaz chose breast implants over a new Jaguar for a high school graduation present from her parents, and then her best friend, Jennifer O'Brien, wanted some, so her parents bought her breasts, too. "This is a gift of love from us, and we see a difference in her," her mother, Doreen O'Brien, told reporters.[4]

The widespread use of financing has enabled even strapped college students to pay for implants, the average price of which is $3,437. In some parts of the country, America's shock jocks and radio station marketers are working hard to attract the teen and young adult market by hosting contests such as "The Breast Christmas Ever," organized by syndicated radio host MJ Kelli, a deejay based in Tampa, Florida, whose real name is Todd Schnitt. The idea is this: women enter radio promotion contests and the winners get free breast augmentations. "The Breast Christmas Ever"—which in Schnitt's case attracted a staggering 91,342 contestants over the 2004 holidays—is one of dozens of radio contests across the country that give away plastic surgery, mostly breast augmentations and almost always for young women. Schnitt claims that his station gave out the first breast augmentation—or "BA," as it is called by the cognoscenti—in the 1980s. His *MJ Morning Show* has also held other cosmetic surgery contests, among them "Pick Your Plastic" and "Boobapalooza."

One former winner, an eighteen-year-old named Ashley Edwards, wrote on the MJ Kelli Web site about her urge to amplify: "When I go jogging, the guys don't stare because my breasts aren't big enough to flop all over the place. I want the boys to drool. . . . I'm a hot piece of ass. New breasts would only double my 'nailability.' " She continued: "If I had new, bigger, firmer, bouncier breasts, I would show them off and shake my new milkers for everyone." Before and after photos are posted on the Web site of the doctor who performs the breast surgeries, Dr. William W. Adams of North St. Petersburg. (According to the Web site for the American Board of Medical Specialties, Adams is not certified by any of their boards. An e-mail request to him for information about his board memberships went unanswered.)

Some radio stations that run these promotions ask listeners to log onto the stations' Web sites to pick the winners. One Atlanta station held its contest at a local nightclub, gathering a crowd of well-endowed women who wanted breast reductions and letting them applaud or boo as judges picked a winner. A Detroit station was so thrilled by the response to its holiday breastathon that it held a "New Year, New Rear" contest that rewarded the winner with $15,000 worth of liposuction. One of the winners, twenty-eight-year-old Kara Cope, had so earnestly wanted to change her figure that she passed a "Boob Job Fund Jar" at parties for years. In Sacramento, a station is reported to have asked its contestants to put photographs of themselves—topless—on the station's Web site. Curiously, many of these contests are held by stations—including WFLZ-FM, MJ Kelli's home station—owned by Clear Channel Communications, the corporate behemoth whose management has often been accused of political conservatism. Clear Channel dumped Howard Stern and owns some stations that refused to play the Dixie Chicks after they said they were ashamed that President George W. Bush is from Texas.

The draw of such contests is not solely for the benefit of breast-obsessed adolescent boys and men: the contests evolved on rock stations aimed at teenagers but, according to radio consultant Alex DeMers, soon became popular in the adult contemporary market, where women make up the largest group of listeners. On the rock stations it was "the voyeuristic appeal to men" but now, DeMers has said, the contests "are directed right toward the woman."

While most cosmetic surgeries are aimed at re-creating the glow of youth and fecundity, most augmentations are intended to make women something they never were: stacked. One of the greatest ironies may be that from a surgical point of view it's virtually impossible to turn a flat-chested woman into a curvaceous bombshell—if she wants to look at all natural, that is. Most small-breasted women simply have too little muscle and tissue to support a 400 cc implant; they wind up as "tits on sticks," no matter how skilled the surgeon. But naturalness, which one might think is the sine qua non of cosmetic surgery, has become a nonissue when it comes to breast jobs. Until the mid-1990s a preternaturally curvy silhouette might have elicited a round of "did she or didn't she" whispers, but in the past few years women have begun to flaunt their surgery and revel in the artificiality. With the flood tide of television makeover shows, the proliferation of celebrity magazines, and the mainstreaming of pornography, breast augmentation has become a rite of passage, and even a badge of accomplishment, in some circles.

A friend of mine, a graduate of a Seven Sisters college, asked me to feel her breast implants recently. They looked soft and pliant. I put my hand on the side of one and was surprised by its turgidity. It had the hard, swollen feeling that human tissue gets after one has been stung by a wasp. These were bosoms that were not going to wobble when she ran for a bus and not do anything but point straight up when she lay on her back. They were awkward, but if you squinted your eyes and pretended to be a man, you could see the appeal: men are visual animals.

Undoubtedly, the widespread embrace of implants and the public acknowledgment that fake is fine are tied to the strange quirks of male sexuality; if large breasts "counted" only if they were God-given and therefore implants failed to arouse sexual ardor, it's unlikely women would get them. But the craze for implants has proven that some men are more aroused by visual cues than by tactile ones; enough men seem to perk up whether the breasts that poke out of that Victoria's Secret camisole are real or synthetic. In fact, many men may have grown to prefer implants, at least unconsciously. Implants, after all, create a female body type that rarely exists in nature but thrives in the pages of comic books, in video games, and on Web sites: huge breasts, wasp waists, gently curved hips, and a high, bubble-shaped butt.

It's the look of a Lara Croft, simultaneously muscular and soft and slender and swollen, a hard body with breasts that is radically different from the ideal of the bosom-obsessed 1950s, a fantasy of lushness embodied by Marilyn Monroe and Jayne Mansfield. Hourglass women had fleshy hips, meaty thighs, and generous derrieres along with their overflowing brassieres, but today's vogue for extreme thinness makes that model déclassé. How to solve the problem of breasts disappearing with all the other body fat when one's BMI falls low enough for one to fit into that Marc Jacobs dress? To many, implants are the perfect, logical fit.

Even on couture runways, where flat chests were once de rigueur, starved-looking models now routinely have implants and have been taught by their handlers to walk so they get the proper "breast bounce," an executive in the fashion industry told me. Each foot crosses in front of the other, as they parade down the catwalk, chests thrust theatrically forward, and as the foot touches the ground, it gives a little body-jiggling stamp that causes the entire physical edifice to tremble tantalizingly.

Sports Illustrated, once proudly implant free, used its first surgically enhanced model in the late 1990s, after a longtime editor (a woman who was opposed to implants on aesthetic grounds) retired. Today, as many as half the women in the annual swimsuit issue, which, with four million readers, is the bestselling single-copy magazine in the world, have had surgery. There is only one magazine left on newsstands that has a strict policy prohibiting models with breast implants. That is *Perfect Ten*, based in Los Angeles and founded by a former math professor turned hedge fund analyst, Norm Zadeh. Zadeh got rich, moved into a 17,000-square-foot mansion in Beverly Hills, and decided to live out his dream, which was to start a pornographic magazine of all-natural, implant-free models, each of whom he personally inspects to establish their organic qualities. He wants readers to know "what real breasts look like, because they've forgotten. They think when a woman lies down, her breasts are supposed to stand straight up, like rockets ready for launch," he says.[5] Of course, authenticity has its price. Each issue of the magazine sells a few thousand copies, as opposed to *Playboy*'s or *Maxim*'s hundreds of thousands.

Breast augmentation surgery has become so pervasive that in regions of the country where augmentation is most popular the wave of implants is changing how department stores stock their racks. Designers who cut with a fuller top and smaller bottom are in favor; designers who cut for women with an A cup are as popular as the flat-chested girl with the size 10 feet at the eighth grade dance. Many department stores work regularly with a tailor to alter clothing that doesn't fit the bountiful new bosoms. A buyer for the Beverly Hills branch of Neiman Marcus told the *New York Times* that the branch sells more dresses in size 12 than any other, while sizes 8 and 10 are the most popular for designer evening wear at other Neiman branches. The buyer said the bigger sizes sell more because more women have surgically increased their cup size.

Brian Bolke, the owner of a boutique in Dallas called 4510 for its address on McKinney Avenue, told the *Times* that about half of his customers have had breast augmentation surgery. "These women have great bodies, but they are not the bodies that designer clothes are made for. There is a ton of adjustments going on, because this area is not known for small chests. Either women are having dresses completely butchered, or we're selling them separates with a top and a skirt in different sizes."[6]

Blending a slender frame with large breasts whips up a strange brew of class issues. To be chicly bone thin and therefore flat was once considered aristocratic (think Slim Keith) just as big breasts were distinctly working class (see Russell, Jane). One of my favorite photographs—I keep a copy of it over my desk—is of Sophia Loren and Jayne Mansfield, taken in 1958 at the swishy Beverly Hills restaurant Romanoff's. Loren, demure in a black evening dress and diamonds, is gazing sideways at the breasts of a goofily smiling Mansfield, whose bosoms are spilling forth from a diaphanous gown like two ripe mangos, one nipple just peeking forth from the flimsy fabric. Loren is elegant in black hair and black dress, her poitrine restrained and her frame slender. Her eyes reflect what must be a state of incredulity. She is the cool Apollonian to Mansfield's Dionysian peroxide blond, an unrestrained, ample explosion of feminine hyperbole. It is a photographic essay on notions of class and femininity: Loren is class, and Mansfield—in Loren's eyes—is trailer park.

But class is a fungible notion these days. In an era when money no longer connotes "good breeding," and Donald Trump is considered a classy guy, tits on sticks make a certain kind of sense. Perhaps they represent the ultimate democratization, as much a part of our collective consciousness as the hip-hopization of Burberry. They are where the highbrow meets lowbrow, a signal that class lines have been blurred to meaninglessness.

They also represent the triumph of pornography. When half the images of women that people with access to computers see every day are of porn actresses or posing sex kittens, the bar on what is acceptably sexy is raised perilously high. On MTV's *Real Life: Plastic Surgery*, girls want to look like Pamela Anderson, not Kate Moss: this is porn talking. And porn talks loud these days. In a 2003 article by Naomi Wolf in *New York* magazine, college women cited their inability to be "porn-worthy" in the eyes of young men. One woman in ten told a 2004 *Elle*/MSNBC.com poll her partner seemed more critical of her body since he started looking at Internet porn. One in five said that as a result she felt compelled to do more to keep her partner sexually interested. And in a recent issue of *Glamour*, an article on body image included "the explosion of porn" on a list of reasons young women suffer from poor self-image. The piece cited a woman who works in a treatment center for eating disorders; she described how her female patients complain about the effect the porn culture has had on their self-image: "They think the guys who look at it are creeps, but also wonder how they can live up to the surgically enhanced breasts on unnaturally thin women. And they say it's hard to find a guy whose standards haven't been distorted by porn or the media." The director of the Masters and Johnson Clinic in St. Louis, Mark Schwartz, told *Time* that pornography's unrealistic images of femininity reach deep into men's brains, turning some of them into erotic automatons. "Men become like computers, unable to be stimulated by the human beings beside them," he said. "The image of a lonely, isolated man masturbating to his computer is the Willy Loman metaphor of our decade."[7]

Breast enhancement may seem a purely modern phenomenon, but it's actually been around in one form or another for more than a hundred years. Beginning in the 1890s, doctors of the shady variety injected some prostitutes and a handful of actresses with paraffin, which, perhaps not unexpectedly, led to infections, hardening of the breasts, and the formation of lumps. Still, this procedure continued on until the 1920s, when fat transplants came into vogue; tissue was surgically removed from the buttock and abdomen and transferred into the breasts. Unfortunately, the fat was quickly and unevenly absorbed into the body, leaving frightening asymmetries in the breasts and nasty scars at the removal site. After World War II, Japanese prostitutes, eager to attract American GIs, began getting injections of silicone, a common crystalline element often used in semiconductors. The technique soon caught on with topless dancers in Las Vegas and San Francisco. But reports of complications poured in: the injections caused chronic inflammation, serious infections, and organ damage due to silicone migration. So doctors experimented with the implantation of polyvinyl sponges, glass and ivory balls, wool, and ox cartilage. They tried Ivalon, a derivative of polyvinylic alcohol, in 1949; Polistan, a derivative of polyethtelene, in 1959; Etheron, made from polymethane, in 1960; and Hydron, from polyglycomethacrylate, in 1961. All produced serious side effects and none created the luscious, low-hanging-fruit effect women craved.

The modern age of breast enhancement began in late 1961, when Houston surgeons Thomas Cronin and Frank Gerow developed the first silicone breast prosthesis with the Dow Corning Corporation. They got the idea after gazing at a plastic sack of blood hanging from a pole during a transfusion; the hint of wanton sag mimicked the human breast. Their discovery came at a crucial time in the zeitgeist; by then breasts had become a national fetish. Lana Turner and her sweater, Marilyn Monroe and her calendar, Jane Russell and her cinematic roll in the hay—these were the totems that haunted average American women. Even the front ends of flashy sedans were sculpted to look like overflowing bosoms. Because pictures of women's breasts were not part of the average cultural diet, women resorted to bra stuffing and complicated brassieres. It was not until the 1960s and the burgeoning popularity of men's magazines, with their soft-porn images, that women realized they could not hide behind fabric and stuffing. There had to be some There there.

Robert Emmons, a public relations executive who has worked in the implant business since the 1960s, told me about one of the first publicity campaigns for silicone breast implants for Dow Corning. "The board of directors said, 'Hey, we just sell the stuff, we don't tell doctors how to use it,' " Emmons recounted. "So they reached down into the bowels of the company and got me and said, 'Hey, we need some good press.' So I write a story, we get some great photographs, and I go to New York and call up every women's magazine. I go see every women's magazine editor. I get nothing. No one is interested. I go back to my hotel room and I am so depressed. So depressed. Then I thought to myself, 'Look, you sell boobs for a living. How seriously can you take yourself?' " Six months later, "*Cosmo*, I think, ran the whole article, word for word, under one of their writers' bylines, with our photos. And suddenly, all the good press started."

Silicone implants were a quantum leap from earlier methods—even Marilyn Monroe got them, shortly before her death—but they caused capsular contracture, a painful and unsightly tightening of scar tissue that occurs in as many as a third of patients, so by the early 1980s the handful of companies that had sprung up to market them began to cover them with polyurethane foam. A decade later, more than 100,000 women carried these rubber-covered sacks of silicone gel in their chests.

In 1992, the FDA issued a report detailing how polyurethane breaks down in the body to form a carcinogen. Worse, the silicone gel often leaked out of the sack, a situation that grew as a concern as more and more women got the implants. Many doctors and the implant makers themselves argued that the leakage carried no long-term health risks, aside from the additional corrective surgeries it required, but women began insisting that their implants had caused serious autoimmune diseases, including lupus and rheumatoid arthritis. In 1988, Dow Corning settled a class-action lawsuit brought by 170,000 women for $3.2 billion. The FDA later ruled that silicone was not linked to autoimmune diseases.

Despite the silicone scandal, hunger for augmentation was unabated. European companies experimented with the Trilucent model, filled with soybean oil, a pleasingly natural-seeming solution to the problem. More than 9,000 European women got such implants during the 1990s—they were never approved in the United States—before they were withdrawn from the market in 1999 because a filler used with the oil became toxic in the body as it broke down. Many of the women described a rancid smell coming from their breasts.

Saline implants, developed by a French surgeon in the mid-1960s, are now the norm. Saline sloshes; it doesn't have the more natural-feeling, densely squishy texture of silicone, and the implants are prone to spontaneous deflation, which can make for additional surgeries, but advocates argue that they are safer than silicone, at least from a long-term health perspective. Teardrop-shaped saline implants intended to be more natural looking were introduced several years ago; they have a tendency, however, to wander within the chest wall, creating spectacular deformities. And hardening of the implants is a problem for a significant minority of patients, as it was with silicone.

Saline implants are far from perfect. According to data presented to the FDA in 2002, almost one-quarter of all cosmetic saline, or saltwater-filled, breast implants will require additional corrective surgery within five years, and few of these types of implants can be expected to last more than a decade. One-third of the participants in a 2000 FDA study reported that they had had to have at least one subsequent surgery in which an implant was removed or replaced. The *FDA Breast Implant Consumer Handbook* warns: "Breast implants do NOT last a lifetime. You should be prepared for long-term follow-up, reoperations to treat complications, and personal financial costs."

Studies have found disturbingly high levels of internal infection, hardening of the tissue around the implanted breast fixture, and implant leakage and deflation. The hardening is perhaps the worst common complication. When any type of breast implant is inserted, the body reacts by forming a wall of scar tissue around it, a lining to protect the foreign object from infiltrating the body. The scar capsule is formed by living tissue and occurs in patients regardless of whether they have smooth or textured implants, saline or silicone. The risk of forming such a scar capsule, according to various studies, is anywhere from 5 to 50 percent.

In some patients, the capsule can shrink down, contracting around the breast implant and rendering it tight and hard. The smaller and more shrunken the capsule, the harder the breast feels. There is in the language of plastic surgery a lexicon devoted solely to the phenomenon of this contracture. Baker grade I means the breast looks soft and feels soft. At Baker grade II, the breast looks soft but feels firm to the touch, which indicates mild to moderate contracture of the scar capsule. At Baker grade III, the breast has begun to take on an abnormal round shape, and the implant may be so tightly constricted it is being choked into an unnatural upward position. At Baker grade IV, the patient is in constant pain, the implant immobile, the breast a hard lump. The patient is at risk for rupture of the implant.

Depending on what doctors view as the cause of the contracture, they may treat the problem with antibiotics or topical vitamin E. Such treatment, I discovered in conversations with several plastic surgeons, is rarely effective. Another treatment is what is delicately referred to in medical terminology as the "closed capsulotomy." The patient disrobes and lies chest up on a table, and the surgeon squeezes the breast with such force that the fibrous tissues surrounding the implant pop or tear. Some surgeons treat patients with the asthma medication Accolate, which comes with its own set of complications.

Breast implants can last anywhere from a few years to a few decades, with most making it ten to fifteen years without problems. The younger the patient, however, the more likely she will need additional surgeries over the course of her life. A woman who gets breast implants at eighteen and wants to keep them for life may have to have surgery twice a decade for the next six decades.

In recent years, there has been a clamor by both patients and plastic surgeons to return silicone to the elective surgery market. (Patients who have lost a breast to cancer are allowed to have silicone implants.) The FDA has waffled, squeezed by potential consumers and pharmaceutical lobbyists on one side and outraged former patients and public health advocates on the other. But many surgeons expect the market to eventually win out, returning silicone to prominence.

Doctors are fiercely argumentative about the notion of breast implants, and differences are drawn along aesthetic and purely financial lines. Dr. Mark Berman of Santa Monica has told reporters that, no matter what kind of breast implants a patient has, she has a good chance for complications; Berman estimates that a third of all artificial breasts in this country are in trouble, with either hard, distorted implants or leakage. But Berman is also trying to sell other doctors on the notion of his "pocket protector," a lining he inserts into the breast cavity that has microscopic pores to which the body attaches fibers instead of walling the implant off.[8]

In the meantime, doctors have also been trying to get approval for anatomic high-cohesive silicone-gel implants, which have already been in use in Europe for a decade. Because of their density and shape-holding design, they have become known to doctors, who like to euphemize the names of medical devices, as "gummy bears."

In the quest for bigger bosoms, there is no dearth of half-baked ideas. In 2001, the Brava Breast Enhancement and Shaping System hit the market. The bralike device, worn ten hours or more a day, has two hard plastic domes ringed with silicone that create a vacuum to induce the breasts to grow. The patient wears the domes, and as the suction causes the breast tissue to stretch, new tissue allegedly grows in to fill the space. I clamped a Brava cone over my breast at a medical conference and couldn't imagine anyone wearing one of these on both breasts for ten hours a day.

How best to measure our fetish for breasts? I decide to register on a Web site called Myfreeimplants.com. It is a "cyber-begging" site, on which women post pictures of themselves and hope that the site's "benefactors"—men who sign in to look at pictures of topless women—will donate money to their cause. The site was founded by an enterprising young man named Jason Grunstra, who lives in Los Angeles. "Have you ever wanted bigger breasts? But couldn't afford the expensive costs of surgery? Here is your opportunity to earn Free Breast implants!" the site's home page reads. On it, a beautiful young woman named Natasha poses in a black and red negligee, showing off her rounded, ample bosoms. Natasha was the inspiration behind My Free Implants. She and Grunstra had had success with a previous Web site on which Natasha earned her breast implant surgery by cyber-begging for the money.

"After seeing the success I saw a niche and a great potential business model that has so far gone untapped," Grunstra tells me. I ask him if, in the interests of journalism, I can register on his site just to see what happens. I don't really want breast implants. In my profile, under "Quote," I enter, "Truth hath a quiet breast—William Shakespeare." And in the body of my profile, "But I'd like louder ones. I am a writer on the East Coast. Why don't we chat on-line?" I enter two goals, "breast augmentation (saline)," which costs $4,000, and "breast augmentation (silicone)," for $5,000. I post a picture of myself. I am smiling but look a bit more writerly than most of the ladies on the site, who gaze beseechingly into the camera, teasing their T-shirts around their waists and licking their lips.

I check my profile every day to see if any benefactors have signed up. Grunstra e-mails to tell me he has figured out which one I am. "The Shakespeare gave it away," he writes. In any event, neither quoting Shakespeare nor my picture helps me out at all. Neither does the fact that I wrote my true age in the profile—thirty-seven—and everyone else on the site is younger and willing to post topless pictures of themselves. Every day for a week I log in and check eagerly to see if I have received any messages from potential benefactors. And then one day, voilà, I have several. I am strangely excited, even though I have no desire for bigger breasts. Most are from men who would donate a dollar or two to any woman's cause so that they could ask to see topless shots of her. "James" writes that I ought to gain weight before getting new "boobs" and that "most husbands would happily forsake the new truck to buy his wife a larger 'rack.' " Another potential benefactor, named Joel, asks what I have written lately. His picture appears with his message: mustached and tan, he poses with his thumbs pointed out and up in between two women in strappy black tank tops that read "Marriage = Death."

Grunstra makes a profit on the site in several ways. "Benefactors pay for message credits in order to be able to communicate with the ladies on the Web site," he tells me. "The ladies get paid $1 per message they receive. So obviously they are encouraged to keep conversations going. The Web site makes a few cents off of each message. Benefactors can also send donations of any amount to the ladies; again the site takes a small percentage. And finally, the average surgery costs $5,000. If it takes one year to raise this much, and there are 200 ladies on the Web site, then in theory after 6 months there is $500,000 sitting in a bank account, so investing that or just earning interest makes a pretty penny." Advertisers are interested in the site, considering how much traffic it gets. But Grunstra says, "I don't want to just throw up any old ad for male growth enhancements though. I want to find the right partner who isn't in it just for the money."

In my correspondence with James—remember, each message is $1!—I ask him if he thinks that fake breasts are just as good as, if not better than, the real thing. "I doubt that men care much about what is filling out the sweater, be it silicone or tissue," he writes. "I have often wondered from where we get our aesthetic. I am attracted to and fascinated by large breasts. Why? Is it nature or culture? There have been arguments about the notion of 'ampleness' and the ability to feed babies. But this notion is false. The size of a woman's breast has nothing to do with her ability to breast-feed. What little research I have done suggests that it is more cultural. The Classical Greeks and Romans preferred the breasts bound. What would Rubens have done if he had lived in Rome at that time? Why were flat-chested flappers the vogue during the excessive Jazz Age, but Mae West and Jean Harlow the rage during the destitution of the Depression? And today we are both fascinated with Tyra Banks's ample chest as well as still following what that scrawny Kate Moss does."

Reading the women's profiles on the Web site, he writes, "both fascinates and saddens me. For the life of me I can't understand why some of the women with D cups want to go up to DD or G. And the A cup women who talk about wanting to boost their self-esteem make me want to start a site called 'My Free

Therapy'!" Joel, the mustached guy, writes to me in more un-equivocal terms. "I don't care if they're real or fake," he said. "Big is good."

After three weeks, I have made $96. It is incredible to me that somewhere out there were ninety-six dollars sitting in men's wallets, waiting to be donated in the tiniest hope of a chance that the benefactors might be able to see a picture of some strange woman's breasts, someday, maybe.

Fourteen

American Geisha

That dark winter night I sat at home moaning over my swollen lip and the funeral reception I missed, you might think that I'd hit rock bottom—one not of alcohol or drugs or co-dependence but of vanity. But I still had a little lower to go.

The next morning, a vicious headache splitting my head, I awoke and walked to the bathroom, tripping over the empty mug ("Happy 29th Birthday—Again!") on my way. There was no moment during which I wondered if the previous day's events had been a nightmare; both the memory and the reality were still too laughably vivid.

The lip—it was difficult to think of it as my lip—was still huge, a generous proboscis jutting out from the front of my face like the broad and welcoming veranda on a southern plantation house. Thanks to the steroids Dr. Michelle had prescribed for the swelling, it had shrunk considerably, but it was still tremendously oversized. Again, I sighed with relief that my husband was out of town and couldn't witness the exploding lip. He is the most understanding of spouses, but a cosmetic procedure gone wrong is,

I imagine, a bit like childbirth, at least in the following sense: a man might convey his willingness to witness the act of giving birth, might even say, "Sure, honey, let me share the miracle with you," but deep down he may not really want to remember what his wife looked like splayed open on a table, grunting like a wild animal, emitting smells and fluids that would make Linda Blair in *The Exorcist* look like a Breck girl at a country club picnic. Several women have told me that after having a face-lift or an eye tuck, they wouldn't let their husbands see them until they were fully healed, lest the memory of the disfigured, swollen, oozing, bandaged face imprint itself in their memory permanently.

The woman who tidies our apartment arrived and told me, Wow, your lip looks very sexy. This is a person who works in a profession that doesn't place much value on pulchritude yet who managed to pay for her own eye lift a couple of years ago (after I checked out her surgeon), during which time we commiserated about scars, which ointments and creams worked best, etc. It didn't occur to me then how odd it was that this delicate Guatemalan grandmother had saved her money to have a cosmetic procedure on her upper eyelids. Now, however, my lip hugely swollen, I stared into her eyes—sparkly and clear, the lids as taut and fresh looking as those of a nineteen-year-old—and realized that she and I had reached a point of curious cultural syzygy: both well-to-do and poor, white and blue collar, housekeeper and employer, had arrived at plastic surgery ground zero.

Back in my bedroom, I turned on the morning news programs and sucked at a glass of orange juice, the straw jammed into the side of my mouth, where it could find purchase. (The rest of my mouth still couldn't form a tight enough seal to grip a straw.) I began the rationalization process: my housekeeper thought my lip looked sexy; this was New York City, land of shut-in writers; I could order in.

My confidence was creeping back. I hadn't done any damage to myself. I would be fine in a couple of days. And, after all, this was expected of me. I was a member of the Sta-Prest, wrinkle-free generation, a group of perpetually youthful-looking women whose number include Sarah Jessica Parker, an actress who despite having advanced to her fifth decade of life still plays the part of the unmarried ingénue girlfriend in movies like *The Family Stone* and *Failure to Launch*. If she gets to play Gidget forever, why shouldn't I?

I flipped through the channels—ogling Katie Couric, Al Roker, Diane Sawyer, Matt Lauer, Charlie Gibson, the local New York anchors—and found myself in a kind of vanity fugue, in which rather than listening to what the talking heads were saying, I merely watched their faces dumbly. Katie, I thought, get some Botox already! Hey, Al, looking great after the weight-loss surgery. Charlie, shall I talk to your producer about some collagen for those droopy nasolabial folds?

The best quality a journalist can have is that of impartial distance, the ability to rise above a situation and study it as if one had no previous opinions or conceptions, no tendency toward easy judgment. I can't say I always have that ability, but at that moment I stopped and listened to my inner monologue tapping out the litany of cosmetic procedures that Katie Couric ought to look into and saw myself, finally and seriously, as a total jerk. Somewhere out of my subconscious swam the memory of my mother remarking on how offensive and outlandish my suggestion was that she get a nose job. I had ricocheted from a preliminary rock bottom the night before to a state of self-hypnosis in which I convinced myself that everything would return to normal, down to a deeper, more permanent sense of spiritual void. My skill at self-deception had finally proved unequal to the occasion.

I put down the remote: I had become Victor Frankenstein, obsessed with reversing the passage of time and the imperfections of nature. And in the process I had become a cartoonish tragedy—a funny tragedy, a temporary tragedy, but a tragedy nonetheless. There is a tremendous passage in *Frankenstein*, when the doctor describes how he approaches his triumphant moment, the act of creating a functioning, breathing creature out of discarded limbs and bones: "One secret which I alone possessed was the hope to which I had dedicated myself; and the moon gazed on my midnight labors, while with unrelaxed and breathless eagerness, I pursued nature to her hiding places. Who shall conceive the horrors of my secret toil as I dabbled among the unhallowed damps of the grave or tortured the living animal to animate the lifeless clay? My limbs now tremble, and my eyes swim with the remembrance; but then a restless, and almost frantic, impulse urged me forward; I seemed to have lost all soul or sensation but for this one pursuit."

I had pursued nature to her hiding places. I had disturbed the secrets of the human frame. I had at least once before asked for the collagen of cadavers to be injected into my face. But most horrifyingly, I seemed to have lost all soul or sensation but for this one pursuit. I couldn't even listen to the morning news, I was so distracted by the anchors' minor wrinkles. And my reward was that I now looked like Bozo the Clown. My greed to remain youthful had delivered me to this moment, along with my willingness to be captured and seduced by images. I was vain, and weak, and easily susceptible to the pressures of a morally debatable, deeply intoxicating subculture.

The exploding lip experience made me hate some part of myself. The qualities I had cherished—fortitude, endurance, practical Yankee good sense—had withered, while I had grown as vain and silly as any teenage pop star with lip implants and a bad boob job. Worse still, my very perception had become warped.

There's nothing new about adoring beauty. Every epoch has nurtured its idea of perfect beauty and developed means for achieving it. What is different about our culture's approach to beauty is the extreme degree to which we believe beauty matters. Advances in medicine and technology in the last century, particularly in the last decade, coupled with the flourishing of mass media in more forms than we could have possibly imagined a quarter of a century ago, have taken our normal animal concerns and magnified them into an obsession.

Women feel very strongly that they must hew to the standard of looking great, performing well, and doing so while looking effortlessly perfect. The phrase *effortless perfection* comes from a Duke University study conducted in 2004 in which the female undergraduates said they believed that more than any other time in history they were held to an unyielding standard of perfection. I first encountered the term in Anna Quindlen's essay against perfection titled "Being Perfect," and it was terrifying. The young women in the study felt compelled to be physically perfect and have great hair and get good grades and be admired for their intelligence and their poise and their social skills, and yet appear as if these exertions required no effort whatsoever. Alarmingly, the study reported that many Duke women were entering as undergraduates and graduating four years later feeling not more confident but less secure.

Effortless perfection is so evocative of the Stepford Wives that it speaks to an eerie geisha-fication of the American woman. And yet that quality of geishalike beauty and steeliness is a vital part of functioning women's lives now.

At a recent conference that *Newsweek* hosted on the subject of women and power, I watched the lunchtime panel with fascination. Engaged in the discussion were a former governor, two CEOs, a lawyer, and a journalist. Each one was as turned out as if she were going for a night on the town: hairdos, diamond studs, makeup, silk. It was *Sex and the City* at age sixty. The audience— a group of hundreds of professional women who held some measure of power, as defined by the *Newsweek* organizers—had seen rivers of Botox and collagen. Chins had been tucked, teeth whitewalled, eyeballs LASIKed, waists trimmed by artifice, diet, or surgery. Several necks had been tightened, eyelids snipped, foreheads planed upwards. In one sense, the gathering put me in mind of a line that the actor George Sanders (playing a sharp-tongued critic named Addison De Witt) delivers to an elegantly dressed woman in the movie *All About Eve*: "From the smartness of your dress, I take it your luncheon companion is a lady."

Somehow, these women were dressing for one another, but they had also beautified themselves in far more intricate ways than mere dress, to show to their contemporaries that they could look more beautiful and younger than they ever had. It was a ritual battle, and the rituals require more money, more time, and more dedication than ever before.

Thirty years ago, an audience of powerful women would have looked decidedly less kempt. These women looked as if they had spent the morning with a professional stylist who chose their clothes and did their hair. At the lunch afterward, the conversation among the group of women seated at my table—lawyers, museum curators, doctors, researchers, executives—gravitated not toward social responsibility or politics or power but to the incredible rejuvenation of one of the powerful women in the audience. A journalist, she had looked slightly haggard in previous years. Her face had sagged with age and fatigue, showing the effects of hundreds of late nights in the pursuit of work and social responsibility. Now, in her midsixties, she was radiant. Her face was that of a forty-five-year-old woman who had never borne children, who had napped all her life, never worked, and never set foot in sunshine. She had lost weight, and her figure—once the body of a dumpy, aging political writer—now belonged to a trim, curvy cheerleader.

She didn't look worked on. Rather, she looked lit from inside by some magical bulb, as if she had taken a youth elixir and it had repaired her face and body.

And then I realized: these women had identities that had to envelop and embrace and present both the masculine (in power) and the feminine (in beauty and presentation). Even women who have proved themselves in many spheres of life feel compelled to hew to this bizarre, unattainable ideal of styled, nipped, serene beauty. The more successful and powerful the woman, the less likely she is to have a husband or child. If she is powerful, she has to be beautiful and feminine, too. Looks are the new feminism. Where once demanding equal rights and pay was a way for us to ask for an equal share of the power, the new way we show we have power is to be styled—from top to bottom, from shoe sole to eye tuck—to prove that we have our act together. This is how we demonstrate to the world we have it all, both the yin and the yang, the masculine and the feminine. Successful women are required to reach both the male and the female markers of success: corporate achievement and success as well as being thin, pretty, and wrinkle-free. And owning a dozen pairs of Jimmy Choos. And don't forget the good hair day: this is a culture in which Tina Brown's predawn mornings back when she ran *Vanity Fair* were described as beginning "when a chauffeur calls for her on Central Park South, whisks her to the hairdresser for a quick comb-out of her Princess Di look-alike locks, then deposits her [at her office]."[1] Later, in an unauthorized biography, Brown was made fun of for once wearing a suit to the office that still had the dry cleaner's silver-foil wrapping on the buttons. It's incredible that Brown had her hair professionally combed each morning before work—after all, she wasn't a news anchor, or a movie star, or someone whose professional aptitude relied on her looks. At least not at first glance. Yet a biographer mocked her for a clothing faux pas. So Brown was indeed supposed to present herself as impeccably coiffed and perfectly dressed every day, even though she was a magazine editor. She was held up to a standard of movie star perfection, even though she lived largely in the universe of words and the imagination.

It is a simple fact of contemporary life that even women who are incredibly successful in their careers do not feel let off the hook with respect to youth and beauty. The sheer time, energy, and anguish that must go into self-presentation at this level are depressing to contemplate. It is almost comforting to harken back to a time when cosmetic enhancement was part and parcel of the film business but not any other.

Of course, the notion of effortless perfection is sick, pointless, and exhausting. The notion of perfection—let alone perfection that appears effortless—no longer works for me. By the time this book comes out, I won't have had a Botox shot or a collagen shot for a year. I've gone cold turkey. I have watched the animation return to my forehead, but it is a slow process. The muscles have been weakened so profoundly by a full decade of Botox-induced paralysis that I wonder if my forehead will ever wrinkle again the way it did when I was twenty-eight. The furrows and lines are struggling to come back. They show that life requires effort and that effortless perfection is a myth. No one can be perfect. Even trying to be just plain okay requires effort.

There are many arguments against cosmetic surgery. Most critics of it say that the desire for physical perfection is vain and immoral, the purview of the ignorant and shallow; that to reward ourselves with perfect breasts or buttocks is unfair to those who can't afford to; and that the entire process of cosmetic beautification is a way of doing violence to human nature—something that is just not natural.

It's easy to see the opposite sides of these arguments, which sound pat and puritan to me. If you had to nail me down on the subject of whether cosmetic surgery is a good thing, I would have to defend it. Not all physically perfect people are necessarily vain, immoral, and ignorant. At seventy-three, William Butler Yeats, not known as one of literature's more shallow poets, wrote this memorable couplet: "You think it horrible that lust and rage / Should dance attendance upon my old age." At the time, he was trying to restore his physical power, youthful vigor, and sexual virility by injecting himself with secretions from monkey glands. Yeats is no different from a man of today who takes Viagra or gets a face-lift or has hair implanted in his scalp.

The economic argument—that it's unfair that the well-to-do get to buy things that make them more beautiful—yields to cold fact. The rich do get things the poor don't: the wealthy send their children to better schools, receive better medical care, wear nicer clothes, and live longer. It's a matter of global economic reality. Unfairness is a part of the human condition.

As medicine and technology stretch the boundaries of biology and threaten to disturb the foundations of human identity, it is important to ask ourselves how much we want to change human nature. But what, exactly, is human nature? Is it a requirement of human nature to resist change? Or is it a defining feature of human nature that we seek change and enhancement? Certainly, some enhancements backfire. But perhaps it is merely part of the evolutionary cycle that those who survive their beautification process, whatever that process entails, flourish and pass their genes on to the next generation or influence the culture in some way.

Ultimately, most arguments for cosmetic surgery pivot on the notion of choice—whether the individual has the choice, and the right, to perform what some perceive to be self-mutilation in the name of happiness. And, really, the most ignorant of human conditions is the act of imposing tyranny over another person. The New York social figure Jocelyn Wildenstein chose to look like a cat and found a surgeon who created a feline expression on her face.[2] It was her choice, and by all accounts she is extremely happy with her appearance. I think she looks frightening. But who am I to say that she should not have had her surgeries? What dominion over her life can other human beings presume? None. It is up to Claudia Lowe to spend her money on a surgery safari and up to Peggy Siegal to spend the amount of time she does each month maintaining her looks. It is up to the man addicted to Botox and the stripper with the enormous breast implants to discover when enough is enough.

In the end, it is our own choice that damns us or elevates us.

I come from a family of writers, professors, doctors, people who focus on the world of ideas, on the world of thinking, rather than on the world of looks. The women in my family generally age naturally, into a refined, slightly wrinkled bohemian wispiness. There is, generally speaking, an elegance to this way of aging, in the spirit of the Japanese notion of *wabi-sabi*, which refers to the imperfections wrought by age, wind, and weather. I don't know why I got temporarily sidetracked, but I think I have a small clue.

I loathe the idea of being the center of attention at a big party or celebration. My wedding was tiny; we were married in our apartment and had a small dinner party afterward. So when my husband and I were discussing our funerals one day—one of those big what-if conversations you inevitably have when you are married and there are children and other lives involved—I shocked him by saying I wanted a huge funeral.

"I want the newspaper to run a black border around its edges," I said. "I want a thousand people to come. I'll leave you a list of names and phone numbers. And make sure your first phone call is to Liz Smith." (Liz Smith is the legendary gossip columnist. To my husband's surprise, I recited her direct phone number to him from memory. "Write it down," I ordered.)

And this is where the anxiety about looking good, about looking young, comes into focus. We want people to look at us and praise our youthfulness, as if it were a quality we worked for. We want them to pat our hands and say, "You have plenty of time to write a book/have a baby/climb Mount Everest. You're so young." The more we believe we're young, the more time we believe we have left and the more ability we believe we'll be able to cultivate. A recent cover story in *New York* magazine titled "Forever Youngish" put forth the idea that people in their thirties and forties no longer believe that there is a definite point at which they must pass into the realm of the adult world. These aging Gen-Xers (i.e., me) don't believe in the former model of being a grown-up, a formulaic existence that entailed the following, in strict order: college, marriage, kids, boring job and boring responsibilities, wearing a suit to work, retirement, death. "It's also about rejecting a hand-me-down model of adulthood that asks, or even necessitates, that you let go of everything you ever felt passionate about," the author, Adam Sternbergh, wrote. "It's about reimagining adulthood as a period defined by promise, rather than compromise."[3]

Sternbergh presents the case of a thirty-two-year-old father who decided one day to learn to skateboard. "I thought, *Too bad I'm too old to do that*," he quotes the would-be skateboarder as saying. "Then I thought, *I'm not too old!*"

This is how I like to approach the world. I like to believe I'm not too old to try anything. But that's an illusion. I'm not so young. As I finish this book, I have just turned thirty-eight, and more than ever I have to learn to confront the notion of Never. There's something deeply sorrowful in the idea that I will never compete in the Olympics or swim the English Channel or serve a hundred-mile-an-hour ball across a tennis court. The idea that certain physical doors are forever closed to me is a reminder that we all simply inhabit these mortal envelopes until they wither. Of course, we can procreate, but this is no guarantee we survive. I was recently pregnant and went to the doctor a couple of times, watching the fetal heartbeat on the monitor. On the third visit, he pointed out a black spot on the ultrasound screen and said he had some bad news. "The heart isn't beating anymore," he said. All possibility for the future, for the continuation of my self into the future, for a creation of a new human being, disappeared into that black hole. No matter how methodically you work at something or how duly you try to correct a situation, the events of human life will not be influenced by effort or education or good will alone. As Edgar says in *King Lear*, "Men must endure / Their going hence, even as their coming hither: / Ripeness is all." Skin loosens. Bones break. Hearts stop. And there is no reversal.

In a sense, preserving my outer carapace was a way to insistently remain an adolescent, to lead myself to believe I remained a fearless adventurer, all without looking like an old lady trying to learn new tricks. It was also a way for me to try to relive my early adulthood the way I should have: taking care of my self, taking care of how I looked, and—as shallow as this sounds—being *pretty*. Youth is wasted on the young, they say, and we all wish we could go back and relive it with the tools we have as adults.

But life is not about endless possibilities. Without limits, it would become a bore. It is only within certain parameters that we find joy and pleasure. The process of constant scrutiny and constant evaluation and constant tuning and touching up—what Nora Ephron calls the endless "patch, patch, patch"—often feels like winning a series of small battles but losing the war. For me, the obsession wound up being tremendously distracting without yielding its ultimate goal: happiness and satisfaction.

I've also discovered that trying to remain beautiful and stay young looking is, paradoxically, a young person's game. By fifty, most people have had to deal with at least one or two significant health crises, and the gravity of serious medical problems highlights the inutility of surgery for beauty's sake. And, by fifty, most successful people have discovered that their reservoirs of self-confidence come not from their looks but from their accomplishments. By that time, and often earlier, they have come to understand that deterioration is an inevitable part of life. No matter how many antioxidant vitamins we swallow or Botox shots we get, we live in a constant state of disintegration. In an era in which we aspire to the constant upgrade—we upgrade our houses, spouses, cars, breasts—we inhabit physical machines that are insistently downgrading us all the time. There is something sweetly, naively comical in the belief that enough trips to the skin doctor can prevent the ruin or that looking young somehow inures us to physical catastrophe of other kinds.

I was on my way to the dentist this morning at 7:30 a.m. A front tooth, dead from an accident, had fallen out of my skull. I had wrapped the tooth in a Kleenex and called my dentist. The sun was shining, and for this I was grateful. There is nothing like having a tooth literally fall from your jaw to make you realize that the human body is a remarkably fragile collection of bones and joints and cartilage, and there is no easier way to transform an attractive woman into a parody of femininity and youthfulness than to remove one of her front teeth. A bus lurched next to the window of the taxi in which I was sitting, and I stared sullenly at the ad on its flank: the back of a woman's head swirled with wavy, shiny hair. The copy read: Every sidewalk is a runway.

The bus pulled away. *If every sidewalk is a runway*, I thought, *I shouldn't be anywhere near a sidewalk.* For a moment, I felt a kind of curious outrage. Every sidewalk shouldn't be a runway. How can we possibly manage to get out the door every morning if that's the case?

Human beings are creatures of context. If we lived in a world where it was okay to have a gap instead of a front tooth, maybe my abstracted, strange new look wouldn't have bothered me. But since the first eyeglasses were invented in the twelfth century, we have fooled ourselves into believing that technology can trump the inevitable defects of time and might someday defeat age itself. This is why the loss of the tooth had so upset my self-perception: no one else on Fifth Avenue this morning had a gaping hole in her mouth. *If my tooth does not exist, a dentist should fashion me a new one. If my face is ravaged by a dog, I should have my face replaced with that of a cadaver.* We live in an era without physical consequence.

Truth be told, I look around at some serious beauty junkies and marvel at my restraint. I had my upper eyelids done and had some fat sucked out of my behind. Over the years, I had a lot of Botox injected into my forehead.

And I had one heck of a wake-up call when I had Restylane injected into my lip.

I know enough to recognize when denial is creeping in. Often, when I see a woman who has visibly had too much plastic surgery, I see in her face a needy quality, a desire to be loved that is never quite fulfilled, the need to be approved that is never quite met, the woman who wants to feel important and be recognized but is never quite valued enough. I don't plan to age into that woman. I did enough to myself to soften some edges, and I try not to regret any of those things. In fact, I did enough to make me realize how grateful I was for the existence of cosmetic surgery. Even the exploding lip. Especially the exploding lip. Because it made me stop and think. And think and stop.

Notes

Chapter One: Beauty Junkies

1. Daphne Merkin, "Mad for Makeup," *Allure,* August 2003. Merkin is a prolific writer on the subject of beauty. For more, see her collection *Dreaming of Hitler* (New York: Crown, 1997), which includes her essays "These Unhappy Breasts," "The Pursuit of Thin," and "Am I Tan Enough?"
2. "Runway Success: Tough-Talking Midwestern Tomboy Adrianne Curry Scores a Life Makeover on *America's Next Top Model,*" *People,* July 21, 2003, p. 74.
3. Elizabeth Leonard, "A Changed Woman: Kathy Griffin Shares the Pain—and Gain—of Her Recent Plastic Surgeries," *People,* July 14, 2003, p. 91.
4. Roni Rabin, "Liposuction Mishap: Patient Hospitalized after Complications," *Newsday,* May 3, 2003, sect. A, p. 4.
5. "Pots of Promise: The Beauty Business," *Economist,* special report, May 24, 2003.

Chapter Two: Surgery Safari

1. Rory Carroll, "Scalpel Safaris," *Guardian,* December 17, 2002, feature, p. 8.

Chapter Three: The Rise and Fall and Rise and Fall of Botox

1. I met Kidman, who won the 2003 award for best actress, at the *Vanity Fair* Oscar party, which I covered for the *New York Times.*
2. Alexandra Wolfe, "Smooth! Docs Say Looks Botoxed," *New York Observer,* February 2, 2004, Front Page sect., p. 7.
3. Deirdre Dolan, "The Kindest Cut: Teens and Plastic Surgery," *New York Observer,* March 3, 2003, Media and Society sect., p. 3.
4. Alex Viega, "FTC Approves Allergan Takeover of Inamed," *Associated Press Online,* March 8, 2006.
5. Alex Kuczynski, "In Quest for Wrinkle-Free Future, Frown Becomes a Thing of the Past," *New York Times,* February 7, 2002, sect. A, p. 1.
6. Ibid.
7. Gina Piccalo, "Taking Aim at Botox," *Los Angeles Times,* September 22, 2003, part F, p. 1.
8. Food and Drug Administration, Department of Health and Human Services, Warning Letter to Mr. Peter A. Kresel of Allergan, Inc., June 23, 2003; http://www.fda.gov/foi/warning.htm.
9. http://www.thesmokinggun.com/archive/medavoy1.html.
10. Ned Zeman, "The Botoxed and the Boldfaced," *Vanity Fair,* May 2003, p. 194.
11. Jennifer English, City News Service (Los Angeles), September 7, 2004.
12. Denise Gellene, " 'Mr. Botox' Case Raises Some Brows," *Los Angeles Times,* August 22, 2004, part C, p. 1.
13. Ibid.
14. Dave Gardetta, "The Skin You're In," *Los Angeles,* January 1, 2002, p. 47.
15. Gina Piccalo, "Stress Lines Show at Botox Trial," *Los Angeles Times,* October 8, 2004, part E, p. 1.
16. Ibid.
17. Meredith Pierce, City News Service (Los Angeles), October 8, 2004.

18. Denise Gellene, " 'Mr. Botox' Case Raises Some Brows."

19. At the Allergan booth at an international conference of plastic surgeons in Houston, Texas, a sales rep detailed the numerous ways in which Botox could improve my life, such as ridding me of neck wrinkles and migraines. None of the uses had been approved by the FDA.

20. Interview with author.

21. Interview with author.

22. Interview with author.

23. Interview with author.

24. Meg Laughlin, Gabrielle Banks, and David Kidwell, "Stricken Physician Was in a Downward Spiral," *Miami Herald,* December 8, 2004, p. 1.

25. Alex Kuczynski, "Is It Botox, or Is It Bogus?" *New York Times,* December 5, 2004, sect. 9, p. 1.

26. Ibid.

27. Ibid.

28. John Pacenti and Jane Daugherty, "Doctor Who Paralyzed Self, 3 Others Charged; May Face Life in Prison," *Palm Beach Post,* February 3, 2005, sect. A, p. 1.

29. U.S. Department of Justice, U.S. Attorney's Office for the Southern District of Florida, press release, January 26, 2006; www .usdoj.gov/usao/fls.

Chapter Four: Forefathers

1. Charles Homans, "Analysis Shows More Soldiers Surviving Injuries than in Earlier Wars," Knight Ridder/Tribune News Service, December 9, 2004.

2. Elizabeth Haiken, *Venus Envy: A History of Cosmetic Surgery* (Baltimore: Johns Hopkins University Press, 1997), p. 31.

3. Michelle Tackla, "Phoenix Born from the Flames: Plastic Surgery Emerges Out of the Horrors of World War II," part I, *Cosmetic Surgery Times,* October 1, 2003, p. 1.

4. Mrs. William K. Vanderbilt, "Miracles of Surgery on Men Mutilated by War," *New York Times,* January 16, 1916, p. 6.

5. Quoted in Haiken, *Venus Envy,* p. 33.

6. Sander L. Gilman, *Making the Body Beautiful: A Cultural History of Aesthetic Surgery* (Princeton: Princeton University Press, 1999), p. 68.

7. Ibid.

8. Ibid., p. 83.

9. Ibid., p. 249.

10. Ibid.

11. Ibid., p. 204.

12. "Old Faces Made New: Plastic Surgery Finishes Its War Task and Looks Around for Further Work to Do," *New York Times,* December 9, 1923, p. xx2.

13. Rose C. Feld, "Facial Surgery Now a Routine: Hospitals Treat Industrial Accidents with Skill Learned in the War," *New York Times,* May 16, 1926, p. x17.

14. Haiken, *Venus Envy,* p. 94.

15. Ibid., p. 93.

16. Lisa Anderson, "The Transatlantic Trade That, for Better or (Often) Worse, Gave American Girls Status and British Royals Wealth," *Chicago Tribune,* December 28, 1989, Tempo, p. 1.

17. Gilman, *Making the Body Beautiful,* p. 255.

18. "City-Run Hospitals Won't 'Lift' Faces: Plastic Surgery Department Will Treat Only Urgent Cases, Dr. Greeff Announces," *New York Times,* February 3, 1930, p. 17.

19. Emily Mayhew, "Flying in the Face of Adversity: Emily Mayhew Tells the Story of the Heroic RAF Pilots Who Overcame Horrific Burns and Formed the Most Exclusive Club in the World," *History Today* (London), September 1, 2004, p. 48.

20. Gilman, *Making the Body Beautiful,* p. 163.

21. Mayhew, "Flying in the Face of Adversity."

22. Haiken, *Venus Envy,* p. 282.

23. "It's No Longer Reserved for the Vain and Rich," *New York Times,* September 27, 1971, sect. A, p. 30.

Chapter Five: Boom

1. Peter Kramer's phrase "better than well" became the title of a recent book by the philosopher Carl Elliott, who teaches bioethics at the University of Minnesota (*Better than Well: American Medicine Meets the American Dream* [New York: Norton, 2003]). Elliott contributes to the *Atlantic Monthly* and I suggest all of his work as excellent, engaging reading on the subjects of bioethics and manip-

ulation of the human body through cosmetic pharmacology and cosmetic surgery.

2. Joan Jacobs Brumberg, *The Body Project: An Intimate History of American Girls* (New York: Vintage, 1997), p. xxi.

3. Ellen Berscheid, "An Overview of the Psychological Effects of Physical Attractiveness," *Psychological Aspects of Facial Form,* ed. G. W. Lucker, K. A. Ribbens, and J. A. McNamara (Ann Arbor: Center for Human Growth and Development, University of Michigan, 1981), pp. 1–23. Berscheid stresses that unattractive children may believe they are not treated as well as other children because they are intellectually inferior or are not as well socially adjusted, when in fact it is because they are unattractive. She adds that beauty is a double-edged sword. As a child, Berscheid was thought of as the less attractive sister of two and therefore as the less social and more intellectual one; she was encouraged to go to college while her "prettier" sister was not. "It was deemed essential for me to go to college, but the emphasis for my sister was placed on her good looks and her native intelligence was never developed," she recalls (Jane E. Brody, "Effects of Beauty Found to Run Surprisingly Deep," *New York Times,* September 1, 1981, sect. C, p. 1).

Berscheid told me about the effect her findings had on an audience of colleagues. Her article on the psychological effects of attractiveness she said, grew out of a speech to participants at a University of Michigan's annual cranio-facial conference (including cranio-facial surgeons, cosmetic surgeons, and orthodontists): "I remember that conference well because after my speech a man who turned out to be the famed cranio-facial surgeon Ian Monroe,"—who trained in France under Dr. Paul Tessier, the first surgeon to find a way to keep patients alive on the operating table long enough to repair such hideous congenital deformities as having only half a face or an eye located near the mouth—"rushed up to me and said, 'Thank God! There is a Jesus!' He was overjoyed to learn that there existed clear documentation of the effects of physical attractiveness on a person's life, including the lives of children. He, like most of the others there, had not known of the research we had done that clearly demonstrated that a person's physical appearance, especially a child's physical attractiveness, made a significant difference in the quality of that person's life—from the very beginning, in the nursery, in school, in employment, in virtually every setting in which people find themselves, including, of course, in relationships with the opposite sex. At that time he had been trying to persuade the powers that be in the Canadian health system (he at that time was at Toronto's Children's Hospital) that surgery to remedy these deformities was worthy of being covered by Canadian health insurance. Further conversations with others in the audience revealed that insurance companies in this country also subscribed to the widespread belief at the time that a person's appearance was superfluous and irrelevant to the quality of a person's life—the 'interior,' such as character and personality, and behavior toward others being of sole importance. Given the emphasis now placed on appearance (perhaps too much emphasis, except in the case of children, who, in their innocence, do not understand that how they are treated, even by their parents, is affected by what they look like and not solely by their actual behavior), it is surprising to me that the belief that 'appearance doesn't matter' was firmly entrenched so recently."

4. Brody, "Effects of Beauty."
5. I. H. Frieze, J. E. Olson, and J. Russell, "Attractiveness and Income for Men and Women in Management," *Journal of Applied Social Psychology* 21 (1991): 1039–57.
6. "In The Money," *CNN Financial News,* July 6, 2003.
7. Brian M. Kinney, "Practice Management," *Plastic Surgery: Indications, Operations, and Outcomes,* vol. 1 (St. Louis: Mosby, 2000).
8. Natasha Singer, "A Doctor? He Is One on TV," *New York Times,* March 16, 2006, Style sect., p. 1.
9. Tom Barry, "Cosmetic Surgery," *Georgia Trend,* November 1997, p. 29.
10. Peter Ames Carlin and Elizabeth McNeil, "Surgical Strike: Cosmetically Enhanced and Proud of It, Jet-Setter Jocelyn Wildenstein Wages a Bitter Divorce Battle against Her Roving Husband, Alec," *People,* January 26, 1998, p. 57.

Chapter Six: What Is Beautiful?

1. Cathy Newman, "The Enigma of Beauty," *National Geographic,* January 2000, p. 94.
2. *The Insider,* CBS, February 20, 2006; http://insider.tv.yahoo.com/celeb/3758.

3. Mary Tannen, "Woman on the Verge," *New York Times Magazine,* February 22, 2004, p. 102.

4. Diane Richie divorce petition against Lionel Richie, http://www .thesmokinggun.com/archive/richiediv7.html.

5. "Lionel Richie's Estranged Wife Charged," *Associated Press Online,* November 17, 2004.

6. Philip Rieff, *The Triumph of the Therapeutic: Uses of Faith after Freud* (New York: Harper and Row, 1966), p. 32. I first encountered Rieff's work in Carl Elliott's *Better than Well: American Medicine Meets the American Dream.*

7. Ibid., p. 261.

8. Daniel Goleman, "Equation for Beauty Emerges in Studies," *New York Times,* August 5, 1986, sect. C, p. 1.

9. Michael Levine, "Why I Hate Beauty," *Psychology Today,* July–August 2001, p. 38.

Chapter Seven: Los Angeles

1. Sandy Kobrin for WomensEnews, "US: More Women Seek Vaginal Plastic Surgery," IPS-Interpress Service, November 17, 2004.

2. Interview with author.

3. Http://www.labiaplastysurgeon.com/dr-stern.html.

4. Deanna Kizis, "Wearing Thing," *Allure,* January 2006, p. 56.

5. Ibid., p. 58.

6. Susan Campos, "L.A. Stories," *T: The New York Times Women's Fashion Magazine,* August 28, 2005, p. 100.

7. Publicity release on behalf of Dr. Anthony Griffin, 5W Public Relations, New York, N.Y., January 9, 2006.

8. Interview with the author.

9. Samuel Wilton Fussell, "Muscle: Confessions of an Unlikely Bodybuilder" (New York: Poseidon, 1991), p. 85.

10. Paul Wynn, "Health Plans Venture into Cosmetic Services," *Cosmetic Surgery Times,* September 1, 2004, p. 1.

11. Interview with the author.

12. Alex Kuczynski, "A Nip and Tuck with That Crown?" *New York Times,* May 16, 2004, sect. 9, p. 1.

13. Ibid.

14. Jordan Rau, "A Knife Fight in Capitol," *Los Angeles Times,* May 27, 2004, sect. A, p. 1.

15. Ibid.
16. Kuczynski, "A Nip and Tuck with That Crown?"
17. Ibid.
18. Ibid.
19. Interview with the author.
20. Kuczynski, "A Nip and Tuck with That Crown?"
21. Ann E. Marimow, "Governor's Chief Fundraiser Defends Dentists' Donation," *San Jose Mercury News,* October 9, 2004, p. 19A.
22. Jordan Rau, "Governor Vetoes 10 Measures," *Los Angeles Times,* August 31, 2004, Metro Desk, part B, p. 1.

Chapter Eight: You Want It, You Need It: Marketing the Dream of Beauty

1. Anderson has a long love-hate relationship with breast implants. In 1999, she announced she was having her breast implants removed and her breasts went from a 36DD to a 34D, according to an article in *People* titled "Nipped, Tucked and Talking" (September 1, 2003, p. 102). In 2003, however, she said that she had had her breasts surgically amplified again. The same year she played a cartoon character on television named Stripperella, whose main feature was exploding breast implants.

Chapter Nine: Fat Is Not Beautiful

1. Ulrica Wihlborg, "Gaining Control: Daughter of a Singing Legend with Pop Hits of Her Own, She Used Food as Consolation for the Love She Was Missing," *People,* April 17, 2000, p. 54.
2. Roni Rabin, "Weight Loss Surgery: A High-Risk Answer to Obesity," *New York Newsday,* May 26, 2004, sect. A, p. 28.
3. "Vast Majority of Adults at Risk of Becoming Overweight or Obese; Future Burden of Obesity-Related Conditions Likely to Be Substantial," press release, National Institutes of Health, October 3, 2005.
4. Leigh Grogan, "If the Shoe Fits: As Americans Get Bigger, the Footwear Industry Needs to Step Up," *Sacramento Bee,* November 10, 2004, sect. E, p. 1.

Chapter Ten: Harvey Weinstein's White, White Teeth

1. Anne Jarrell, "Doctors Who Love Publicity," *New York Times,* July 2, 2000, sect. 9, p. 1.
2. Tama Janowitz, "Oral Fixation," *Vogue,* September 2002.
3. Julia Reed, "Smile! How to Buy Cover Girl Teeth," *Vogue,* November 1998.
4. Rick Marin, "Polishing Their Image," *New York Times,* January 31, 1999, sect. 9, p. 1.
5. Richard Johnson, "Star Dentist Drilled for $20 Million," *New York Post,* August 7, 2004, p. 10.
6. Ibid.
7. Heather Gilmore, "Rules' Writer's Dental Disaster," *New York Post,* September 19, 2004.
8. Http://aboutbaddentist.com.

Chapter Eleven: My Love Affair with Dr. Michelle

1. Nora Ephron, "On Maintenance," *O, The Oprah Magazine,* October 2005, p. 304.
2. "Beauty Maintenance," *O, The Oprah Magazine,* October 2005, p. 308.
3. Michael Sims, *Adam's Navel: A Natural and Cultural History of the Human Form* (New York: Penguin, 2003), p. 59.
4. Kathryn Pauly Morgan, "Women and the Knife: Cosmetic Surgery and the Colonization of Women's Bodies," *Sex/Machine: Readings in Culture, Gender, and Technology,* ed. Patrick D. Hopkins (Bloomington: Indiana University Press, 1998), p. 279.
5. Mary Tannen, "Botox Babies," *T: The New York Times Women's Fashion Magazine,* August 28, 2005, p. 200.

Chapter Twelve: The Fatal Quest for Beauty

1. The source for some material in this chapter on Susan Malitz and Olivia Goldsmith is Alex Kuczynski and Warren St. John, "Why Did They Die in Cosmetic Surgery?" *New York Times,* June 20, 2004, sect. 9, p. 1.

2. Http://www.ninds.nih.gov/disorders/myasthenia_gravis/detail _myasthenia_gravis.htm.

3. Christopher J. Gearon and Helen Fields, "Medicine's Turf Wars," *U.S. News and World Report,* January 31, 2005, Science and Society.

4. Ibid.

5. Richard Oakley, "Dead Woman Abandoned after Face-Lift, Says Lawyer," *Times* (London), January 8, 2006, Home News.

6. Russ Buettner and William Sherman, "He Specializes in Noses—and Litigation: Plastic Surgeon Has Paid Millions in Settlements, but Has Never Faced Sanctions," *Daily News,* March 6, 2000.

7. The citation, dated February 13, 2004, reads: "Action: License limited precluding the physician from performing complex nasal procedures except when assisting or being assisted by a surgeon who is either board certified by the American Board of Plastic Surgery or the American Board of Otolaryngology and who also has completed a fellowship in facial-plastic surgery and has at least ten years of experience in performing such complex nasal procedures. For the purposes of the limitation the term 'complex nasal procedures' means those procedures requiring multiple operations (more than two planned procedures) and serial reconstructive procedures including those involving congenital malformations. The physician is not precluded from performing without such assistance routine nasal-septal procedures, including but not limited to routine nasoplasties; open rhinoplasties and cartilage or synthetic grafts for structural and functional purposes with probation commencing upon the active practice of medicine in New York State for three years. Misconduct Description: The physician did not contest the charge of negligence on more than one occasion." *Professional Misconduct and Physician Discipline.* Consumers can search this database to find out if doctors in New York have been reprimanded.

   The Web site is http://w3.health.state.ny.us/opmc/factions.nsf/physiciansearch.

8. Sally Morgan, "We Spent £35,000 to Stay Young," *Mirror* (London), November 19, 1998, Features.

9. Warren St. John, "The Irish Patient and Dr. Lawsuit," *New York Times,* April 24, 2005, sect. 9, p. 1.

10. Http://www.michaelevansachs.com.

11. "Nurse Charged with Practicing Health Care without a License," *Associated Press State and Local Wire,* August 10, 2004.

12. Scott Williams, "Fighting for Surgical Safety: Waukesha Couple's Daughter Died during Plastic Surgery in Florida," *Milwaukee Journal Sentinel,* December 15, 2005, sect. B, News.

13. Todd Ruger, "Dead Woman's Kin Wants Grand Jury to Investigate Dangl," *Sarasota Herald-Tribune,* December 6, 2005, Sect. A, p. 1.

14. Michelle Nicolosi, "Death Cases Closed Quietly: The Histories of Many Dentists and Doctors Are Hidden from Consumers. Surgeon Had a String of Lawsuits before Fatal Case," *Seattle Post-Intelligencer,* October 4, 2005, News.

15. Ibid.

16. "Beware Fake Doctors: Guests Tell Their Experiences with Phone Physicians," *Montel,* transcript, August 30, 2004.

17. Michelle Green and Allison Adato, "Dying to Look Good," *People,* March 22, 2004.

18. Nancy Shute, "Makeover Nation: Americans Are Opting for Cosmetic Surgery in Record Numbers. But Do They Know the Risks?" *U.S. News and World Report,* May 31, 2004.

19. David Hafetz, "Fatal Eye Op Suit," *New York Post,* March 19, 2006, News.

Chapter Thirteen: The Breast

1. Teresa Riordan, *Inventing Beauty: A History of the Innovations That Have Made Us Beautiful* (New York: Broadway Books, 2004), p. 63.

2. Marilyn Yalom, *A History of the Breast* (New York: Ballantine Books, 1997), pp. 162–63.

3. Carolyn Latteier, *Breasts: The Women's Perspective on an American Obsession* (New York: Haworth Press, 1998), p. 4.

4. *20/20,* ABC News, June 24, 2005. When John Stossell, the host, told Jennifer O'Brien that according to the FDA about 40 percent of augmentation patients have at least one serious complication within three years, O'Brien replied, "Well, then I had one to three years of my life where I felt great about myself, and you can't take that back."

5. Dana Calvo, "New Magazine Features Topless Models Sans Implants," *Associated Press,* August 21, 1997.
6. Eric Wilson, "Fashion Refigured," *New York Times,* May 12, 2005, Sect. G.
7. Pamela Paul, "The Porn Factor," *Time,* January 19, 2004.
8. Natasha Singer, "Busted," *W*, April 2005.

Chapter Fourteen: American Geisha

1. Elizabeth Mehren, "Road to the Fair: For Tina Brown, a Decade of Detours," *Los Angeles Times,* January 30, 1985, View, part 5, p. 1.
2. Adam Nichols, "Catwoman Finds a Purr-fect Partner," *Daily News,* May 1, 2005, News, p. 3.
3. Adam Sternbergh, "Forever Youngish," *New York,* April 3, 2006.